Ben-Ami Scharfstein was educated at Brooklyn
College, the Teachers Institute of the Jewish
Theological Seminary, Harvard, and Columbia.
Now Chairman of the Department of Philosophy at Tel-Aviv University, he previously taught
at Brooklyn College and at the University of
Utah. Books by Professor Scharfstein include
The Roots of Bergson's Philosophy, *The Need
to Believe* (with M. Ostow), and *The Mind
of China*. He is currently at work on a study
of how rationality and irrationality mingle in
philosophers.

BEN-AMI SCHARFSTEIN

MYSTICAL
EXPERIENCE

Penguin Books Inc
Baltimore • *Maryland*

Penguin Books Inc
7110 Ambassador Road
Baltimore, Maryland 21207, U.S.A.

First published by The Bobbs-Merrill Company, Inc.,
Indianapolis/New York, 1973
Published by Penguin Books Inc, 1974

Printed in the United States of America

TO HY AND SHULA

Contents

I

On the Understanding of
Mystical Experience

Seen very broadly, mysticism is a name for our infinite appetites. Less broadly, it is the assurance that these appetites can be satisfied. Still less broadly, it is some particular attitude towards 'reality' and a view as to how someone or anyone can come into perfect contact with it. And mysticism is also, of course, a name for the paranoid darkness in which unbalanced people stumble so confidently. It is therefore a quality of the life of each of us, beginning with our infinite appetites, continuing with the rise and fall of our hopes that they will be satisfied, and ending with the precarious balance we keep as we stroll, or plod, or stride, or shuffle along the way of sanity, the darkness of self-hatred on one side, and the darkness of self-love on the other.

Mysticism can be painstakingly defined, but such a definition, especially when it precedes the attempt to understand, is apt to limit the attempt to verification of what has been decided in advance. I think it is best to begin, not with a definition that aims at exactness and completeness, but with a rough criterion.

The usual criterion for the mystic state is the certainty that one is undergoing the direct, previously veiled touch of reality in itself; and that this reality more nearly resembles our internal experience than our simply external environment. Since it is like the internal experience of a single person, the reality may be considered spiritual and essentially unified. As it is felt more and more strongly, it penetrates the self more and more deeply, or the self swells endlessly, until self and reality become identical or at least very close. To use another common metaphor, the mystic climbs up the ladder of comparatives until he reaches the superlative, where all pain, fear, guilt, and anxiety vanish and he enters into an indescribable state of rapture, equanimity, or wholeness.

So much is usual, and I accept it. But it is less usually realized that mystical experience, or something quite close to it, characterizes every intense effort to create, including that of the scientist who analyses and theorizes anxiously in order to solve an impersonal problem which has somehow become personal to him. By means of the solution, he arrives at a simultaneous outer and inner harmony. Perhaps our very desire to understand mysticism in its breadth and depth is tinged with a mystical hope.

We meet mysticism or its differently-named analogues everywhere, among primitives and, more elaborately developed, in the Far East, the Near East, and the West. We find it not only in religion and philosophy, but, obviously, in art and literature, and, less obviously, in science; and I am convinced that, in our own mechanized world, it is still prevalent—contemporary philosophy and art show that mysticism and mechanization do not necessarily exclude one another.

Mystical experience may come and go for no clear reason, and in the West we are inclined to regard it as inexplicably spontaneous; but it has also been sought and arrived at systematically, as if it too were the goal of a difficult though purely internal creation; and it has been defended in systematic and sometimes highly interesting ways. Whether true, false, or neither, mysticism has utilized intellects as acute as any in the history of thought, and practical, though dogmatic psychologies of great insight.

Mysticism concerns us all, and it is worth trying to understand. If I might choose a motto for the attempt, it would be: no fear and no pretence. With the help of what we already know of religion, psychology, and the history of thought, we can understand mysticism fairly well, provided that we look at enough evidence, and that we assess it carefully, with a minimum of preconceptions, and without any fear. But we ought not to pretend to know more than we actually do. The evidence we use is often ambiguous, the sciences by which we judge it are themselves uncertain and changing, and the evaluations we make, whether implicit or explicit, have an incorrigible note of subjectivity. Rhetorical solutions are all too easy. The words are all there for the asking, pretty, pious, poetic, logical, complacent, harsh. The words are cheap; understanding comes more expensive.

Perhaps I should say, at the outset, that I reject the metaphysical claims of mysticism of any sort. But I am also writing for those who accept them. I do not think that the more reasonable mystics, non-mystics, and anti-mystics need part company before they have exchanged ideas with one another. I have read that the White Stork and the Black Stork, both of Europe, are different in their habits. The White Stork claps with its beak when pleased, the Black Stork when it feels great tenderness. The White Stork is social and breeds in communities of its own kind, and the Black Stork is solitary and builds its isolated nests in the marshy forests of Poland, Roumania, and Russia. But human beings are not quite storks.

2

The Superlative States of Mysticism

Before we begin to analyse and argue, we ought to make out exactly what we are analysing and arguing over. This chapter is therefore an anthology of mystical experiences, described, for the most part, in the irreplaceable words of those who had them. The ideal men of the mystics, designed to embody the effects of mystical experience, are also here. Because of their social importance, I have chosen classic examples, such as have influenced large numbers of people; but because there are examples relatively unfamiliar in the West, I have at times added some explanation. Doctrinal descriptions of mystic ideals have not been avoided, for they are a part of the training mystics often undergo, and mystics are necessarily influenced by them. But I have favoured descriptions given by identifiable individuals out of their own experience.

Apart from presenting the examples, I have done nothing but classify them. I have made a crude, bold, and yet revealing division of mystical states into three different types: the type of passion or involvement; the type of passionlessness or detachment; and the type of both passion and passionlessness, which is the union of involvement and detachment.

The ideal of passion raised to a superlative degree is common enough in our literature. It can include every passion, whether pleasant or, in the ordinary sense, unpleasant. The broad ideal, which includes every superlative passion, has been held by some mystics, but these, as far as I know them, fit more easily into the third type, and so I shall confine the type of passion to the one passion that dominates it, which is love. Such love naturally tends to personify its object, which is imagined as the divine father, mother, or spouse. Love mysticism, with its yearning for union, sees the divine Beloved most usually perhaps as the spouse, though union with a divine Mother is a frequent ideal. In his imagination, the human lover often inverts his sex to complement that of his divine Beloved. There has even been a rather bitter debate in India as to whether the human partner in mystic marriage should play the role of the ideal wife or the ideal mistress.

We may begin with the tradition of mystic love most familiar in the West, the Christian, and, among Christian mystics, with Origen, the third-century theologian who died a martyr's death.

Origen was convinced that he experienced the actual presence of Christ, the holy Spouse, to his 'spiritual' hearing, sight, touch, and taste. In his *Homilies on the Song of Songs* he has Christ say:

On your account have I risen from the dead, and removed the sting of death and broken its bondage. That is why I say to you, 'Arise and come, My love, My beautiful one, because the winter is past and the rains are ended and flowers have reappeared in the land.'

Origen feels that the human lover suffers a love-wound far more glorious than that which could be inflicted by a human partner, for God shoots a superlatively precious, glowing dart.[1]

The metaphor of marriage is also dominant in St. Bernard of Clairvaux. God, he says, demands to be honoured and feared, but love is better than honour and fear, especially the love of the bride for her groom, for she is nothing but love for him and love alone. When the soul, says Bernard, conforms to God's Word, it becomes His bride. This relation is holy matrimony. 'It is an embrace—an embrace surely, where to will and not to will the same thing makes one spirit out of two. . . . They are bride and Bridegroom. . . . But his Bridegroom, remember, is not only loving; he is Love itself. . . .'

Unlike Origen, St. Bernard testifies that God's loving presence to him has not been by means of the senses, 'spiritual' or otherwise:

The Bridegroom-Word, although He has several times entered into me, has never made His coming apparent to sight, hearing, or touch. . . . Not by His movement was He recognized by me. I could not tell by any of my senses that He had penetrated to the depths of my being. It was, as I said, only by the movement of my heart that I was able to recognize

His presence, to know the might of His power by the sudden departure of vices and the strong constraint placed upon all carnal affections.[2]

St. Mechtilde of Magdeburg, the thirteenth-century nun, prays that God and the soul, two lovers, should be brought together to speak long of love. When the soul complains, in one of her poems, that Love has captured, bound, and wounded her beyond healing, Love, which is Christ, answers that he has hunted her for his pleasure, caught her for his desire, bound her for love, and made her his with cunning blows. And she, the Bride of God, asks that His breath draw her effortlessly into Himself, for, she says, 'Nothing can satisfy me save God alone, without Him I am as dead.'[3]

Walter Hilton, the fourteenth-century Englishman, describes God's love, which he experienced, as neither bodily nor not bodily:

All men that speak of the fire of love know not well what it is . . . it is neither bodily, nor is it not bodily felt. A soul may feel it in prayer . . . but he feeleth it by no bodily wit. For though it be so, that if it work in a soul the body may turn into a heat . . . nevertheless the fire of love is not bodily, for it is only in the ghostly desire of a soul.[4]

St. Teresa of Avila, to whom God's love came in a rapture that, by contrast, caused loathing for all worldly pleasures, also finds that God's love is spiritual but not merely so. This she says, in transparently sexual imagery, when she tells how God's love once appeared to her in the form of an angel:

He was not tall but short, and very beautiful; and his face was so aflame that he appeared to be one of the highest ranks of angels, who seem to be all on fire. . . . In his hands I saw a great golden spear, and at the iron tip there appeared to be a point of fire. This he plunged into my heart several times so that it penetrated to my entrails. When he pulled it out, I felt that he took them with it, and left me utterly consumed by the great love of God. The pain was so severe that it made me utter several moans. The sweetness caused by this intense pain is so extreme that one cannot possibly wish it to cease, nor is one's soul then content with anything but God. This is not a physical, but a spiritual pain, though the body has some share in it—even a considerable share. So gentle is this wooing which takes place between God and the soul that if anyone thinks I am lying, I pray God, in His goodness, to grant him some experience of it.[5]

As a coda to the Christian descriptions, we may merely recall those of Teresa's pupil, St. John of the Cross, especially the poem in which he keeps a night-time tryst with God, whose gentle hands wound his neck and stupefy him with love. Then, in the words of too literal a translation, he says:

I remained, lost in oblivion; My face I reclined on the Beloved.
All ceased and I abandoned myself, Leaving my cares forgotten among
  the lilies.[6]

Among the Moslems, the ideal of superlative, mystic love was developed by the Sufis, so called, it is generally assumed, because of the robe of rough wool (*suf*) they wore. Love was particularly the theme of the Persian Sufis, to whom God, beautiful beyond reason and imagination, had an indescribably intense magnetism. The encounter with Him was a shock, a stupor, a painful ecstasy (*wajd*). This ecstasy, one of them said, 'is a flame which is born in the interior of being; it springs out of a passionate desire, and when it comes the limbs are shaken by joy or sorrow'.[7]

The Sufi resents the most minute distance between himself and God, the veil, at last, which is nothing other than his own, human personality. He wishes then for 'annihilation' (*fana*) into the onto-logical density of God. The lover vanishes into the Beloved, for 'one who does not become an expert in annihilation shall not dis-cover the beautiful face of the bride. Such a one shall neither today nor tomorrow have a share among the Sufis.'[8] Whether this annila-tion was total or not was a matter for debate, and so the poet, Rumi, says of the 'annihilated man':

The essence of his being survives but his attributes are merged in the attributes of God, like the flame of a candle that in the presence of the sun *exists* because if you put cotton on it it is burnt away; *it does not exist* because it gives you no light: the light of the sun has annihilated it.[9]

According to Sufi theory, annihilation is paralleled by the 'subsistence' (*baqa*) of the unity of everything. One contemplates, at the ultimate, God as the essence of the universe. The veils of the world removed, reality is there naked, the soul is freed.

The greatest of the Sufi poets is Jalal al-Din Rumi, whose image of the candle-flame in the sunlight has been quoted. He was lean and hypnotic-eyed; peaceful, tolerant to everyone, and infinitely modest; and eager to pass the time with the simplest men. On 28 November 1244, an elderly wandering dervish, Shams al-Din of Tabriz, arrived at Konia, and Rumi fell in love with him. Rumi 'was so transported and smitten', says a contemporary, 'that for a time he was thought insane'. When, to Rumi's great sorrow, Shams finally vanished, Rumi fell in love with one of his own pupils, and then, when this pupil died, with another, who was to succeed him as head of the Sufi order he founded.

Rumi loved Shams as the 'annihilated' ideal man, that one in an age who has become identical with God and allowed God to become conscious, in him, of himself. Rumi wrote a collection of poems which he attributed to Shams, by a fiction that was transparent but not superficial. Of Shams and to Shams, God incarnate in his eyes, Rumi wrote:

> I have put duality away, I have seen that the two worlds are one;
> One I seek, One I know, One I see, One I call.
> He is the first, He is the last, He is the outward, He is the inward. . . .
> If once in this world I win a moment with thee,
> I will trample on both worlds, I will dance in triumph forever.
> O Shamsi Tabriz, I am so drunken in this world
> That except of drunkenness and revelry I have no tale to tell.

Rumi's allusion to drunken dancing was more than a figure of speech. We are told that, intoxicated with love, he would take hold of a pillar and turn himself around it and improvise poetry, which others took down; and that he taught his Sufis the ecstatic circular dance that made 'whirling dervishes' of them. He valued the closeness of these dervishes as if he and they were a single man:

The dervishes are in the situation of a single body; if one of its members feels pain, all the other parts are diseased. The eye gives up its seeing, the ear its hearing, the tongue its speaking; all assemble in that one place. The condition of true friendship is to sacrifice oneself for one's friend, to plunge oneself into tumult for the friend's sake. For all are directed towards one and the same thing; all are drowned in the same sea. That is the effect of faith, and the condition of Islam.

Rumi advised to love so constantly that it would become impossible to stop:

Wherever you are and in whatever circumstances you find yourself, strive always to be a lover, and a passionate lover at that. Once love has become your property you will be a lover always, in the grave, at the resurrection, and in Paradise for ever and ever. When you have sown wheat, wheat will assuredly grow, wheat will be in the stook, wheat will be in the oven.[10]

In spite of these Christian and Sufi examples, it is in the Indian tradition that the theme of mystic love has had its greatest flowering. One of its sources is a tenth- or eleventh-century compendium of stories, the *Bhagavata Purana*. Its hero is Krishna, the dark-skinned, lotus-eyed incarnation of the god, Vishnu, who descends to the world periodically to help the righteous against the evil.

Born into a human family, Krishna, even as a babe-in-arms, begins ridding the countryside of its demons. As he grows up, the girls, who are occupied with cow-herding, fall altogether in love with him. Neither moral rules nor husbands can hold them back; when a husband tries, his wife is so avid that her spirit hurries out of her body to Krishna. When autumn comes, his flute sounds in the forest, and the cowgirls beautify themselves and rush to him. They find him, crowned in peacock feathers, his long yellow loincloth bright against the blue-black of his skin. Mockingly, he reproves them for leaving their husbands. They cry. Then he says, as they respond wildly and immodestly, 'Dance and sing with me.' But Krishna thinks the girls now suppose he is in their power, and he vanishes. They search for him, and finally he relents and reappears, explaining that he, who is the fulfiller of all desire, cannot be judged like others; and he has been testing their love.

Now he divides himself magically and dances with them all, one Krishna to each girl:

Each thought he was at their side and did not recognize him near anyone else. They put their fingers in his fingers and whirled about with rapturous delight. Krishna in their midst was like a lovely cloud surrounded by lightning. Singing, dancing, embracing and loving, they passed the hours in extremities of bliss. They took off their clothes, their ornaments and jewels and offered them to Krishna. The gods in heaven gazed on the scene and all the goddesses longed to join. The singing mounted in the night air. The winds were stilled and the streams ceased to flow.

The stars were entranced and the water of life poured down from the great moon. So the night went on—on and on—and only when six months were over did the dancers end their joy.[11]

This story arouses religious fervour, *bhakti*, in its listeners. A historian writes of its effects:

Bhakti in this work is a surging emotion which chokes the speech, makes the tears flow and the hair thrill with pleasurable excitement, and often leads to hysterical laughing and weeping by turns, to sudden fainting fits and to long trances of unconsciousness. We are told that it is produced by gazing at the images of Krishna, singing his praises, remembering him in meditation, keeping company with his devotees, touching their bodies, serving them lovingly, hearing them tell the mighty deeds of Krishna, and talking with them about his glory and his love. All this rouses the passionate bhakti which will lead to self-consecration to Krishna and life-long devotion to his service. Such devotion leads speedily to release.[12]

In the course of time, Krishna, the force of love, was paired especially with the beautiful Radha. The love between them was celebrated by artists of every sort. One of the most inspired was Jayadeva, who in the late twelfth century wrote his powerful erotic verses, which were sung and danced for centuries at religious festivals.

In Jayadeva's *Song of the Cowherd*, Radha is pictured as jealous, neglected, and bitter. Krishna asks her to come to him, but she is too lovesick to move. He comes to her, but now she turns on him in anger and orders him to leave. He leaves, he returns, she is mollified and yields, and then she and love make love:

Their love play grown great was very delightful, the love play where thrills were a hindrance to firm embraces,
Where their helpless closing of eyes was a hindrance to longing looks at each other, and their secret talk to their drinking of each the other's nectar of lips, and where the skill of their love was hindered by boundless delight.[13]

This religious and mystical poetry influenced a number of sects. One of the most influential was founded in Bengal in the sixteenth century, by a man who took the name of Krishna Chaitanya. He and his followers would sing Radha-Krishna hymns together, and march in procession through the city, dancing and singing to the point of rapture. The memory alone of Krishna, or his image alone, would awaken Chaitanya's passion; and he used the story of Radha and Krishna as the basis of religion because, as he said, nothing else could touch men so deeply.

Like the ideal of passion, the ideal of passionlessness or detachment may be selective, or it may attempt to be complete. The ideal of superlative dispassion is hardly natural to us now, but it was at least approached in ancient times by the Stoics, and by the Epicureans when they worshipped the impassive self-contained gods they imagined living in the spaces between the worlds.

Plotinus is still selective, because he does compare the mystic union to the union of lovers, and he does find beauty, suggesting transcendent beauty, everywhere. But he instructs us in negation and in the thinking away of space and time and every shape and pleasure they contain. 'This,' he says, 'is the life of gods and divine and blessed men, deliverance from the things of this world, a life which takes no delight in the things of this world, escape in solitude to the Solitary.' It is not easy to forget that Plotinus, as his disciple tells us, 'seemed ashamed of being in the body'.[14] Plotinus ashamed of his body was akin to the more drastic men, who were becoming as visible in the Greco-Roman world as they had long been in India, who hated their bodies and who valued, not love, but perpetual virginity, sometimes to the point of self-castration. Such passion directed against passion is surely apt to lead to the dispassionate ideal.

The Hindus who followed the ninth-century philosopher, Shankara, adopted an ideal which, like that of Plotinus, has some muted suggestions of passion. The passion lay in their view that reality was, at bottom, pure consciousness and pure bliss. But the purity of this bliss led them to reject every pleasure, including sexuality, as a delusion. They too wished to annul everything spatial, temporal, moving, limited, shaped. In their eyes, the only ordinary experience that could suggest the ideal was deep, dreamless sleep. They shunned involvement, or rather the passion of involvement, and sought only the fixed inner Self, the Atman. What this might mean in simple human terms we see in a description, plausibly attributed to Shankara himself, of the ideal man, still dressed in the body for which he had lost all concern:

He is the greatest of the great. The things perceived by the senses cause him neither grief nor pleasure. He is not attached to them. Neither does he shun them. Constantly delighting in the Atman he is always at play with himself. He tastes the sweet unending bliss of the Atman and is satisfied.

The child plays with his toys, forgetting even hunger and physical pain. In like manner, the knower of Brahman takes his delight in the Atman, forgetting all thought of 'I' and 'mine'.

He gets his food easily by begging alms, without anxiety or care. He drinks from the clear stream. He lives unfettered and independent. He sleeps without fear in the forest or on the cremation-ground. He does not need to wash or dry his clothes, for he wears none. . . .

The knower of the Atman does not identify himself with his body. He rests within it, as if within a carriage . . .

The man of contemplation walks alone. He lives desireless amidst the objects of desire. The Atman is his eternal satisfaction. He sees the Atman present in all things.

Sometimes he appears to be a fool, sometimes a wise man. Sometimes he seems splendid as a king, sometimes feeble-minded. Sometimes he is calm and silent. Sometimes he draws men to him, as a python attracts its prey. Sometimes people honour him greatly, sometimes they insult him. Sometimes they ignore him. That is how the illumined soul lives, always absorbed in the highest bliss.[15]

This ideal of non-attachment is formally acknowledged by many Hindus. They crave for a wisdom of emotional disinvolvement consummated 'when one draws in, on every side, the sense-organs from the objects of sense as a tortoise draws in its limbs from every side'. Withdrawal is something they assume must be learned, by means of yoga, as a result of which 'one's properly controlled mind becomes steadfast within the Self alone' and one is freed from all desire and pain and enjoys supra-sensory bliss.[16]

In the classic system of Yoga, one arrives at the goal slowly. The goal is 'isolation' from anything material, incomplete, changing, or attractive. Such 'passionlessness is the consciousness of being master on the part of one who has rid himself of thirst for either seen or revealed objects—thirst for objects that are seen, such as women, food, drink, or power; thirst for objects revealed in the Vedas, such as heaven or its discarnate state'. The final means for arriving at this state is a graded series of forms of concentration on more and more subtle objects, ending in an indeterminate, supra-consciousness of self, for the mind with an imperceptible object is itself as if non-existent. Rid of all psychic 'fluctuations', whether they are the unconscious but powerful residues of experience in earlier lives or the conscious experiences of the present life, 'the Self's Energy of Thought becomes isolated, since it is grounded in itself. . . . Its continuance thus for evermore is Isolation.'[17]

Like believers in classic Yoga, the Jains and the Buddhists, whose religions developed simultaneously in India, accepted the ideal of detachment, though, with what consistency we need not now ask, they also stressed sympathy and helpfulness. Like the believers in Yoga, they held that life in its cycles of transmigration must always be painful. To the Jains, everything was inhabited by souls, so that mere existence was in every way the suffering and infliction of pain. They identified themselves, by means of what I should consider mystic self-extension, with every pain and all pain:

> Helpless in snares and traps, a deer
> I have been caught and bound and fastened, and often I have
>   been killed.
> A helpless fish, I have been caught with hooks and nets;
> An infinite number of times I have been killed and scraped,
>   split and gutted . . .
> A tree, with axes and adzes by the carpenters
> An infinite number of times I have been felled, stripped of my
>   bark, cut up, and sawn into planks.
> As iron, with hammer and tongs by blacksmiths
> An infinite number of times I have been struck and beaten, split
>   and filed . . .
> Ever afraid, trembling, in pain and suffering,
> I have felt the utmost sorrow and agony . . .
> In every kind of existence I have suffered
> Pains which have scarcely known reprieve for a moment.[18]

Such are the pains of the transmigratory life! The 'isolation' of pure happiness, infinite perception, and pure and infinite knowledge must be better.

The most stringent passionlessness was that, I think, aimed at by the Buddhists. I say 'stringent' because they so often refused to think of the ideal, Nirvana, as a state of bliss or consciousness or anything else. Simply and solely an ending, and yet not death, Nirvana is defined as 'the stopping of becoming', 'the getting rid of craving', 'the going out of the lamp', 'the going out of the flame'. At somewhat greater length and more picturesquely, it is characterized in this way:

Where is no-thing, where naught is grasped, this is the Isle of No-where. Nirvana do I call it—the utter extinction of ageing and dying.

As Ananda, Buddha's favourite pupil, is said to perceive:

This is the real, this the excellent, namely the calm of all the impulses, the casting out of all 'basis', the extinction of craving—dispassion, stopping, Nirvana.[19]

This is difficult to interpret and aroused endless disputes among the Buddhists themselves. Buddha, wisely, refrained from much interpretation, preferring, it is said, to heal than to engage in metaphysics. But we can explain the early Buddhists' Nirvana with some plausibility. As idealists of dispassion, self-conscious bliss appeared to them undesirable or impossible. If pain and desire were diminished, they thought, to the vanishing point, then the painful cycle of life and death and life again would be broken. This was a usual Indian approach; but the Buddhists showed unusual restraint in almost consistently refusing to say just what the vanishing point, Nirvana, might be. They could only say what it was not. The favourite initial image was the extinction of a flame. But the ancient Indians did not believe that a flame was ever either absolutely lit or absolutely extinguished. They thought that quiescent fire, a kind of essential fire, was present practically everywhere, but especially in inflammable substances. A flame when lit was simply fire become visible, and when extinguished, become invisible again. It is therefore plausible to suppose that an extinguished self was not, in the Buddhists' imagination, absolutely destroyed, but remained in some inexpressibly quiescent state. Certainly Nirvana, as freedom and dispassion, is not non-existent. In a later, scholastic work we read:

> According to ultimate meaning, Nirvana is the Ariyan Truth of the stopping of suffering. But because, when that—Nirvana—is reached, craving detaches itself, besides being stopped, it is therefore called Dispassion and it is called Stopping. And because, when it is reached, there is renunciation, and there does not remain even one sensory pleasure that is clung to, it is therefore called Renunciation, Surrender, Release, Lack of Clinging. . . . Because it is attainable by means of the special cognition perfected by unfailing effort, because it was spoken of by the Omniscient One, because it has existence in the ultimate meaning, Nirvana is not non-existent.

Yet though the most positive thing that could be said of Nirvana was that it had the flavour of peace or was not non-existent, there were Buddhists who thought that it might be compared or even identified with empty space. Nirvana and space are both supreme no-things, both eternal, omnipresent, and infinite, both luminous and calm and peace-inspiring; and Nirvana and space neither impede nor are impeded by anything, neither hurt nor are hurt by anything. Hence empty space may be nothing other than Nirvana.

Whatever the doctrinal difference, it is easy for the imagination to move from Nirvana as empty space to Nirvana as simple emptiness, and to say of the ideally dispassionate man, 'One who is convinced of the emptiness of everything has no likes or dislikes. For he knows that that which he might like is just empty, and he sees it as just empty.'[20]

The mystic state, then, is uninterrupted not non-existent emptiness.

The ideal of both passion and passionlessness, or of involvement in life that is also detachment from it, is not only more subtle than the others but, to my mind, more interesting (this is not an appraisal of the *truth* of any of the ideals). The attitude by which psychic opposites can be integrated suggests certain themes in modern philosophy and psychotherapy. It is characteristic of China, Japan, parts of India, and, in varying degrees, of the cultural tributaries of these countries.

In China, the most obvious early sources are the classic books of Taoism. There are signs in them of yogic-like breathing techniques and of great mystic 'awakenings', but the dominant emphasis is on an unforced participation in the rhythms of nature, as if man and nature are each the movement and the breath and the bones, blood, and flesh of one another. In this world of come and go, of harmonic oppositions, the ideal man does not wrench himself out of the natural context or need the artifice of evaluation or the goad of words:

> Something and Nothing produce each other;
> The difficult and the easy complement each other;
> The long and the short off-set each other;
> The high and the low incline towards each other;
> Note and sound harmonize each other;
> Before and after follow each other.

Therefore the sage keeps to the deed that consists in taking no action and practises the teaching that uses no words.[21]

The universe does not suffer, the Taoist says, from trying to do anything. It, so to speak, happens itself with perfect spontaneity, and he therefore describes it as the synthesis of inactions. He says:

I take inaction to be true happiness, but ordinary people think it is a bitter thing. I say: the highest happiness has no happiness, the highest praise has no praise. The world can't decide what is right and what is wrong. And yet inaction can decide this. The highest happiness, keeping alive—only inaction gets you close to this!

Let me try putting it this way. The inaction of Heaven is its purity, the inaction of earth is its peace. So the two inactions combine and all things are transformed and brought to birth. Wonderfully, mysteriously, there is no place they come out of. Mysteriously, wonderfully, they have no sign. Each thing minds its business and all grow up out of inaction. So I say, Heaven and earth do nothing and there is nothing that is not done. Among men, who can get hold of this inaction?

And who is the ideal, who the man that aims not at utility but life, the man who aims, without aiming, at exactly his own fate and nature? Who can be perfectly one and yet not one?

The True Man of ancient times knew nothing of loving life, knew nothing of hating death. He emerged without delight; he went back in without a fuss. He came briskly, he went briskly, and that was all. He didn't forget where he began; he didn't try to find out where he would end. He received something and took pleasure in it; he forgot about it and handed it back again. This is what I call not using the mind to repel the Way, not using man to help out Heaven. This is what I call the True Man.[22]

Unlike Shankara's ideal man, this man finds that keeping alive is the highest happiness. He walks *briskly*, he takes pleasure in what he receives; but he has neither hopes, demands on himself, nor regrets. Briskness, spontaneity, and all, this man is assimilated into Ch'an, that is, Zen Buddhism, which may be crudely described as the mingling of Buddhism with Taoism. We find the same elusive point, which is always somewhere else as long as we search for it too logically. It is neither here nor there:

'If you want to catch 'it' in the moving, it will go to the unmoving and if you want to catch 'it' in the unmoving, it will go to the moving. It is like a fish concealed in the water which it can stir into ripples through which to skim . . . The moving and unmoving are two kinds of state but the man of Tao can make use of both the moving and unmoving states.[23]

The Zen emphasis against detachment alone is particularly strong in Hakuin Zenji, the gifted, humane, and practical mystic who revitalized Japanese Zen in the eighteenth century. He tells us that he was misguided in his youth, when he thought that Buddhism required nothing other than keeping the mind in absolute calm. Calm meditation succeeded at first, but not for long. He writes:

On the very first day that I went into the mountains to study and practise meditation I made up my mind to be strenuous and bold in faith, and to work hard at carrying on the refining discipline of the Way. But after only two or three frosts had passed over me, suddenly one night I received an enlightening experience. The many doubts which I had felt up to this time were brought into harmony with the root principles of the inner spirit and they melted away like ice in water.

But there came a night, Hakuin says, when

those two conditions of life, activity and non-activity had become entirely out of harmony. The two inclinations in me towards finiteness and in-finity had become indistinct in my mind. I could not make up my mind to do or not to do. So that thought occurred to me that I would like to clothe myself in a lustrous glow and throw off my present life and depart from this world.

Finding myself in such a state of mind, I set my teeth, fixed my eyes clearly and determined to forgo sleep and food. But, before I had spent many months in that strenuous way my heart began to make me dizzy, my lungs became dry, my limbs felt as cold as if they were immersed in ice and snow. My ears were filled with the ringing as of the rushing waters of a swift river in a deep canyon. My inward organs felt weak and my whole body trembled with apprehensions and fears. My spirit was distressed and weary, and whether sleeping or waking I used continually to see all sorts of imaginary things, brought to me through my six senses. Both sides of my body were continually bathed in sweat, and my eyes were perpetually filled with tears.

The illness seemed hopeless; but Hakuin was told of a wise hermit, Haku-yu, who lived in a mountain cave. Hakuin found him there, sitting on a soft straw mat and staring straight ahead, his hair down to his knees, and his face 'ruddy and beautiful as the fruit of the jujube tree'. The hermit told Hakuin that he had been meditating too strenuously. Zen was the cure. 'When suddenly it starts working', he told him,

you will find yourself laughing. For surely meditation through non-meditation becomes true meditation. Too much meditation must be said to be heretical meditation. Sir, facing your previous over-meditation, you are now seeing these severe sicknesses. Now, in order to save yourself from these, it must be by non-meditation, do you not think so?'

In keeping with Chinese medical principles, Haku-yu explained that Hakuin's 'meditation sickness' had been caused by the rising of the vital heat to the upper part of the body and the resulting dangerous coldness of the lower part. To restore unity and to drive the 'heart-fire' down, Hakuin was told to abandon absolute meditation for a while and attend to breathing exercises, and to the relative meditation that fixes the mind on the protecting fire.

Hakuin took the hermit's advice. Within three years he was completely healed and also further advanced in his search for reality:

Not only were my illnesses healed, but also those things which are difficult to enter into or penetrate and which until then I had not been able to grasp with my hands or feet or get my teeth into—these things I now penetrated intuitively, right to their roots and to their depths. And I have experienced this joy six or seven times. And besides all this, I forgot how many times I have experienced the 'little vision', those joys which make one dance.[24]

In Zen training, Hakuin favoured the use of certain koans, that is, intractable riddles that increased tension up to the breaking point, the Great Doubt which, he thought, infallibly preceded enlightenment:

If a person is confronted with the Great Doubt, then in the four directions of heaven there is only wide, empty land, without birth and without death, like a plain of ice ten thousand miles in expanse, as if one sat in an emerald vase. Without there is bright coolness and white purity. As if devoid of all sense one forgets to rise when he is sitting, and forgets to sit down when he is standing. In his heart there remains no trace of passion or concept, only the word 'nothingness', as if he stood in the wide dome of heaven. He has neither fear nor knowledge. If one progresses in this fashion without retrogression, he will suddenly experience something similar to the breaking of an ice cover or the collapse of a crystal tower. The joy is so great that it has not been seen or heard for forty years.

Hakuin taught that there were no special abilities or circumstances needed to arrive at the Great Doubt, but only the right exercises practised with enough energy. He also taught that there were different stages of mystic insight. He knew this from experience. Once, for example, as he sat reading the *Lotus Sutra*, a favourite scriptural text, he grew aware of the humming of an insect. 'Suddenly', he says, 'I saw through the perfect true mystery (of the sutra) and broke through all initial doubts. I comprehended the error of my earlier greater or lesser enlightenments. Unexpectedly I called out and wept. One must realize that the practice of Zen is by no means easy.'[25]

Hakuin is remarkably candid. His candour of course opens a way for the sceptic, who might ask him what immediate certainty could ever, in itself, prove that no overriding certainty might not replace it some day, and so on ad infinitum. How Hakuin would have answered I do not know, but the very efforts he had made, the fears he had suffered, and the joys of illumination he had experienced, were no doubt enough to convince him. Of the difficulties of the search he says:

Whatever way one ventures along this way to the secret, bone-shaking, life-taking search—so hard to penetrate, too hard to explain—especially while one is still held by the karma of false ideas of ignorance and of the cycle of life and death, one cannot fail to be alarmed.

As a result of his experiences, Hakuin argues against the commitment of one's life to solitary meditation. He asks what would become of the world if princes, warriors, merchants, farmers, and artisans all did nothing but sit in meditation. He recalls that the early Zen masters used to haul stones, move soil, carry water, cut firewood, peel vegetables, and build. They sought inward strength, he says, within the 'way of activity', for their activity was their meditation. In this spirit, anyone's clothing are monk's robes, anyone's words are a meditation table, anyone's saddle a meditation cushion.

The hills, the streams, the plains will be the floor of your meditation hall. The four corners of the earth and its ten directions, the height and the depth of the universe will be to you the great 'cave' in which you are performing—they will be, in very truth, the substance of your real self.

In discriminating the absolute reality, Hakuin says, one must always allow the whole truth to dominate the two opposite states that it transcends. If one succeeds, the greatest of joys will come:

What is of absolute importance, is that the two states—activity and calm, order and contrariness, vertical and horizontal, must have the pure, unmixed, complete and whole truth in the forefront. It must be such, indeed, that even if one were surrounded by ten thousand people one would be as if one were dwelling alone in a wide open space of thousands of miles, and as the ancients said—'one's ears as if they were deaf, one's eyes as if they were blind'. Thus should it be all the time. This is the time which is called the season of sincere and real correctness and great doubt actually present. If, when that time comes, you do not go back, but deliberately go forward, then there will come to you such a joy as has not been seen in all the forty years of your life, nor will you have heard anything so joyous—it will be as if you had broken through a large pack of ice, or had breached a veritable fortress of precious stones.[26]

In spite of Hakuin's liberality, the involvement of Zen in life, or of life in Zen, remained limited, especially as regards sex and the family. Zen was centred on the ordinarily celibate monk. The Indian mysticism to which we now turn, the so-called 'Trika' of Kashmir, regarded sex, both as a symbol and in fact, as an essential means to awaken the absolute within men. Trika's sacred books go back as far, perhaps, as the beginning of the Christian era, while its greatest thinkers—for it was a philosophical mysticism—belong to the ninth and tenth centuries A.D.

The techniques used in Trika for mystical experience are drawn from a variety of Indian sources, and its metaphysics of reality and illusion is of a common Indian variety. What is less common is its combination of intellectuality, spontaneous emotion, love for life, and an acute psychological, aesthetic awareness.

The god of this mysticism is Shiva. Ultimately, he is the absolute beyond unity, difference, or both together. As in Shankara's philosophy, the absolute is regarded as pure self-consciousness, which is the same as pure joy. Consciousness in itself is also the light, lodged in our hearts, by which we see and know. Under the illusion that we are separate individuals, we decompose light prismatically into visible colours, we break up reality intellectually into fragments, we isolate things perceptually in space and time; and so we lose that perfect liberty native to self-consciousness, the truth that I am I and that besides me, who repose in my own self, there is nothing.

The truth is that we are all this I, which is Shiva, Shiva the radiant infinity against which the colours of prismatic illusion flicker on and off. Shiva is the painter who, with no brush or pigment, paints the universe on the wall of his own consciousness. He is the actor who plays every part in existence, so intensely, sometimes, that he forgets who he is. Shiva is the dancer who dances the universe, in harmony or in destructive violence. He is the lover enlaced with his goddess in an eternal act of love. He is the god of the third, fiery eye that projects felicity and consumes duality. He is the ascetic who burns the god of carnal love to ashes. And Shiva is his own terrifyingly naked self absorbed in his primordial absoluteness.

To know this Shiva, who is hiding from himself in order to enjoy the cosmic game he is playing, we do not need to go any further than ourselves:

There is neither You nor I, neither contemplated nor contemplation, but only the creator of the universe who is lost in self-forgetfulness.[27]

To know ourselves as Shiva we need sensitivity and vitality enough to enter into every experience at its most extreme or spontaneous, so that we *become* that experience and move, as it were, in a single vibration. Penetration to the real is by means of paroxysm, intensity, and the confusion of boundaries. We penetrate to it in the paroxysm of love, the paroxysm of sneezing, and the paroxysm of terror. The shudder at the edge of the precipice, the pang of anxiety or of hunger, the stir of curiosity, the shock of recognition, the stagger of exhaustion, all cause that sudden influx of virility that unifies our consciousness. Even seeing something new may cause it, or hearing good or bad news. It comes at the moment of freedom, when the sperm is ejaculated or speech is released. It can come too in uninterrupted concentration, as when we fix our eyes intently on something, such as the cloudless sky. Memory can bring it, as when a man recalls intensely the pleasure aroused by the kisses, caresses, and embraces of a woman. It can be born of art, as when a man identifies himself completely with the music he is hearing, though he must be the kind of man who can rise above aesthetic to mystical pleasure. Confusion of a sort may help. For example, if one recites a poem too quickly for the thought to follow the words, one remains momentarily suspended between concept and intuition, and this suspension may bring on the mystic experience. Likewise the moment of falling asleep that confuses without effacing the difference between self and world may bring it on.

The mystic experience begins, then, in our spontaneous self-unification. Suddenly, the usual thread of psychic continuity may snap and one's egoistic preoccupation and consciousness disappear. The ecstatic instant ends, and one falls back empty, desireless. One is in a void between past and future, in the pure, timeless present where subject and object are no longer two. The ordinary man allows this precious void to pass; but the truly lucid man continues to live in it, for it is the energy of all being, and he lives on in a more-than-human intensity of self-consciousness.

In this mysticism there is no revulsion from ordinary life. The lover is regarded as having a great advantage over the Yogin. The Yogin has to struggle to maintain his concentration, while the lover keeps his mind on love-making without the least effort. Yoga, asceticism, ceremonial, and the other usual religious methods are condemned as separating men from Shiva, 'because even in usual affairs (purchases, sales, etc.), the Lord by his free will enters into a body and manifests as external the objects which shine within him. The functions which he displays in the cosmos (creation, grace, etc.) are the same as those he exercises in the course of ordinary or artistic life.'

Therefore walking, eating, and going about one's ordinary business are all, for the liberated person, the same immortal pleasure. The liberated person will never be reborn. He is all-powerful, for, as he knows, reality is made by his thought just as the dream is made by the dreamer. 'All the realities of the universe which he wrongly took for limitation will appear to him thereafter as the overflowing play of innate joy' and the expansive freedom of his consciousness. Because everything is the same undifferentiated plenitude, he no longer cares for anything—clothing, food, or place—in particular. He is and acts free. His worship is that given in the temple of his own body; his sacrifice is duality and its seeds.[28]

Resembling, and perhaps including the Trika mysticism of Kashmir, but often more inclined to magic and more profuse in its symbolism and extreme in its techniques, there is what is loosely known as Tantrism. The holy books of Tantrism are, as usual with holy books in India, supposed to be eternal. Their language is veiled, for they transmit esoteric traditions into which one must be initiated, with every precaution, by the right teacher. The aim of their symbolism and ritual is transcendental experience. The ritual union of male and female is generally supposed to grant it, provided that breath, thought, and semen can be held 'immobile'.

One of the principles common to Tantrism is that 'perfection can be attained by satisfying all one's desires'.[29] It is also often supposed that one can learn to become dispassionate by indulging in passion so as to turn it, by one's attitude, against itself:

A man who is poisoned may be cured by another poison, the antidote. Water in the ear is removed by more water, a thorn in the skin by another thorn. So wise men rid themselves of passion by yet more passion. As a washerman uses dirt to wash clean a garment, so, with impurity, the wise man makes himself pure.[30]

When 'more passion' means wine and meat, only abstainers are likely to be disturbed. The use of sexual ritual and of women regarded as low may go further; and the recommendations sometimes found to eat excrement and commit incest go far enough to disturb almost anyone, as is no doubt relevant to their purpose. All of the recommended extremes have been practised at times. But Tantric rituals are often accomplished in the mind rather than in fact, so the mere language of a text may not suffice to tell its reader, even if he understands it, what actually was done. In any case, salvation was supposed to come by means of the body.

One of the important figures of Tantrism in its Buddhist form is Saraha, or Rahulabhadra, who lived about the seventh century A.D. A Brahmin by birth, he lost caste because he drank and lived with a low-caste woman. It is said that he recognized her at first glance as his predestined, holy partner, for she, the arrow-maker's daughter, was able to guide him 'in respect of the nature of things'. He took up arrow-making himself and wandered through many lands with her. 'As his wisdom grew steadily, he received the name of Saraha, or "he who hits with the arrow".'[31]

Saraha is worth recalling here because his mystical couplets have been preserved. In these couplets, he mocks at the Brahmins with their prayers and offerings, at the money-hungry, ash-smeared ascetics, and at the dirty Jains, whose holy nakedness is as effective as the nakedness of a dog. The Yogins concentrate and squint at the ends of their noses, and the ordinary Buddhists wither away in concentration, meditate on sacred diagrams, and try to define the indefinable Nirvana. These acts are all defiling, he says. 'Do not defile in contemplation thought that is pure in its own nature, but abide in the bliss of yourself and cease these torments. Eat and drink, indulge the senses, fill the mandala with offerings, by things like these you'll gain the world beyond.' He says:

Look and listen, touch and eat, smell, wander, sit and stand, renounce the vanity of discussion, abandon thought and be not moved from single-ness. . . . Abandon thought and thinking and be just as a child. . . . Enjoy-ing the world of sense, one is undefiled by the world of sense. One plucks the lotus without touching the water. So the yogin who has gone to the root of things, is not enslaved by the senses although he enjoys them.

In the state of highest bliss, says Saraha, there is no beginning, middle, or end, no cycle of birth and death, no Nirvana, no self and no other. 'Wherever you see it, that is it, in front, behind, in all the ten directions.' One holds one's thought and breath immobile and 'now it is a matter of self-experience, so do not err with regard to it. To call it existence or non-existence or even stage of bliss would impose a limitation.' In this great bliss 'all forms are endowed with the sameness of space, and the mind is held steady', ceases to be mind, and the Innate shines forth.

Saraha wonders at the great effect of the woman, the ritual partner, who consumes the mind till neither passion nor absence of passion is left. Here the man's opposite natures lose their difference, he comprehends that everything is of his own nature and at the moment of the embrace wins the great bliss. 'When the sun of suffering has set, then arises this bliss, this lord of the stars.'[32]

Orthodox Buddhists would say, of course, that to eat and drink, indulge the senses, and lie with a woman in ritual embraces, could bring only misery and rebirth. Saraha's disciple repeats this argument and then answers:

This is true, but only in so far as those who have no spiritual friends or advisers are concerned. By indulging in passion and other emotional outbursts they will surely suffer . . . But he who is utterly loveless will suffer much more, because he hates love. It is for such people that passion-love has been taught . . .

'And Saraha declared: Some are fettered by renouncing things; others by these same things gain unsurpassable enlightenment.'

Therefore, to induce passionate people to be dispassionate, to teach loveless people passion-play as a mediator, and to bring people who have passion-love as a mediator to genuine love, this unsurpassable and extremely profound teaching of 'transcending awareness in and through discrimination and appreciation' is given to highly developed beings.[33]

From 'passion-play' one goes to its purely spiritual analogue, and from there to the final 'instantaneous awakening to Buddhahood', in which all veils of instability and wrong belief have been torn and the 'immaculate effect' revealed.

3

Personal and Pragmatic Defences of Mysticism

Having surveyed a few kinds of mystical ideals, we can begin to explore the defences of mysticism in general. It is best to avoid the systematic, abstract defences for a while, and to turn instead to the personal experience that lies behind them and that motivates the first and most candid ventures into argument. A mystic who remains intellectually alert, will accompany his emotional experience, as we may non-committally call it, by persistent reasoning. He will ask himself whether his mystical experience is no more than a terribly persuasive illusion, he will reflect on the consequences of its truth or illusoriness, he will compare it with the experiences of other mystics, and he will try to persuade at least his intimates that he has become aware of a precious reality to which they are still blind. He engages, that is, in self-persuasion and the persuasion of others at the same time.

This process of persuasion and self-persuasion takes the natural form of a biography or autobiography. Rather than put the arguments in my own way, I should therefore prefer to rely upon two unusually instructive examples, the one, going back to the late eleventh century, of the Moslem theologian, al-Ghazali, and the other, almost contemporary, of William James. Both men make excellent examples because they were well-educated in the conventional sense and yet continued to educate themselves out of an almost unrestrained curiosity; because they were both intelligent and sensitive and had mastered the technical philosophy and much of the science of their times; because they underwent personal crises to which mystical experience and conviction, or what verged on these, provided the cure; and because they were gifted writers who related their convictions to their personal experience in a way that allows us to see them realistically and to judge them fairly enough.

Al-Ghazali owes his importance in Moslem life to his ability to create a viable union of dogma, reason, and emotion. Thanks to him, it became easier for Moslems to infuse their traditional practices with Sufi warmth, and easier, conversely, for Sufis to feel at home in orthodox tradition.

Our interest here in al-Ghazali is of course in his mystical experience and in his arguments for the validity of mysticism. Our source is his *Deliverance from Error*, a schematic autobiography in which he intersperses an account of his spiritual development with various defences of his position at the time he wrote the book. He begins by telling how he went from orthodoxy to a painful but concealed scepticism. The process began, he tells us, out of an overpowering intellectual venturesomeness. He poked and pried because he could not help himself. He says:

To thirst after a comprehension of things as they really are was my habit and custom from a very early age. It was instinctive with me, a part of my God-given nature, a matter of temperament and not of my choice or contriving. Consequently as I drew near the age of adolescence the bonds of mere authority ceased to hold me and inherited beliefs lost their grip upon me, for I saw that Christian youths always grew up to be Christians, Jewish youths to be Jews and Muslim youths to be Muslims. I heard, too, the Tradition related of the Prophet of God according to which he said: 'Everyone who is born is born with a second nature; it is his parents who make him a Jew or a Christian or a Magian.' My inmost being was moved to discover what this original nature really was and what the beliefs derived from the authority of parents and teachers really were. . . .

I therefore said within myself: 'To begin with, what I am looking for is knowledge of what things really are, so I must undoubtedly try to find what knowledge really is.' It was plain to me that sure and certain knowledge is that knowledge in which the object is disclosed in such a fashion that no doubt remains along with it, that no possibility of error or illusion accompanies it, and that the mind cannot even entertain such a supposition.

Having thought the matter over, al-Ghazali decided that he could be sure only of direct sense-perception and of obviously necessary truths, such as those of mathematics. With a gleam of humour, he supposed that someone, in order to persuade him that three was more than ten, transformed a stick into a snake before his very eyes. But that bit of magic has nothing to do with the relationship between the numbers three and ten, and all it could do was to arouse his wonder about the turning of sticks into snakes.

So far, so sure; but the serpent of doubt insinuated itself into his certainties. Once he had believed many things that he now knew to be untrustworthy. Could the senses really be trusted? The most powerful of them was sight, yet he learned that though the shadow on a sundial seems motionless, it must in fact be moving slowly and steadily by imperceptible distances. And the sun, which looks about the size of a coin, could be proved, by geometrical computation, to be larger than the earth. He saw that the sense made its judgment, but that another judge, the intellect, overruled it repeatedly and irrefutably.

Al-Ghazali's doubt then spread to intellectual principles. It was not that he could deny that ten is more than three, or deny the basic principles of logic. It was only that he had learned that the fact that a judge appeared trustworthy did not make him so. Perhaps behind the intellect there was another judge who could overrule it just as the intellect had overruled sense-perception.

Al-Ghazali hesitated. But sense-perception, with the jealousy of a discarded favourite, pressed him and reminded him that dreams are discovered to be unfounded and ineffectual only when we wake up. Maybe, it suggested, men were as if dreaming relative to a state they had not yet entered. It said to him:

It is possible that a state will come upon you whose relation to your waking consciousness is analogous to the relation of the latter to dreaming. In comparison with this state your waking consciousness would be like dreaming! When you have entered into this state, you will be certain that all the suppositions of your intellect are empty imaginings. It may be that that state is what the Sufis claim as their special 'state', for they consider that in their 'states' (or ecstasies), which occur when they have withdrawn into themselves and are absent from their senses, they witness states (or circumstances) which do not tally with these principles of the intellect. Perhaps that 'state' is death; for the Messenger of God (God bless and preserve him) says: 'The people are dreaming; when they die, they become awake.' So perhaps life in this world is a dream by comparison with the world to come; and when a man dies, things come to appear differently from what he now beholds. . . .*

Al-Ghazali tried to repel these thoughts but could not, for in order to repel them he would have had to assume the very principles of demonstration that were being put in doubt. It was, he says, a baffling disease that lasted almost two months, during which he was a sceptic in fact though not in theory or outward expression. But then, he tells us, God cured him, his being was restored to health and an even balance, and he regained his confidence in the certainty of the basic principles of the intellect. He says:

This did not come about by systematic demonstration or marshalled argument, but by a light which God most high cast into my breast. That light is the key to the greater part of knowledge. Whoever thinks that the understanding of things Divine rests upon strict proofs has in this thought narrowed down the wideness of God's mercy.

At this point, al-Ghazali said to himself that he could no longer return to the level of naïve and derivative belief. He investigated orthodox theology and found it inadequate. Then, during solitary hours snatched from his work, for he was engaged in teaching over three hundred students in the religious sciences, he taught himself philosophy. He found that not only did the philosophers disagree with one another, but that they were essentially irreligious.

By the conceptions then current, philosophy was taken to include mathematics, logic, natural science or physics, theology or meta-physics, politics, and ethics. Mathematics, al-Ghazali agreed, made genuine demonstrations and, once grasped, was impossible to deny. But the clarity and cogency of mathematics created a problem. The student of mathematics was led to assume that all the philo-

---

* A humorous Chinese equivalent, in Chuang Tzu, compares the present life to that of a girl who weeps despairingly when a king takes her captive, but who repents her tears when she discovers the pleasures of his bed and the luxuries of his palace. How do we know that we shall not one day wake up and repent our craving for the unroyal life we now lead?

sophers' sciences were equally clear and cogent, and, knowing that the philosophers despised revealed truth, he too rejected it out of confidence in these mentors.

The truth is, that accomplishments are usually specialized:

It is not necessary that the man who excels in law and theology should excel in medicine, nor that the man who is ignorant of intellectual speculations should be ignorant of grammar. Rather, every art has people who have obtained excellence and pre-eminence in it, even though stupidity and ignorance may characterize them in other arts. The arguments in elementary matters of mathematics are demonstrative, whereas those in theology (or metaphysics) are based on conjecture. This point is familiar only to those who have studied the matter deeply for themselves.

The truth is that mathematics is irrelevant to religion. It is powerless to attack Islam, just as Islam cannot be defended by means of a denial of the mathematical sciences. Logic too, which is the study of formal methods of demonstration, is irrelevant, that is, in itself it denies or affirms nothing of religion. As in the case of mathematics, however, its practitioners may be admired blindly and their opinions accepted in the field of religion, where their standards of proof are decidedly relaxed. The general difficulty is that people with less intellectual ability, who cannot judge for themselves, 'take the men as criterion of the truth and not the truth as criterion of the men'.

Al-Ghazali, having tested all the other positions and found them wanting, turned to Sufism. He studied it and found it comprehensible. 'It became clear to me, however,' he says,

that what is most distinctive of mysticism is something which cannot be apprehended by study, but only by immediate experience (*dhawq*—literally 'tasting'), by ecstasy and by a moral change. What a difference there is between knowing the definition of health and satiety, together with their causes and presuppositions, and *being* healthy and satisfied? What a difference between being acquainted with the definition of drunkenness— namely, that it designates a state arising from the domination of the seat of the intellect by vapours arising from the stomach—and being drunk! . . . Again, the doctor, when he is himself ill, knows the definition and causes of health and the remedies which restore it, and yet is lacking in health . . .

I apprehended clearly that the mystics were men who had real experiences, not men of words, and that I had already progressed as far as was possible by way of intellectual apprehension. What remained for me was not to be attained by oral instruction and study but only by immediate experience and by walking in the mystic way.

Al-Ghazali saw that he would have to become more selfless, and that nothing he was doing, even his teaching, was contributing to the attainment of eternal life. His motive in teaching, he realized, was the desire for an influential position and public recognition. He saw before him the fires of hell. He found himself in a quandary, one day deciding to leave Baghdad and his public life, and the next day reversing his decision. He put, he says, one foot forward and drew the other back. Now the crisis was upon him:

For nearly six months beginning with Rajab 488 A.H. (=July A.D. 1095), I was continuously tossed about between the attractions of worldly desires and the impulses towards eternal life. In that month the matter ceased to be one of choice and became one of compulsion. God caused my tongue to dry up so that I was prevented from lecturing. One particular day I would make an effort to lecture in order to gratify the hearts of my following, but my tongue would not utter a single word nor could I accomplish anything at all.

This impediment in my speech produced grief in my heart, and at the same time my power to digest and assimilate food and drink was impaired; I could hardly swallow or digest a single mouthful of food. My powers became so weakened that the doctors gave up all hope of successful treatment. 'This trouble arises from the heart,' they said, 'and from there it has spread through the constitution; the only method of treatment is that the anxiety which has come over the heart should be allayed.'

Al-Ghazali decided to turn away from everything he had, position, wealth, family, and friends. Keeping only a little for himself and his children, he distributed most of his property to others. He travelled secretly to Damascus, where for two years he lived in solitude, occupied with religious and ascetic exercises. Sometimes he would shut himself up, alone, for a whole day in the minaret of the mosque. He went to Jerusalem, where he lived similarly. He made the pilgrimage to Mecca. Finally, his children's entreaties and 'various concerns' drew him back home, where anxieties about his family and the necessities of his livelihood impaired, he says, the quality of his solitude and allowed him to experience pure ecstasy only at times. In his own words:

I continued at this stage for the space of ten years, and during these periods of solitude there were revealed to me things innumerable and unfathomable. This much I shall say about that in order that others may be helped: I learned with certainty that it is above all the mystics who walk on the road of God; their life is the best life, their method the soundest method, their character the purest character; indeed, were the intellect of the intellectuals and the learning of the learned and the scholarship of the scholars, who are versed in the profundities of revealed truth, brought together in the attempt to improve the life and character of the mystics, they would find no way of doing so; for to the mystics all movement and all rest, whether external or internal, brings illumination from the light of the lamp of prophetic revelation; and behind the light of prophetic revelation there is no other light on the face of the earth from which illumination may be received.

He who goes on the mystic way must sink his heart completely in the recollection of God. This is the beginning of the way.

With this first stage of the way there begin the revelations and visions. The mystics in their waking state now behold angels and the spirits of the prophets; they hear these speaking to them and are instructed by them. Later, a higher state is reached; instead of beholding forms and figures, they come to stages in the way which it is hard to describe in language; if a man attempts to express these, his words inevitably contain what is clearly erroneous. . . .

Now this is a mystical 'state' which is realized in immediate experience by those who walk in the way leading to it. Those to whom it is not granted to have immediate experience can become assured of it by trial (*i.e.*, contact with mystics or observation of them) and by hearsay, if they have sufficiently numerous opportunities of associating with mystics to understand that (*i.e.* ecstasy) with certainty by means of what accompanies the 'states.' Whoever sits in their company derives from them this faith; and none who sits in their company is pained.

But though the possibility of mystical experience can be rationally demonstrated, known by immediate experience, and accepted on faith, the ignorant deny all this, 'they are astonished at this line of thought, they listen and mock. "Amazing," they say. "What non-sense they talk!" ' God has made these people deaf and blind.

We may finish here with al-Ghazali's narrative; but his arguments are not completed. He tends to equate mystical experience with prophetic revelation, the basis of Islam. He argues again that there is a stage beyond the intellectual. Remember, he says, the nature of perception. By touch, we perceive heat and cold, roughness and smoothness, moisture and dryness; but not colours or noises. So far as touch goes, these might not exist. By sight, we sense colours and shapes; by hearing, all the various sounds. Add taste, and the world of sensible things is completed. At about the age of seven, the child begins to discern relationships, which are beyond mere sensation. Then he comes to think with explicit logic and grasp that which is necessary, or possible, or impossible. He is at the stage of intellect; but there is still another, that of prophecy, 'in which there is an eye endowed with light such that in that light the unseen and other supra-intellectual objects become visible'. But just as the child who discerns nothing beyond relationships might disregard and reject the objects of the intellect, so some intellectuals disregard and reject the objects of prophetic revelations. Because they have not reached this stage, they suppose that it does not exist. 'When a man blind from birth, who has not learned about colours and shapes by listening to people's talk, is told about these things for the first time, he does not understand them nor admit their existence.' But he who has some mystical experience finds it easier to have faith in the principle of prophecy, which reason cannot apprehend any more than hearing can apprehend colours, sight apprehend sounds, or all the senses apprehend the objects of reason.

The intellect, al-Ghazali insists, is at ease only with familiar things and arrogant towards all that does not fit its preconceptions. Experience teaches us that a few grains of opium make a deadly poison that freezes the blood 'through its excess of cold'. A physicist who has not made the experiment and who is equipped with no more than the usual scientific concepts would say that opium cannot do what in fact it does, and he would give his theoretical proof of the impossibility. Philosophers, of whom al-Ghazali's physicist is one, suppose impossible anything they are not familiar with. If you say to a philosopher, ' "Is it possible for there to be in the world a thing, the size of a grain, which, if placed in a town, will consume that town in its entirety and then consume itself, so that nothing is left of the town and what it contained nor of the thing itself?"; he would say, "This is absurd; it is an old wives' tale." Yet this is the case with fire, although, when he heard it, someone who had no acquaintance with fire would reject it. The rejection of the strange features of the world to come usually belongs to this class.' Everything is in a sense surprising, miraculous, but the philosophers insulate themselves against the unknown and measure the enormous, incredible shape of the universe with their own short and rigid intellects.[1]

There is much in al-Ghazali's contentions to which we cannot now respond. There is, first, his belief in purely Moslem dogma. His visions confirm Moslem truths as such, but this confirmation, which lends him strength in his own culture, is a weakness outside of it. There is, then, the matter of his mental and physical disturbance, which invites a psychiatric explanation, but this kind of response we defer, in order to meet his contentions, as far as possible, on their own level. There is also the immediacy of mystic experience, the 'taste' al-Ghazali speaks of, which we leave for later consideration because, while it is essential to all mysticism, it requires factual preliminaries before anything useful can be said about it.

We are left with a few reasonable points and one persuasive but unsound argument. His reasonable points are, I take it, truisms, if not in his own time, then certainly by now. It is true, as al-Ghazali says, that we often follow eminent men from the fields of their eminence to contiguous ones, and then to the distant. Their ability has a resonance that is difficult to escape, and so we follow men instead of reasons. But al-Ghazali also asks us, and this too is a resonance difficult to escape, to believe in the mystics' insights because their characters are impressive and their conduct noble.

Al-Ghazali is also right, and it has also become a truism, that mathematics and logic, however they may be used to support or clarify arguments, are not in themselves relevant to the truth of mysticism. As for science in general, I think and shall try to show that it has some relevance, but only when it is empirical and therefore relatively inexact.

It is true, furthermore, as al-Ghazali says, that men tend to be blinded to whatever escapes the meshes of their favourite abstractions. Al-Ghazali stresses this blindness so as to favour the possibility of supra-intellectual revelation, which the philosophers he knew denied, he thought. Mostly he puts what might be called 'the argument of the third eye', the third eye of which Indian mystics speak, or the third in al-Ghazali's progression, which goes from the sensory, to the intellectual, to the supra-intellectual eye.

The argument of the third eye, a favourite among mystics, is the one I have called persuasive but unsound. There are times, in ordinary experience, when we make natural miscalculations. Experience teaches us how to use the evidence that it presents. We learn that a stick in water looks but is not crooked, as we learn that what is black in the near-darkness may be red in the light, or as we learn that something large may not be as heavy as something small. But in ordinary experience the testimony of any one sense does not on the whole contradict that of any other, nor do the senses on the whole contradict the 'discernment', as al-Ghazali calls it, of relations or the conclusions of the intellect. The senses and the intellect influence and supplement one another in an extraordinarily subtle, complex way. Together, they slowly constitute a coherent world for each and all of us. The normal human world is a cumulative accomplishment. It includes the blind, the deaf, and the dumb. We know that a person blind from birth learns to get along by means of touch and hearing. I shall later say that space is not the same to him as to others, and yet in the gross, practical sense, it is just about the same, and he and we live in the single space in which we walk about and meet and sometimes bump. The man blind from birth can learn to make rather realistic sculptures. If it is not right to suppose that he sees with his fingers, it is right that his fingers feel and his mind assimilates the same textures and volumes that our eyes see. Obviously, his fingers cannot make out colours as such. But blind scientists might well arrive at a structural equivalent of light and colour, just as scientists who do see discover invisible radiations. There are, after all, plenty of clues to light and colour in heat, transparency, degrees of reflectivity—in everything that a scientific instrument as well as another sense might make perceptible to the blind. Attempts are being made, and are in principle certainly possible, to create an instrument that will read print to a blind man, and an instrument might be constructed—for all I know it may already exist—to read colours aloud as musical tones. In any case, the mystic's analogy between his presumed insight and the presence of a sense lacking to others is unsatisfying because this sense would apparently not complete but negate the testimony of all the others, an unprecedented situation which all our ordinary experience cannot serve to make likely.

What I have said is true for the usual mystic claim that all ordinary experience is 'unreal'. A modified claim, which is all that al-Ghazali seems at times to make, but which is not adequate for Sufism, that mystical experience merely corrects or adds to ordinary experience would not be as unprecedented. But mystics tend towards absolutism rather than a modest and coherent 'correction' hypothesis. In a peculiar and, I think, unsatisfactory way, the correction hypothesis is present in some forms, which have been and will be referred to, of Hindu and Buddhist mysticism. But we must stop the third-eye argument before it engulfs us.

Unlike al-Ghazali, William James did not accept any detailed religious tradition. But James, too, passed through a crisis of doubt and illness and emerged with faith and with a defence of mystical attitudes. The physical illnesses, neurosis, and hypochondria of his young manhood reached the critical point in the hallucination he reported in *The Varieties of Religious Experience*. Attributed to an anonymous Frenchman, the hallucination was the image of a greenish epileptic idiot he had seen in an asylum. James's own sudden terror joined the image. In his own words:

That shape am I, I felt, potentially. Nothing that I possess can defend me against that fate, if the hour for it should strike for me as it struck for him. There was such a perception of my merely momentary discrepancy from him, that it was as if something hitherto solid within my breast gave way entirely, and I became a mass of quivering fear. After this the universe was changed for me altogether. I awoke morning after morning with a horrible dread in the pit of my stomach, and with a sense of the insecurity of life that I never knew before, and that I have never felt since. It was like a revelation; and although the immediate feelings passed away, the experience has made me sympathetic with the morbid feelings of others ever since. It gradually faded, but for months I was unable to go out into the dark alone.

In general I dreaded to be left alone. I remember wondering how other people could live, how I myself had ever lived, so unconscious of the pit of insecurity beneath the surface of life. My mother in particular, a very cheerful person, seemed to me a perfect paradox in her unconsciousness of danger, which you may well believe I was very careful not to disturb by revelations of my own state of mind. I have always thought that this experience of melancholia of mine had a religious bearing.[2]

Interestingly, James's crisis resembled an earlier one his father had undergone. James, we know, recovered. He remembered the moment at which his recovery began, when he determined that his will was free and that, believing so, he could help himself. His father described the transformation in a letter:

He came in here the other afternoon when I was sitting alone, and after walking the floor in an animated way for a moment, exclaimed 'Dear Me!' what a difference there is between me now and last spring this time: then so hypochondriacal' (he used that word, though perhaps in substantive form) 'and now feeling my mind so cleared up and restored to sanity. It is the difference between death and life.' He had a great effusion. I was afraid of interfering with it, or possibly checking it, but I ventured to ask what specially in his opinion had promoted the change. He said several things: the reading of Renouvier (specially his vindication of the freedom of the will) and Wordsworth, whom he has been feeding upon for a good while; but especially his having given up the notion that all mental disorder required to have a physical basis. This had become perfectly untrue to him. He saw that mind did act irrespective of material coercion, and could be dealt with therefore at first-hand, and this was health to his bones. It was a splendid confession, and though I knew the change had taken place, from unerring signs, I never was more delighted than to hear it from his own lips and so unreservedly.[3]

James entered a long period of relatively good health. Though energetic and prolific, he was still rather a hypochondriac, and, as his biographer writes, 'There was always a ghost or a premonition of disability.'[4] He was by nature mercurial, distractible, and subject to crises and dramatic regenerations. He did not regard himself as a mystic. In *The Varieties of Religious Experience* he wrote, 'Whether my treatment of mystical states will shed more light or darkness, I do not know, for my own constitution shuts me out from their enjoyment almost entirely, and I can speak of them only at second hand.'[5] He said he had no more than a 'mystical germ', and towards the end of his life he made himself out to be a defender of mysticism out of sportsmanship. 'I think', he wrote, 'you overdo my personal mysticism. It has always seemed to me rather a matter of fair play to the various kinds of experience to let mystical ecstasy have its voice counted with the rest.'[6]

But James did describe a number of 'abnormal' experiences of his own, and it is hard to resist the conclusion that they at least helped to make him favour mysticism. Otherwise, why should he have attacked 'articulate reason' for its inability to translate into words 'a kind of experience in which intellect, feeling and will, all our consciousness and all our subconsciousness together melt in a kind of chemical fusion'?[7] His 'over-belief', as he called it, was clearly mystical. He said:

The further limits of our being plunge, it seems to me, into an altogether other dimension of existence from the sensible and merely 'understandable' world. Name it the mystical region, or the supernatural region, whichever you choose. So far as our ideal impulses originate in this region (and most of them do originate in it, for we find them possessing us in a way for which we cannot articulately account), we belong to it in a more intimate sense than that in which we belong to the visible world, for we belong in the most intimate sense wherever our ideals belong. Yet the unseen region in question is not merely ideal, for it produces effects in this world. When we commune with it, work is actually done upon our finite personality, for we are turned into new men, and consequences in the way of conduct follow in the natural world upon our regenerative change. But that which produces effects within another reality must be termed a reality itself, so I feel as if we had no philosophic excuse for calling the unseen or mystical world unreal.[8]

William James really believed that 'there is a continuum of cosmic consciousness, against which our individuality builds its accidental fences, and into which our several minds plunge as into a mother-sea or reservoir'.[9] But though he thought that 'mystical states may possibly be . . . windows through which the mind looks out upon a more extensive and inclusive world', he took the cautious position, not typical of mystics, that mystical states do not contradict ordinary experience and do not free us from the liability to error, for, 'as a rule, mystical states merely add a supersensuous meaning to the ordinary outward data of consciousness. They are excitements like the emotions of love or ambition, gifts to our spirit by means of which facts already objectively before us fall into a new expressiveness and make a new connection with our active life. They do not contradict these facts as such, or deny anything that our senses have immediately seized.'[10]

To the experiences which tempted him to believe in mysticism, James added the pragmatic arguments typical of his philosophy. Properly understood, he claimed, all our thinking is aimed at helping us to succeed in life, by which he also meant to succeed in fostering our higher values. The truth of ideas is nothing other than their effectiveness. When ideas can be tested scientifically, they should be, for science gives us the most rigorous methods for testing effectiveness. But there are ideas that are neither testable nor trivial, ideas that sustain the life of at least the 'tender-minded' among us. The tender-minded must believe that there is something in the universe, something perhaps itself limited and fallible, that sustains human values. Much like a scientific theory, this fundamental optimism is proved by its results. It can make the difference, as James knew from his own life, between health and illness, between a vegetative dependence and an active humanity. Its truth is the conclusion drawn from the long experiment which is an individual human existence. If a man lost in a blizzard believes that he can save himself, he will keep moving and increase his chances for survival, and so his will to believe may justify itself.* If a man lost in life finds himself by means of a mystical faith, that faith justifies its own content; nothing else can.

---

* Rumi says, 'Expectation is a wing, and the stronger the wing the longer the flight' (*Discourses of Rumi*, pp. 87–8).

Like those of al-Ghazali, the arguments of William James are candid
and simple. He does not conceal his personal involvement in them,
and yet he draws extensively on the experiences of others. Again,
I refrain from a purely psychiatric reaction, though I cannot resist
pointing out the obvious—that James relived his father's crisis and
regarded it as a mission to 'understand a little more of the value and
meaning of religion in Father's sense' and 'to help it to its rights'
in the eyes of uncomprehending people.[11] His sportsmanship was
in his father's behalf, just as his incomplete surrender to mysticism
was, I suspect, the degree of freedom he retained from his father's
influence. It is also striking that James, who was so surprised by
his mother's unconsciousness of danger, should find his own safety
in a 'mother-sea' of cosmic consciousness.

James did not suppose that his arguments were coercive, but he
may not have realized how weak they in fact are and how little fit
to persuade anyone who is not already persuaded. The cases he cites
are interesting, but the accumulation of more and more evidence
does not improve its quality if it is doubtful to begin with. That many
people have had mystical experiences we know beyond the shadow
of a doubt; but, as should become especially clear in the discussion
of psychosis, the frequency and 'certainty' of such experiences
cannot demonstrate their truth or have the cumulative force of
inductive evidence. From the standpoint of inductive reasoning,
James's worst failure is his lack of serious interest in negative
instances, such as, cheerful, active, humane persons without his
faith in a cosmic consciousness. Is there any good evidence that the
degree of one's immersion in the 'mother-sea' is directly propor-
tionate to one's optimism or decency? Granted the characterization
of mysticism that we have accepted, I see no reason to believe that
there should be a larger number of generous than selfish mystics,
nor should I be surprised to find as many mystical scoundrels as
mystical saints. As for peace of mind, the mystic finds it, but sometimes only fitfully, and always, I should think, after a depth of
suffering that the non-mystic may never have to undergo.

James thinks that the helpfulness of a belief may be equivalent
to its truth. But it is psychologically impossible to accept a belief
in full consciousness only on the grounds that the belief is helpful.

In relation to himself, James was rationalizing—he believed as much as he did because he could not help himself, and his pragmatic defence is wilful and could easily be reversed, as it was, approximately, by John Dewey. How can we lift ourselves by our own belief-straps?

As far as the evidence goes, James's saving faith may as easily have been the result of some shift in psychic balance as its cause. There was, as usual, a long subterranean preparation for it. I say this not at all in derogation, for we are all streaked with irrationality, but to point out that James's reasoning was indecisive. All he really tells us is that in certain men vital optimism accompanies a mystical faith.

4

Logical and Metaphysical Defences of Mysticism

So far, the arguments in favour of mysticism have been of the informal kind that suggest themselves to a mystic as the result of his own experience. Even when they are not persuasive, it is difficult to judge them as simply right or wrong, for they express something of our incessant ambiguity, the puzzles or vagueness that reason finds in or around us, or perhaps our straining towards incompatible goals. These arguments may not be acceptable, but to dismiss them with a curt 'Yes' or 'No' seems harsh, even towards ourselves. But there is a quite different kind of argument, sharp-etched, abstract, meant to be coercive, which dissociates itself from individual experience and insists either on the formally provable truth or on the failure, by its own standards, of such truth. This is the kind of argument, which solicits the conclusive 'Yes' or 'No', to which we now turn.

It need not be emphasized that mystics often look on reason as their enemy. They sound, sometimes, as if they should like it abolished, though I do not know if there has ever been a mystic with enough self-restraint never to reason. The more humane mystics are moderately negative. They regret not reason but its excesses or its eventual barrenness. Rumi compares formal disputation with autumn, when the warmth of emotion has vanished and flowers can no longer blossom. The rose, he says, pulls its head back into its stem, and when autumn dares it to come out, it answers, 'In your presence I am a barren branch and a coward. Say what you will!'[1] The Taoist confronts reason with his smile and his images. 'The fish trap exists because of the fish,' he tells us;

once you've got the fish, you can forget the trap. The rabbit snare exists because of the rabbit; once you've got the rabbit, you can forget the snare. Words exist because of meaning; once you've got the meaning, you can forget the words. Where can I find a man who has forgotten words so I can have a word with him?[2]

In spite of the frequent rage of mystics against reason, many of them have used it just as freely as their opponents. In India, where formal disputations were held, skill in debate might attract the patronage of kings and princes. The biography of Naropa, for example, tells how he celebrated his choice as abbot of Nalanda, the most famous Buddhist institution of higher learning, by disputing against and defeating all the non-Buddhist scholars. To immortalize his success, he composed some immodest verses, in which he recalls how he scattered his enemies like sparrows, how with his axe or lamp or battering ram of grammar, logic, and precept, he cut down their trembling tree, illuminated their dark ignorance, and battered down their city of bewilderment. Naropa's biography emphasizes the social importance of his triumph. It says:

At that time 100 learned Hindu teachers shaved their heads, were converted to Buddhism, and were followed three days later by another 600. The inmates of Nalanda university hoisted the great banner, beat the big drum, blew the conch of the Dharma and were full of joy and happiness.

The biography adds that the great king who was present bowed repeatedly to Naropa, saying 'I am happy to be your patron.' Such words had, of course, political and financial implications.

It is only right to add that although this grandiose debate was over what might fairly be called mystical doctrine, Naropa suffered a terrible vision which led him, after eight years, to search for further enlightenment at the hands of a teacher he had not yet met. And so the man who 'gave superworldly explanations', who was 'unsurpassable in grace', and who was 'especially gifted in explaining the experiences and realizations' of Buddhism left his despairing students like fish, his biography says, on dry land. The fire of his craving had to be extinguished, he explained.[3]

The reasons for developing a pro-mystical logic have not been

sociological alone, but have stemmed at times from the very principles of mysticism. The varieties of mysticism that identify reality
with consciousness and consciousness with intelligence are by nature
disposed to use and even glory in intelligence, though they point
out the limitations of its merely human use. In the West, Plato,
his disciple Plotinus, and Plotinus's disciple, Proclus, have, with
Aristotle, fathered the idea that reality and intelligence are the same.
In India, Shankara and his followers, and not they alone, accept
it. In Islam, the 'philosophers' and the 'metaphysicians of light'
have been identified with it, and in medieval Christianity, the
Augustinians.

Yet I think that the most pervasive cause of the argumentativeness
of the argumentative mystics is a personal one. By their own canons,
most mystics should be content with their visions, illuminations,
paradoxes, and concentrating exercises, and not argue. But the
human mind is an incurable organ. Who with the wit to use it can
keep it still for long? A daydreaming pianist will hammer with his
fingers on invisible keys, a poet will mutter with fragmentary elo-
quence, a bright man will reason, quietly if he must, but impatient
to express himself aloud. And just as a rationalist may sometimes
break out into mystical poetry, mystics, unable or unwilling to
check themselves, break out into reason, and some of them, after
they have tasted the forbidden pleasure, go on enjoying it until one
is led to suspect that they are anti-rational mystics by name but
reasoners by nature, with the normal, unmystical lust to defeat the
enemy.

It does not take a more reasonable mystic long to discover that,
if he wishes to avoid ascetic dumbness, he cannot avoid reasoning.
Shankara complains that logicians do not agree. 'It is notorious', he
says, 'that what one logician establishes to be right knowledge, is
demolished by another who, in his turn, is ousted by a third.' But
Shankara acknowledges both the practical and theoretical necessity
for reasoning. 'If all reasoning were unfounded practical life would
be impossible', he says, to which he adds, 'the assertion that reasoning has no foundation is itself based upon reasoning'.[4]

And so it happens that mystics compound facts with logic and
engage in system-building and detailed polemics. It is to be expected

that the mystics who specialize in elaborate reasoning should be looked at askance by the others. The Buddhist 'logicians' were condemned by fellow-Buddhists as practitioners of a quite profane science. They were accused of lacking tolerance for humankind, a cardinal sin among Buddhists, and of preferring argument and merely conventional truth over mystic realization and absoʌute truth. Besides, their logic could not, in the end, dispense with the revelations of the Buddhas.[5]

Opposition or no, the logic was spun out at length. It retains a genuine interest for us, though, unlike its inventors, we do not need it to convert ourselves, convert infidels, impress patrons, or establish one or another mystical doctrine. This logic is interesting as a matter of history and sociology, and as a formal game, its goal almost as fixed as the checkmate in chess, and its tactics exhibiting more and more virtuosity. Sometimes there is the shock of recogni tion of an idea we have come to regard as characteristically modern, and there is always, to my mind, the charm of a precisely told ontological fairy tale. But there is something more important, which has hardly been recognized as yet. These technical arguments are expressions of certain basic ways of grasping experience. The Buddhist, for example, usually expresses a granulating or dissociating temperament—he would prefer all ropes to be made of sand— and both he and the Hindu use logical negation with the ease of men who love denial. Polemic, consistency, inventiveness, and temperament do not allow the mystical logicians to accept the timid realism of common sense. They are by nature ontological radicals, and they project different models of existence or non-existence for the far-out meditator. We appreciate the ability of an independent mathematical invention to give a more calculable form to something problematic in, say, physics. But there is another, no less necessary kind of invention in advance—of exact and yet radically imaginative schemata, like those in the technical defences of mysticism, which are forms readied for any exact radical thinking, but most obviously for science. Mystical dissociation and mystical negation have made forms in advance for science. The Neo-Platonist's dynamic world structure is another possible example. Infinity, which has given mathematics such infinite headaches, is still another. We must, however, leave this theme merely suggested and face the logical and metaphysical arguments themselves.

If we are to exhibit the technical qualities of the arguments in a few pages, we must shorten and limit them. We must, first, ignore the superstitions or religious dogmas that enter them, and free them, as far as possible, from their distinctly local conditions. In doing this, we risk falsifying them. It is extremely easy to mistake ancient for modern reasoning that sounds like it, or to give a somewhat incongruous Greek, French, or American ending to a Hindu beginning. Furthermore, the arguments cannot be given completely or considered in detail. The most that can be done is to explain the basic mechanisms of the arguments and to give examples of their use.

For the West, I have chosen a single representative, Proclus, the Neo-Platonist of the fifth century A.D. Proclus was intimately familiar with Euclid's *Elements*, and his own *Elements of Theology* is the one really systematic exposition we have of Neoplatonic philosophy. Proclus links ancient with medieval thought, and I would hazard the statement that much of our traditional metaphysics, even that which is not considered mystical, stands or falls together with his proofs.

Proclus begins with two basic characteristics of everything within the range of our experience. Everything, he says, since it is recognizable as some one thing, has its own unity; and everything moves or tends or strives in some direction. On further thought, we discover that the unity and the movement or striving are identical. Unity is coherence and survival and so it is good. And movement or striving, which is always towards rest, peace, completion, towards, that is, the good, unifies that which moves or strives. Oneness is therefore goodness, and goodness oneness. We know this unconsciously; but Proclus hopes that if we recognize it consciously we will strive better to join the One-Good in mystic union.

Having telescoped Proclus's beginning into a few sentences, we may try to follow something of his reasoning in more detail.

First we show that a world without unity is inconceivable. Suppose we try to conceive it. Suppose we say that there is nothing that is not simply and purely plural. But a plurality is made up of members, and what are we to say of them? At least that they are each not one. But if to be not one means to be nothing, then there can be no plurality either, for no collection of nothings is more than nothing. But if each of the members of a plurality is not one, and if it is impossible that 'not one' should mean 'nothing', then each must itself be plural. By the same reasoning, each member of the plurality that is a member of the original plurality must also be plural; and so on, I am afraid, ad infinitum. If this is the case, then every member of every plurality is an infinity. But this is impossible. An infinity is by nature that which cannot be exceeded; it is an absolute maximum. How then could there be a plurality that contains an infinite number of infinities? The conclusion is, necessarily, that the world cannot be purely plural—at a basic level, every plurality consists of 'ones'. In Proclus's terms, every plurality participates in unity.

Next we show that everything unified is such because it participates in the absolute One. How so? The unified things we have been speaking of are not simply ones. They can be broken up physically, or analysed intellectually, and they are not-ones in the sense that they have characteristics other than their unity. Because they are other than one, more than simply one, we may say that they have no reason inherent in them to be unities. Not being only and inherently one, their oneness must have been imported into them; and the only possible cause of their oneness is the One as such. Without it, things could never get to be unified. Otherness or plurality can exist only if unity exists; but the opposite is not true.

Next we show that unity is superior to plurality. Unity, we already know, is the cause of plurality. If unity is not superior to plurality, it must be either equal or inferior to it. If it is equal, if, that is, productive causes are equal to their effects, then everything in the world would be equal to everything else, and nothing either better or worse, and we know that this is not the case. If, at any point, there were something unequal, we should have a violation of the approximately Euclidean principle that equal powers create equals. It is also impossible that the productive cause should be inferior to its effect. Everything tends, as far as possible, to increase its own power. If anything had the power to create another thing better than itself, why should it not have used this power to better itself? And so, because it cannot be either equal or inferior, every productive cause is superior to that which it produces; and the one is superior to the many.

Next we show that all that exists has the Good as its principle and its first cause. Movement or striving is always towards something absent, something that attracts or is craved. Goodness, that which attracts or is craved, therefore exists. Now we already know that all that exists proceeds from a single first cause, which we have called the One. If the first cause is not the Good, but superior to it, it would affect the nature of things. Why, otherwise, should we consider it a cause? But by the word 'superior' we mean 'better', that is, more good, or more nearly absolutely good. So how could anything be better than the Good, which is the best?

Next, and last, we show that the good unifies; that unification is good; and that the Good is identical with the One. Everything, we know, desires to maintain its being, and it does this by striving towards its good, by which it is one. Conversely, unity keeps each thing together, and therefore is good. If goodness is the tendency towards unity, and unity is maintenance of goodness, then the superlatives of goodness and unity are identical. Q.E.D.[6]

Q.E.D.? No one now thinks so, but to state the reasons carefully would be to review a great part of traditional metaphysics. I therefore confine my response to two critical, obvious points. Unity and plurality are fundamental to both our perception and our thought. I do not know what metaphysical status should be granted to either, I cannot see how either can be made metaphysically prior to the other, nor can I conceive by what magic the world could be created and sustained by the absolute One. There are, it is true, problems here, perhaps such as cannot strictly be solved. However, Proclus's paradox of infinity has long ceased to be obviously paradoxical. It takes little knowledge of mathematics to recall that an infinite collection is now considered to contain an infinite number of collections equal in quantity to itself. Proclus's view is not unreasonable, but neither is it necessary. We have found it more useful to transform the paradox into a definition.

In relation to the Good, Proclus is anthropomorphic. To him, the simplest physical motion is a 'striving' and any stopping point a 'goal' and a 'good'. There is nothing in his universe without an at least unconscious motive. It has become obvious that an assumption of this kind cannot be used to prove anything.

Proclus is by no means a negligible thinker; but it appears to me that some of the Buddhist and Hindu mystics to whom we now turn are more consistently sharp and harder to dismiss.

The first of the Buddhists is Nagarjuna, who lived, mostly in South India, it seems, about A.D. 200. Nagarjuna begins with a Buddhist assumption shared by many philosophers. It is that something that exists in the full sense of the word must be fully independent, that is, dependent only on itself, must have, in a Buddhist term, its 'own being'. Its independence means that it can neither be caused nor destroyed by anything else, and it must therefore be eternal. But nothing we can think of in our ordinary, phenomenal world has such independence. The phenomenal world is certainly here in a sense, but it is empty of being, it does not stand alone. It cannot be truly said either to exist or not to exist.

To prove this, Nagarjuna makes use of 'argumentation demolishing all possible alternatives'. He is willing to accept any thesis, along, in principle, with the rules of argument his opponent thinks are right, and tries to show that its opposite is equally true, but that the thesis cannot really be abandoned, and that no combination of thesis and anithesis is possible. If he succeeds, we recognize that we speak and think and even perceive incoherently, and we take our final refuge, as he wishes, in silence, or in speech tempered with the insight of silence.

A person, says Nagarjuna, for example, has physical and emotional reactions. But the possessive verb here is not accurate. If we think of what the person might be, deprived of all his reactions and states, we find that he has disappeared. No laughing, anger, walking, sleeping, no living—nothing is left, because he *is* these and cannot be conceived apart from them. But if he *is* these, they cannot be all of him; they must be the reactions and states *of* someone. Both views are right and also wrong, and we cannot correct them or put them together successfully.

If we generalize this problem, we have come upon the old one of substance and attribute. Philosophers tell us that attributes exist only as the manifestations of a substance. We agree, until we try to think of a substance without attributes and see that it is as dependent on them as they on it. The conclusion is that neither is independent, that both together are not independent, and that nothing we can think of is independent.

If this conclusion seems unpleasantly drastic, we might try running away from it. A useless tactic, in Nagarjuna's eyes. Not only can we not escape the truth, the truth is that we cannot run or even move. To move, we must cover a certain distance in a certain time. This is what it means to move. But our distinctions of space and time depend upon motion. If nothing moves, we cannot measure, sense, or think of space and time. Motion arises and continues in space and time, space and time depend upon the arising of motion. This is too difficult, so we had better rest. It is too late. If nothing moves, nothing stops; if nothing stops, what can it mean to be at at rest? All these distinctions, space and time, motion and rest, are misleading.

Nagarjuna levels the same kind of attack on the idea of cause. This is, perhaps, his main target, and so we follow his reasoning in more detail. If we are to distinguish cause and effect, there must be a difference of nature between them and a difference of time; that is, according to his dialectic, that there must but cannot be. Cause and effect must be different in nature because the effect, by definition, is something new. But where could the novelty have emerged from? What could have caused the cause to change from potential to actual, from where does the increment or difference come? If the change in the cause is the result of another cause, the question is simply shifted to the cause of the cause, as it can be shifted to any possible coordination of partial causes. Perhaps there is true spontaneity in the world, and this is what makes the difference. But if there is spontaneity, anything can come from anything, and the idea of cause loses its meaning.

The difference in time between cause and effect is equally necessary and impossible. Without the difference, we lose an essential concept of cause and lose our ability to understand the processes of nature. But when, exactly, do cause and effect meet? If there is no interval of time between them, then they coincide in time, and, at the time they meet, cannot be distinguished as cause and effect. But if there is time between them, what bridges the gap? An activity, an energy? But an activity or energy of what? The problem is insoluble, and the existence of cause and effect, as fundamental descriptions of reality, made wholly doubtful. Cause and effect are experienced as coordinations, but they are coordinations of nothing.*

Nagarjuna applies the same ruthless dialectic to the Buddhist goal of Nirvana, and with engaging audacity to Buddha himself. Not that he speaks ill of them, but he denies that they exist or can be reached or known or rationally distinguished from anything else. Nirvana is not a being of any kind, because beings have causes and a substratum and are not independent. Of course, Nirvana is not a non-being, because non-beings, like beings, cannot be independent. Nor is Nirvana a mixture of being and non-being; the two cannot

---

* Nagarjuna's type of dialectic was later cultivated by opponents of Buddhism as well. One eminent cultivator was Shriharsha, a twelfth-century follower of Shankara. He demonstrates, by his own lights, that all concepts are involved in self-contradiction, and he concludes that the realities the concepts appear to distinguish cannot be what they seem.

Here is a fragment of Shriharsha's attack on the concept of 'difference':

A book, we say, is different from a table. The book's quality of 'being different from' has no locus, and therefore no meaning, until the idea of 'the table', or something else, completes it. 'Difference' cannot, in other words, be confined to the book, and therefore the table must enter into the nature of the book—and the book must likewise enter into the nature of the table. But then everything distinguishable must enter into the nature of everything else, and the concept of difference loses its meaning. That is, things with differences must be different from one another, but to be so they must be the same.

And yet, the concept of difference is external to that of things as they are actually understood or perceived. Even the idea of 'difference' is itself different from the idea of the book and the table. This is true whether we think of the book and table together or separately. And the joint idea of book and table is different from the idea that 'the book differs from the table'. To know the nature of a book we do not have to know beforehand that it differs from a table. We see and know what a book is. This shows that the grasp of individual things does not require any idea of difference as its constituent. Et cetera. (See S. Dasgupta, *A History of Indian Philosophy*, Vol. II, Cambridge U.P., 1932, Chap. 11.)

be simultaneously present. But if Nirvana is neither a being nor a non-being, it cannot be understood. For that matter, Buddha, the source of all wisdom, cannot be understood to exist, not to exist, or both, or neither. Briefly, he cannot be understood. More wonderful still, there is no distinction between Nirvana and the world of appearances. The limit of the two is the same, and we cannot find the slightest shade of difference between them. Since the relative and the absolute are not different (or the same), and since all these thoughts, like the world itself, are so troublesome, it is best to stop thinking. Plurality will then cease (and unity), and we (though not we exactly) will remain (in a non-temporal sense) in a state of bliss.[7]

Nagarjuna having precipitated us into the inconceivable, we may shift our attention to another Indian Buddhist, Vasubandhu—presumably the Elder—who lived during the fourth century A.D. Philosophically speaking, Vasubandhu was an Idealist, who believed that pure intelligence or consciousness was the ultimate reality, which split in each of us into an apparent subject and an apparently external object. He was therefore concerned to show that consciousness could produce an apparently external world and that a truly external world was impossible.

An opponent of Idealism may say that we recognize objects to be external by the fact that they are localized in space and time. But this is no proof, because the objects in a dream, this village you see, or garden, man, or woman, are not at every place and time, but at a certain place and time. The opponent may object that only external objects have 'physical' effects; but dream-objects may have them too. A dream may, for instance, cause the loss of semen.

Vasubandhu now turns to the attack. If there is an external, physical world, it is either a physical multiplicity or unity. If it is a multiplicity, it must be made up of atoms, that is, indivisibly minute particles. Otherwise we could not conceive how the material world is constructed. But the notion of a partless atom is paradoxical. To grasp this, think of a number of atoms surrounding a central atom. If the central atom faces towards all the others, it must have as many different points or surfaces as there are atoms surrounding it. Having different points or surfaces, it is theoretically divisible and not the atom that is needed. But if it does not have them, it has no dimensions and cannot separate the other atoms from one another. In this case, they would all be at the same point and could not reach the dimensions that would make them visible in the mass. And atoms that lacked surfaces would not obstruct or exclude one another and ought not to be called material. Evidently, the central atom cannot be a point, that is, a pure unity, or more than a point, that is, a space-occupying and divisible object.

We are left with the second possibility, that the material world is a pure unity. The notion is immediately absurd. A single step, if it could be taken, would lead everywhere, anything grasped would include everything, any one place would be all places, and nothing would be different from any other thing.

It may be objected that there must be an external world, since we perceive external things immediately, the colour I now see, for example. But seeing, as we know, is a process that takes time. By the time the intellect discriminates objects and we are conscious of seeing, the object we assume to have initiated the process already lies in the past. Lying in the past, it no longer exists, and we therefore cannot immediately perceive anything external.

On awakening from a dream, we realize that nothing in it was externally real. On awakening from this world, we can arrive at the transcendent knowledge in which we are no longer split into the knower and the known.*[8]

It would be a pity to leave the mystical metaphysics of Buddhism without pausing at the doctrine, as it has been called, of momentariness. It was held by a number of the Buddhist logicians, Dharmakirti, for example, who lived in the seventh century A.D., and who studied at Nalanda. Like most Buddhist thinkers, these men practised the dissociation of everything into many elements. Most of them believed in the normal Buddhist absolutes, but they thought that, apart from these, the only ultimately real things were the pure instants or the point-instants, unnameable 'thiscs' and 'nows' that

* To illustrate this possibility, Fa-tsang, a seventh-century Chinese Buddhist, 'arranged ten mirrors, eight at the eight compass points, one above, and one below, all facing each other. He put a Buddhist figure in the centre and illuminated it so that its image was reflected from one mirror to the other' and the finite world appeared to pass into infinity. (Fung Yu-lan, *A History of Chinese Philosophy*, Vol. II, pp. 339 ff.)

stimulated our imaginations to construct this world of objects in space and time.

Dharmakirti even believed that we could become indirectly aware of these pure instants. He suggested an experiment in introspection that he had evidently undertaken on himself. 'Now,' he said, 'if we begin to stare at a patch of colour and withdraw all our thoughts on whatsoever other objects, if we thus reduce our consciousness to a condition of rigidity (and become as though unconscious), this will be the condition of pure sensation. If we then (awakening from the condition) begin to think, we notice a feeling that we had (but did not notice or name) an image, because it was pure sensation.'

Everything that seems to be continuous in space and time is really constructed from or around successive, absolutely minimal flashes of sensation. The flashes die as soon as they are born. They are not in space and time, which do not really exist, and they have no qualities—qualities are made out of them. Therefore 'reality itself is called annihilation . . . The momentary thing represents its own annihilation.'*

The Buddhist with full insight, the Saint, is not deceived by the world imagination has constructed. He sees reality pure and strong, for the object of his meditation is the instantaneous flash. He occupies the pure, vivid, timeless moment. In it, he is cut off from the past, with its accumulated guilts, and from the future, with its endless anxieties. He is in a state of ecstatic contemplation, the life of the unattached moment, the dimensionless paradise.[9]

* Anyone familiar with current physics will recognize some analogy between this Buddhist 'momentary thing' and the physicist's 'virtual particle'. Researchers into perception sometimes make use of a further analogous idea, that of the 'perceptual moment'. They debate 'the theory that sensory data reach consciousness in discrete packages rather than in a continuous flow.' They come on such Buddhist-sounding problems as the following: 'If everything falling within a discrete package (of perception) is treated by the higher centres of the brain as *simultaneous*, then does the perception of time itself stand being broken down into "atoms" or moments? If so, then during the span of one of these moments there can be no cognizance of temporal order.' And the researchers may specify that 'perceptual moments need not necessarily always be of the same duration, but the general concordance of obtained estimates puts the size of the moment at about 100 msec.' (See A. J. Sanford, 'A Periodic Basis for Perception and Action', in W. P. Colquhoun (ed.), *Biological Rhythms and Human Performance*, Academic Press, London and N.Y., 1971, pp. 179-80, 189.)

Since we ourselves are not yet there, we may glance at one more mystical metaphysician, the Hindu, Shankara. Shankara uses logic, but mainly to attack opponents. In direct, at least apparent contradiction to the Buddhists, he does not dissociate the self into bits of consciousness, but accepts it as permanent and as identical with the absolute intelligence he knows as Brahman. The rest, the world of 'names and forms', is a kind of superimposed illusion that follows its own shadow-logic.

Against the Buddhists, Shankara argues that unless the self were continuous and fundamentally unchanged, it would be impossible to explain memory and recognition. The knower persists, though the man's body it is joined with sleeps deeply, faints, and grows insane. The lapse of consciousness is only apparent. As light in space is invisible when nothing reflects it, intelligence is invisible when no objects of thought reflect its presence.

This self, reflected or not, cannot be proved to exist. The existence of other things is proved by perception, logic, testimony, and so on; but how could these prove the perceiver, the giver and taker of testimony, and the logician. The self can neither be proved nor denied because it is self-evident. Shankara says, 'To refute such a self-established entity is impossible. An adventitious thing, indeed, may be refuted, but not that which is the essential nature; for it is the essential nature of him who refutes. The heat of fire is not refuted by the fire itself.'

If we ever could experience things apart from consciousness, we would know that they are separable. If we never do experience them separately, why not conclude that they cannot be separated, because they are identical? In Shankara's words:

From the fact of our always being conscious of the act of knowledge and the object of knowledge simultaneously, it follows that the two are in reality identical. When we are conscious of the one we are conscious of the other also; and that would not happen if the two were essentially distinct, as in that case there would be nothing to prevent our being conscious of one apart from the other. For this reason also we maintain that there are no outward things.

Yet there is a difference, the difference between form and substance. The form of our consciousness, except in the deepest sleep, keeps on changing; only its substance, the consciousness itself, remains always the same. We are, if we can only realize it, the object-less, blissful light of pure interiority.[10]

These are the ways that mystical metaphysicians argue. I might have put their arguments more fully or etched them more sharply, but we now owe them the 'Yes' or 'No' they demand. I am tempted by the 'No', in part because I feel that these metaphysicians are making an unrealistic and prejudiced use of logic, by which I mean, primarily, thinking in some rational order. We use such logic consciously and unconsciously, and it is fairly obviously natural to us, as the mystics themselves testify in practice.

Logic, however, is also a formal technique, and we have learned to build many kinds of logical systems, even to conceive of a logic of logics, a formal system that embraces all formal systems, including those of both mathematics and logic. Logic, or logics, are devices for creating order in thought, and thus for finding or confirming order everywhere. But having many kinds of order at hand, we have to experiment with them. We can never be sure which kind we will meet when we look through a microscope, send up an observation balloon, or give a drug to a schizophrenic. Humanly conceived logics do not fit nature perfectly. They are like shoes that pinch or hats that fall off when the wind blows. We have learned to expect that eventually, at some extreme of size, pressure, complexity, or time, the formal structures we have built to represent natural structures will show serious weaknesses. Even that indispensable rule of thought, the rule of excluded middle, may show its usual self to be *empirically* inadequate, and require at least a special inter-pretation. Nagarjuna did not so much deny the concept of identity, without which clear thought would be impossible, as say that when applied to anything real it was inadequate and had to be thought of together with the concept of difference, at every point.

Now it is easy to think on purpose so as to arrive at contradictions, and this is what Nagarjuna does; but, except for poetry and mysticism, it is much more useful to avoid them. When self-contradictions arise, we assume that something has gone wrong with the reasoning, and we try to cure it. A contradiction in logic or science is the sign of a critical defect in them, but not of a defect or essential unintelligibility in nature. This conclusion is simply the optimism bred in us by our increasing ability to explain the world and to replace one logical structure by another. If the hat blows off too easily, we may stop wearing it, and get soaked in the rain; but we may also buy a hat that fits better.

This is a general response to the mystics' arguments, but to be fair we should consider the more purely logical contentions by themselves. I have chosen four, which are:

(1) Everything is relative to something else. Relative things have no independent, that is, real existence. The sum of relative things has no independent existence. That which has independent existence must be other than anything.

(2) There is no real distinction between cause and effect. At the moment of supposed contact they are simultaneous. But if neither then precedes the other, neither of them can be the cause of the other. But if they are really successive, there is no contact between them and no relation of cause and effect.

(3) All concepts of difference are hopelessly unclear. A 'difference' is either an essential part of the different things or is separated from one or all of them. Both suppositions lead to absurdities.

(4) The world is nothing but consciousness. We must think so because we cannot separate the supposedly external world from the conscious perceptions that reveal it.

Consider the first argument, that everything is relative and therefore unreal. But what would it mean to say, for example, that 'up' and 'down' were not real because each implied and needed the other? We map the world in terms of directions, which are contrasts of a sort, and which are most easily put as verbal opposites. That opposite terms imply one another makes them 'unreal' only if reality has been defined, as Nagarjuna or Shriharsha defines it, so as to exclude them. But I could suppose in an uncontradictory way, that the reality of 'down' was proved by the fact that when I walked on my hands my ears began to ring, my arms got tired, and my hands got bruised. Contrary numbers with opposite signs may add up to zero, but 'up' and 'down' are not numbers with opposite signs. They are simply the words that express the fact that we stand upright, are affected by gravity, and make many useful analogies with the resulting relationship between our heads, our feet, and the earth. For reasons such as these, 'distance' in Chinese is 'far-near', 'length' is 'long-short', and 'size' is 'big-little'. The Chinese are a practical people.

Consider the second argument, that we cannot distinguish the priority of cause to effect. On close inspection, our ideas of cause and effect are tangled and inexact. Science surely alters them; they remain problematic. But temporal succession is a perceived fact, to which we must adjust our concepts and terminology as well as we can. It does not help to define 'touching' in time or space so that the things that touch are considered identical. The physicist explains the action and reaction we see, the mystic, that we cannot really be seeing them. Both jobs are difficult, but only the physicist's is possible.

Consider the third argument, that all concepts of difference are hopelessly unclear. To begin with, there is the fact that we perceive differences or contrasts. In the ordinary senses of 'part of', it makes no sense to ask if 'difference' is or is not part of the things that are different from one another. Abstractions such as 'difference' cannot be glued together or cut apart or inserted into a physical object. If, nevertheless, it seems useful to say that an object 'has' the 'quality' of difference, it should be clear that this 'having' is different from physical possession and this 'quality' different from qualities like shape or texture. Relationships are not objects or physical parts of them. Relation-words mimic the language of physical possession and containment, but why should we confuse them any more than we confuse a parrot and a man?

Consider the fourth argument, that the world is nothing but consciousness. The object of the mystics who say this is not alone to abolish the physical world, but to abolish the difference between subject and object. They want only the pure subject to remain, or, to a Buddhist, something even less. This, I think, is an impossible notion. The mystics admit the *apparent* existence of a perceptible and plural world. Most of them, when asked to explain the workings of this illusion, decline, on the grounds that it is an insoluble mystery.

Or, if they do conceive of a special illusory physics, physiology and psychology, its relation to the inconceivable 'truth' or 'emptiness' remains an equal mystery. The mystic continues for the most part, as he admits, to perceive and act as if ordinary perception were true. He fails to explain in any coherent and not immediately circular way the nature of the necessity of his 'illusion'. The non-mystic may be naïve in taking the world as it looks, yet if he does, he can begin to explain himself, the mystic, and the world. In ordinary experience, the world is more or less one; in mystical experience it is split, it lacks the possibility of at least intellectual coherence. Mystics try to sweep the world under the rug. Then they try to ignore the lumps in the rug.

In the end, the mystic's claim that everything in ordinary experience is illusory comes down to one of two things. It either expresses an actual quality of his experience, a quality we shall consider at length, or it expresses his dissatisfaction with ordinary experience. He may try to persuade us to see and feel with him, but no one else is rationally compelled to agree. This is my point. I have not tried to lay down the rights and wrongs of the ancient controversies reflected in mystical arguments. I have simply said that the reasoning of the mystical philosophers is inconclusive.

To end this chapter of arguments and counter-arguments, I should like to cite three near-parables, all well known to those who know them. The first is from an Upanishad of about 500 B.C., the second from a ninth-century Zen master, Nansen, and a third from Wittgenstein. The near-parables are, respectively, about a frog in a sealed well, a goose in a bottle, and a fly in a fly bottle.

In the Upanishad, a king complained to a sage of the human predicament and asked his advice. The king said:

We see the passing of other beings: the drying up of the oceans, the collapse of the mountains, the wandering of the polar star, the tearing of the windcords, the flooding of the earth, the fall of the gods from their seats. In such a world what good are the enjoyments we see coming back repeatedly? Therefore deign to rescue me: I am trapped in this world like a frog in a sealed well. You are my refuge, revered sir!

The sage, Shakayana by name, was pleased and explained to the king how to depart from his body and go into and become 'the supreme light', the self, 'the immortal, the freedom from fears,' Brahman.

The Zen story goes this way:

Riko, a high government official, said to Nansen, 'A long time ago a man kept a goose in a bottle. It grew larger and larger and it could not get out of the bottle any more; he did not want to break the bottle, nor did he wish to hurt the goose; how would you get it out?'
The Zen master called out, 'O officer!'
Riko answered at once, 'Yes!'
'There, it is out!'
This was the way Nansen freed the goose from its imprisonment.

Wittgenstein's parable goes on:

A man with a philosophical problem is like a fly buzzing about in an open bottle, unaware that it is open. 'What is our aim in philosophy?— To show the fly the way out of the fly bottle.'

In comparing the frog, goose, and fly, we may begin with Wittgenstein's recommendations. He contends that his problem, or the fly's, is solved by the discovery of the ways in which the logic of language has been misunderstood. He says, 'The philosopher's treatment of a question is like the treatment of an illness.' The problem appears to have no solution because it is not an empirical one. The philosopher appears to be saying something that cannot be right. His problem has the form, 'I don't know my way about.' But philosophy ought not to interfere with the actual use of language:

It can in the end only describe it. For it cannot give any foundation either. It leaves everything as it is. . . . Philosophy is a battle against the bewitchment of our intelligence by means of language. . . . For the clarity that we are aiming at is *complete* clarity. But this simply means that the philosophical problem should *completely* disappear.

Oddly, or perhaps not oddly (or perhaps oddly and not oddly), the Upanishadic sage and the Zen master could agree with every one of Wittgenstein's quoted words. They too look on the philosopher or sage as a physician, they too agree that the problem appears to have no solution because it is not an empirical one—the Zen master gives an unrational answer to emphasize this—but a problem of vision. The sage and the master would both agree that the problems we try to solve are attempts to find the way, the very Way that appears in mystical literature by this name. They too hardly want to interfere with the normal use of language and intelligence. They too aim at perfect clarity and want the problems to disappear completely.[11]

What then is the difference between frog, goose, and fly?

Observe, first, that the predicaments of the frog and the goose seem worse. The frog is in a sealed well, the round of life and death which is sealed off from escape. The goose is growing and imprisoned in a bottle that must not be shattered. Only the fly is in an open container. Well, the frog solves his problem by discovering, intuitively, experientially, logically, or all together, that there really is no well at all, and therefore, *a fortiori*, no sealed well. This he does by means of reasons such as were elaborated by Shankara and Shriharsha, tending to demonstrate that except for his witness-self there is nothing at all. His external froggishness and the well are both only momentary shadows superimposed on an identical absolute self of intelligence that is bliss. As for the goose in the bottle, the Zen master certainly wants to imply that in the last analysis there is neither goose nor bottle. But he wants to believe that they are there all the same. Perception, language, and reason all have created this misunderstanding; and reason cannot find the way out of its bottle, nor even grow inside it. The solution means that we should leave things alone, language too, but see them in the light that makes the problem simply vanish. The sameness and the difference of reality are paradoxical to reason, and one can at best see that this paradox is a form of self-injury by reason, and then see and say, 'There, it is out!' meaning, 'Poor language! But we can see and experience what we can't say—so here, you're out!'

In other words, Shakayana and Nansen have less faith than Wittgenstein in the ability of reason, and of language, its self-expression, to help itself. Their use of language and reason becomes, at crucial moments, negative, or, if not, becomes a fingerlike pointing. But all agree that reason and language are at least something of a help; and all agree that, looked at properly, the problem vanishes.

But Wittgenstein's soluble problem is the verbal and intellectual difficulty itself. Shakayana's and Nansen's is that of life and existence. I do not know if, towards the end of his life, Wittgenstein would have agreed with them; but given his sentiments earlier in life, I do not know if he would have disagreed either. Maybe all heroic philosophers and mystic sages are alike, or at least not very different in the stories they tell.

5

Everyday Mysticism

The arguments for and against mysticism may be sacred, sophistical, or logical; but they rarely touch on the psychological reality, which, unlike arguments, cannot be escaped. The psychological reality is such that everyone is potentially subject to mystical experience, although, when had, it may be dismissed or called by another name. Mystically-toned feelings arise rather easily and under fairly usual circumstances. The exaltations of extreme mysticism are paralleled, I think, by the more ordinary ones of everyday mysticism.

Everyday mysticism expresses the power of each human self to assimilate whatever lies outside it, that is, to abolish the otherness of other persons and things. This stripping off of differences is almost the power to return to the indifferentiation of early infancy. An infant, they say, lives in a world of flickering immediacies, not unlike the Buddhist moments we have spoken of. To an infant, things are not clearly different from one another or from himself—the very notion of 'things' is not clearly applicable. His experience is peculiarly hard to describe because it is antagonistic to our own *accumulation* of experience, and to the fixity of our words and grammar. The difference between ourselves and infants is so great that if we had not, in fact, once been infants, we might not know or remember how to be mystics, even everyday ones.

Granted our difficulty in entering into the world of an infant, how, nevertheless, might we try to describe it?

At first the world is a succession of different sensations and feeling states. What varies is the quality and distribution and intensity of sensations. Except for the difference in the nature of the sensations involved, hunger, which we say originates from within, and a sharp sound or cold breeze, which we cannot imagine except as something that reaches us from the outside, are indistinguishable. There is no awareness of such things as approach, withdrawal, or direction of any sort. Even if the baby turns his head towards the nipple and grasps it, his sensation is that the nipple comes or is; no other state with which to contrast this exists. Light and darkness; harshness and softness; cold and warmth; sleep and waking; the contours of mother's face as seen from below, vis-à-vis, or even from above; being grasped and released; being moved and moving; the sight of moving people, curtains, blankets, toys; all these recede and approach and comprise the totality of experience in whatever constellation they occur at each split second in time. With recurrence, there develops islands of consistency.*[1]

If we, with our adult consciousness, could for a moment inhabit a tiny child and that child's perceptions, we should feel plunged into a kaleidoscopic chaos. Every fresh appearance, every blink, every new perspective, would be something else again. There would be no spatial quality to most objects and very little direction. Our experience would be, I think, like that of a man blind from birth to whom sight is given by means of an operation. Sight is given to him, and yet he cannot see anything clear or stable, but only 'a painful chaos of forms and colours, a gaudy confusion of visual impressions none of which seems to bear any comprehensible relationship to the others'. Only slowly and with great effort does this blind man, like the infant, come to see visual shapes located in visual space. It is often easier for him to shut his eyes and go back to his familiar dark world.[2]

To understand how we make the world real by looking at it, we need only recall the experience of blind children. For a short while, they are roughly like all the others. But an ordinary child beginning to move purposefully discovers that his eyes are his best guide—they are better than ears at locating things, and they reach so much

* Clever recent experiments make this description seem too indiscriminate. Even in newborn infants, the interaction of hand and eye is observed and may therefore be assumed to be built into the nervous system. But infants below the age of about four months seem unable to identify an object in motion with the same object at a standstill. For them, 'An object becomes a different object as soon as it moves to a new location.' The object concept itself seems not to be built into the neural system, but to be developed or discovered. This conclusion obviously does not take into account the possible effects of maturation of the neural system in the months following birth. (See T. G. R. Bower, 'The Object in the World of the Infant', *Scientific American*, October 1971.)

further than hands do. A blind child, however, is neither so richly stimulated nor so well guided. Using sound alone to guide himself, he fails much more often to get what he is reaching for. He stumbles more often. The things around him are harder to handle, less predictable, and more malicious. It is easier for him to stay where he is, to rock back and forth, to touch and play with his own body, to remain still and centred in himself.[3]

To return to the infant we are trying to inhabit, we discover that he has no sense of continuous time. To him, out of sight is out of mind, and out of mind, out of existence. Only *he* is always there, his past shrouded in a fitful amnesia, his present equivalent to his acts, sights, pleasures and pains.

Slowly, of course, the world takes shape to him as well. He makes it, so to speak, by moving, which brings him up sharp against its protrusions and teaches him the possible results of the sequences of his movements. He makes it by his demands, to which it responds by giving and withholding. And he makes it by trying repeatedly to assimilate it to himself, as if it were his thumb, his crust of bread, or his idea. He uses the world and collides against it until, by an enormous number of mutual touchings and definings, the world detaches itself from him and is slowly distinguished into things and persons, and the things and persons into friendly and hostile. A person bearing food and a smile elicits the child's true, non-automatic smile, which is his recognition of the friendly other. He learns to exploit his difference from the other by means of shaking his head Yes or No. In doing this, he is becoming conscious of his own self as separated from others and as able to reject and refuse, on the one hand, and accept and agree on the other.[4]

Sometimes, tragically, the child fails to separate his self and remains psychologically fused with his mother, or half-merged in things as in the fantasies of a Surrealistic painter. If he is to be a sane, separate person, his physical birth must be followed by a later, psychological one that separates him, first of all from his mother, and gives him a clear inward shape (a shape, that is, to himself), and a clear outward boundary. Lacking such clear limits, which are those of his individual selfhood, his humanity is qualified —he is 'autistic' or 'psychotic'.[5]

We exist as individuals by virtue of our clear boundaries and selves. This is less metaphorical than it may sound. A variety of neurological disturbances has made it clear to psychiatrists. For example, a brain lesion may disorder or destroy the experience of part of one's body, and so change one's experienced shape. There are people who believe, contrary to the evidence of everyone's eyes, that they are able to move their paralysed limbs as well as their healthy ones; and there are others who are not able to perceive that their paralysed limbs belong to them.

Even more strikingly, there are people who have lost the ability to find the parts of their own body, and having lost the directions of their body, they have trouble finding the directions of anything else. Such cases were described by the German neurologist, A. Pick, in the early twentieth century:

When Pick saw his first case of this kind, the patient first sought her left ear on the table. Only upon the repetition of the order did she grasp her left ear. She did not succeed in finding her left eye and finally said: 'I don't know, I must have lost it.' When she was asked to show her hands, she tried to find them on the table and said: 'Nowhere, for heaven's sake; I have lost them, but they must be somewhere.' But the orientation of right and left was also lost. She did not know if there was right or left on her own body.

Such difficulty in finding the left and right sides of one's own body is also a difficulty in finding left and right in general.[6]

Observations of this kind have led to the conception of the 'body-image', which is a useful one for the understanding of mystical experience. It seems that each of us gradually constructs an inner image of himself, by which all postures and movements are judged. To construct the image, we use the look of our bodies to ourselves, that is, our optic images; we use the sense of our posture and the changes it undergoes; we use our feelings of our own symmetry; and we use the sense of our touch and our skin, which contains us.

This last, the skin that surrounds and bounds us, is not always as sharp a boundary as it may seem. If we close our eyes, we feel it here or there as warm or cold, but not as a smooth and complete and clear boundary. When we touch something and look at it, we see finger and object together, but we feel them as separate, a psychological space intervening between them. What is fused by the eyes is sensed but separated by touch. It is precisely the touch on the skin that makes us feel the skin distinctly and that defines us exactly in relation to what we touch. The less we touch, the vaguer we grow. Untouched, we grow vague as a colour which is not that of any surface.

As touch helps define our surfaces, movement helps to define our structures. Our shifting weight and moving limbs and expanding and contracting chest allow us to feel the parts of ourselves in their working relationships to one another. Perceiving our bodies more completely as we move, we have a feeling of completeness and perhaps reality. The feeling of reality is more or less concentrated in certain parts of the body. As we walk, it is concentrated in the soles of our feet, for then our changing contact with the ground tells us where and how we stand. We are realistic when we have our feet on the ground. The less we feel our heaviness and its shifting balance, the more vague we grow.

But the feeling of reality is also defined by our eyes. Our consciousness is focused with them, and although this may be a strange way of speaking, our egos, our own reality in our own eyes, seem to be located between our eyes, and to shift somewhat as we look far away, close by, or within ourselves.

Because the sense of reality joins the eyes, attempts at self-perception may cause actual shifts of the real and unreal. One experimenter reports the creation of something like the mystic third eye, and an apparent emptying of the body. He writes:

Some years ago, when I was interested in the phenomena of autoscopy (seeing one's own self), I made some experiments with normal subjects. I gave them the order to imagine themselves with closed eyes standing or sitting in front of themselves. The second instruction was to imagine themselves, but without an optic image in addition to the body which they felt. They were to imagine themselves as they saw themselves when they looked at their body, but they were also to imagine their face. All subjects could easily imagine themselves. They saw themselves more like a picture, sometimes a little smaller. At any rate the picture is not very plastic. It is not very different from any other picture we may imagine.

When one tries to imagine oneself according to the second instruction, there is very often a spiritual eye, which is in front of the subject and looks all over the body. This spiritual, inner eye need not be outside. It can be inside. It is like a psychic organ, which wanders round in the body and sees the outside of the body from the inside. It looks through the body, which is in some ways empty, yet it does not see the inside of the body, but the surface. This immaterial eye wanders according to the point of the surface that has to be observed. The impression of emptiness which occurs in these experiments is very queer. We are led here . . . to the problem of the perception of the inside of our body.[7]

There has not been much detail in what I have said of the child and his unity, and of the adult and his unity as expressed in the body-image. But I hope I have made it plausible that we begin life in a type of discontinous perceiving that bears some resemblance to mystical experience—not because it is discontinous, but because nothing in it is clearly distinguishable from the self, and because it hardly contains space, time, or stable objects of any sort. I hope it is also plausible that our sense of reality depends on a complicated sense of ourselves, which depends, all the time, on touching, moving, and seeing, and which is quite subject to change even in a sane and ordinary man. The same point is made, out of ordinary experience, by a psychologist, who describes the rise and fall of his sense of reality:

To begin with, how, from the introspective standpoint, shall the feeling of reality be defined? It is, as it were, psychical solidity: not merely vividness of experience but, rather, density of experience whether that experience be perceptual, ratiocinative, or emotional. With the loss of the sense of reality, tangibility and meaning evaporate from experience.

In my own experience the feeling of reality rises and falls. . . . Lack of sleep reduces the feeling of reality; so too, in even greater degree, does muscular fatigue of the eyes. . . . At such times the external world seems to lack solidity: it awakens no interest; people appear as trees walking; thought moves sluggishly; indifference to the consequences of actions ensues; consciousness of self ebbs. . . . The haze of an autumn day that makes objects seem far-off, immense, veiled, has the same effect upon mental experience. . . . The roar of a big city, the presence of a crowd of people reduces the sense of reality. . . .

Not only do sense stimulations bring on a feeling of unreality that extends from the sense world to the world of thought and emotion, but the reverse may happen. Prolonged reading or thinking on philosophical topics has the same results. Not only do conclusions seem to lack validity, but the world of daily experience also grows thin, dreamlike. This state, which is rather unpleasant, seems more akin to emotional than to mental fatigue. Again, the reading of certain sorts of poetry ... reduces the sense of reality.[8]

But when ordinary reality grows thin, another reality may grow visible. The shadow of unreality and the glitter of ecstasy coincide, the kind of mood Virginia Woolf often expressed, as when she described Mrs. Ramsey sitting alone at night:

She could be by herself, by herself.... All the being and doing, expansive, glittering, vocal, evaporated; and one shrunk, with a sense of solemnity, to being oneself, a wedge-shaped core of darkness, something invisible to others. Although she continued to knit, and sat upright, it was thus that she felt herself; and this self having shed its attachments was free for the strangest adventures. When life sank down for a moment, the range of experience seemed limitless. . . . Beneath it is all dark, it is all spreading, it is unfathomably deep; but now and again we rise to the surface and that is what you see us by. . . . Losing personality, one lost the fret, the hurry, the stir; and there rose to her lips always some exclamation of triumph over life when things came together in this peace, this rest, this eternity. . . .[9]

Sometimes, reality changes faces, and its objectivity becomes subjectivity:

The thing happened one summer afternoon, on the school cricket field, while I was sitting on the grass, waiting my turn to bat. I was thinking about nothing in particular, merely enjoying the pleasures of midsummer idleness. Suddenly, and without warning, something invisible seemed to be drawn across the sky, transforming the world about me into a kind of tent of concentrated and enhanced significance. What had been merely an outside became an inside. The objective was somehow transformed into a completely subjective fact, which was experienced as 'mine', but on a level where the word had no meaning; for 'I' was no longer the familiar ego. Nothing more can be said about the experience, it brought no accession of knowledge about anything except, very obscurely, the knower and his way of knowing. After a few minutes there was a 'return to normalcy'.[10]

Sometimes the 'subjectivity' is sensed as illumination. One's eyes project selfness and transform everything to a single brilliance:

Upon that instant the luminous haze engulfing me and all around me became transformed into golden glory, into light untellable. . . . The golden light of which the violet haze seemed now to have been as the veil or outer fringe, welled forth from a central immense globe of brilliancy. . . . But the most wonderful thing was that these shafts and waves of light, that vast expanse of photosphere, and even the great central globe itself, were crowded to solidarity with the forms of living creatures . . . a single coherent organism filling all place and space, yet composed of an infinitude of individuated existences. . . .

But this vast spectacle of heaven and earth was succeeded by an even richer experience; one in which everything in time and space and form vanished from my consciousness and only the ineffable eternal things remained. . . . And as the point of a candle-flame leaps suddenly upward, when an object is held just above it, so the flame of my consciousness leapt to its utmost limit and passed into the region of the formless and uncreated to tell of which all words fail.[11]

'Subjectivity', we see, can grow ecstatic and overwhelm the world's otherness. For the moment, our ecstasy lights and our love warms everything. Everything narrows and deepens to infinite fulfilment. It concentrates to a point at which reality and illusion are the same, Nirvana and the round of birth and death have no shade of difference. The ecstasy is the tool by which we make the world into something more nearly ourselves. It does not yield to the transformation for long. Suddenly it bruises us. We try a harsher transformation. We make it into anger, despair, or enmity. But again it does not yield for long. It caresses us. It threatens to turn quite dumb. Then we mould it, we paint it, we build it, we move it, we juggle it, we retell it, we rhyme it, we whistle it, we create it again and again.

6

Creators' Mysticism

The person who creates the world most effectively is the scientist
or artist. But the scientist is himself an artist, the artist is a mystic,
and the mystic is a scientist and an artist. If I have said this too
bluntly, I am willing to make amends with the all-powerful words,
'in a sense'. Because they are all creators, the scientist, artist, and
mystic are, in a sense, fundamentally alike. The likeness between
them is Buddha's smile.

I do not think that my exaggeration can be rescued by this obscure
metaphor alone. To make my meaning clear, I will describe Buddha's
smile. In the hope that the reader trusts me to be relevant in the end,
I will describe the smile, not in general, but in its repeated embodi-
ments in the 'Smiling Temple' of Angkor, the old capital of Cam-
bodia. This temple has fifty-four quadrangular towers, and each
side of each tower is a great face of the Buddha of Mercy. As usual
with Buddha, each face is dominated by a smile; but it cannot be
perceived as a clearly smiling face. Except for the mouth, it is impassive. Even the sensuously curved lips smile only with their very
ends, and the smile is accentuated or abolished by the angle from
which it is seen and by the direction from which the light falls on it.

The disappearing and reappearing smile of Buddha seems
comforting, and yet not exactly happy. It expresses two antithetical
states of emotion, profound pity and utter calm, whose union is
essential to Buddhism. We find it roughly the same antithesis in
the inscriptions left by the king, Jayavarman VII, who had the
temple built. This Jayavarman identified himself with the Buddha
of Mercy, and it is supposed that the Buddha who appears everywhere on the temple bears the King's features. One of the King's
inscriptions says that he has espoused his capital city, which is

centred on the temple, in order to procreate the happiness of the universe. Another inscription says that the physical illnesses of his subjects become a spiritual illness of the King, the harder to bear because not merely his own. The same king who procreates universal happiness, suffers more than anyone else. With respect to Buddha or the King, however, no incompatibility is allowed to be felt. The people are, essentially, the King, the King is Buddha, Buddha is both the temple and all reality, and the smile is their union. By the ontological stubbornness of its fellow-feeling, the smile abolishes the distinctions between every living thing and every degree of enlightenment. All beings are contained in it, just as, on the purely human level, worshippers are everywhere confronted with and bounded by the temple's two hundred and sixteen smiles, or one smile in different simultaneous illuminations.[1]

The Buddha's smile is the balance held between his opposite passions. It is the deliberate end result of his fears, his experiments, practical and intellectual, to overcome them, and his insight into all suffering. It is an impersonal compassion, offered to everyone at once, for its giver and receiver have no need to meet. Buddha has, so to speak, left his smile behind him, as the Cheshire cat did in *Alice in Wonderland*. It is as detached from him, personally, as a theory from the scientist who invents it, or a painting from its painter.

The Buddha's smile may be read as containing three essentials of creative effort. The first is a certain intensity of suffering in a certain kind of sufferer; the second is a certain passionately constructive answer to the suffering; and the third is a need, likely to be obscure, to atone for one's suffering and distance by a gift able to transform the suffering into a certain pleasure and the distance into a certain intimacy.

I have repeated the word 'certain' five times, not, I hope, out of pedantic caution, but because the words qualified by it ought to be explained in ways particularly relevant to creative effort. I know that I shall hardly be able to explain them so. Furthermore, I allow myself to speak of 'the' scientist, 'the' artist, and 'the' mystic, as if we were dealing with homogeneous and immutable species. I have no excuse except that I have been able to learn only enough to allow me to aim at crude approximations of the truth. Because I should be happy to arrive even at these, I shall ignore most of the sceptic's doubts, though I share them all.

Of the factors that will not be considered, the most important is heredity. The child who is to become creative may well begin life endowed with especial sensitivity. He may have literally keen senses, and react more strongly to their evidence. His imagination may more easily endow objects with quasi-human emotions. His emotions may have depth of saturation and delicacy of hue. Perhaps for this reason, he may have been born to have more intense relations with the members of his family—and greater difficulty, therefore, in resolving them without pain. He may be sensitive to symmetry or form in general; that is, he may derive pleasure from the balancing of objects and ideas, and the absence of balance between them may be actually painful to him. Considering all these sensitivities, it is not surprising that he may find himself engaged, while quite young, in what has been called 'a love affair with the world'. In such an affair, yearning and satisfaction are both great. Touch, hearing, sight, movement, or formal thought then give the child the same self-forgetful warmth and absorption that the scientist, artist, and mystic enjoy, and the same climactic exhilaration that is their internal reward.[2]

This is all plausible, and I myself believe it; but not much is known of the hereditary factors apart from their existence as such. They are not easily conceived in the absence of the external conditions that evoke them in different ways. The external conditions, especially the suffering to which I have referred, have been more clearly identified. There certainly is no contradiction in supposing that the need to create is evoked only in the sensitive, but first as an answer to continued pain, the most effective answer possible, because it transmutes the pain into pleasure.*

* Rumi, himself such an extraordinarily creative man, said:

'It is pain that guides man in every enterprise. Until there is an ache within him, a passion and a yearning for that thing arising within him, he will never strive to attain it. Without pain that thing remains for him unprocurable, whether it be success in this world or salvation in the next, whether he aims at being a merchant or a king, a scientist or an astronomer . . . The body is like Mary. Every one of us has a Jesus within him, but until the pangs manifest themselves in us our Jesus is not born. If the pangs never come, then Jesus rejoins his origin by the same secret path by which he came, leaving us bereft and without portion of him. (*Discourses of Rumi*, p. 33.)

However it may really be, this is the way I see the empirical evidence. The evidence which is personally most convincing is itself personal, and is drawn from the biographies of creative men. Since I am trying to suggest an idea rather than prove it, this is the evidence that will be cited. It has, of course, one ineradicable defect, the ease with which counter-evidence may be ignored. Before I give my personal instances, I should therefore like to recall the evidence of the few relatively objective and adequate inquiries of which I know.

To be relatively objective and adequate, an inquiry must, I think, be based on men who are still alive and whose co-operation has been enlisted. It is not that the dead are uninteresting; but unless we are able to raise their spirits, we remain without crucial information, because the evidence that has been left us is too often thin and always too uneven in quality. To be adequate, an inquiry must judge the power of creation by genuine and exceptional accomplishments, and not merely by standard tests.* It is not unknown for accomplished artists, successful by every obvious criterion, to get a low grade in 'creativity' on a test. Not every artist in fact is also a questionnaire-artist or Rorschach-artist. I think that experience also shows that such research, to be even relatively adequate, must deal with small numbers of men. The most immediate reason is that, by high standards, there are not many who qualify as creators. Besides, each individual must be examined as deeply as possible, and always in the light of his highest accomplishments. And yet, in spite of the intensiveness of the research, it must be broad enough to make some statistical generalizations possible.

* This conclusion has been reached by some among the testers themselves:
'The biographical items and past achievements are our most efficient predictors. Self-rating and direct expressions of goals and aspirations are next. Originality and personality inventories run a very poor third. Aptitude and intelligence measures rank fourth (except where restriction-of-range corrections are really applicable), followed finally by parental attitudes.' (C. W. Taylor and J. Holland, 'Predictors of Creative Performance', in C. W. Taylor, *Creativity: Progress and Potential*, N.Y., 1964, p. 41.)
My impression is that inquiries that include all successful professionals in a 'creative' profession, emerge with a more 'normal' composite creator than when only exceptionally successful men are included. Anne Roe has said that the more exceptional an exceptionally creative scientist, the more 'abnormal', i.e. driven or neurotic he is likely to be.

The few researches that qualify seem to show that strikingly creative men share their independence of character and a necessary minimum of intelligence, but otherwise not much beyond their creativity itself. Sometimes a composite picture is made of traits abstracted from many different individuals; but the individuals remain almost as different from their statistical average as they are from one another. They are social or unsocial, married or single, happy or unhappy, psychologically healthy or ill. In spite of all their differences, however, they have undergone some decisive experiences of the same general kind.

What are these decisive experiences? One of them is absence of a parent, or estrangement from a parent, especially a father. Among the forty creative scientists included in one study, nineteen had never known their fathers well, either because the fathers had died early, had been divorced, had usually be absent from home, or had been absorbed in their work alone. The scientists tended to dislike their fathers, whether or not they knew them well, and to emphasize their faults, particularly their sternness and aloofness. Of a similar group of artists, writers, and the like, a full half had lost their fathers in childhood. Business men chosen to compare with the scientists and artists had been much luckier or happier with their fathers.

For some reason, so runs the testimony, whether the nature of parents, the death of parents, illness, or social discrimination, both scientists and artists had felt painfully isolated during part of their childhood. It was then that they had first discovered that they could be their own society and find intense pleasure in their own thoughts and activities. The scientists, I know, and the artists, I think, did not feel lonely when they were alone with their work. Their work was the medium by which they were related both to themselves and to others. They took great satisfaction in recognizing themselves as parts of an ideal community made up of the creators, past, present, and future, whom they respected. But when their work was going badly, or when they had stopped work for a time, they felt alone even when in company.

To test the truth of what I have just said I scanned a collection of brief autobiographies of contemporary English writers. Of the thirteen persons included, nine refer explicitly to loneliness or isolation as crucial to their having become writers, though some regard the loneliness as self-imposed. Norman Nicholson says, 'When I was sixteen my health broke down, and I went to the New Forest and spent most of the next two years in bed. That was my university.' He came back to his home town, but found that 'a sore, a split, was opening up' in his mind. Slowly he was reabsorbed into the town and its people. 'Out of that healing', he says, 'came my poetry, and, at the same time, the writing of the poetry was itself part of the process of healing.' William Sansom remembers an illness. He writes, 'Perhaps this was for me a period not only of fever isolation but also mental isolation of the first order. An advanced course in egocentricity. Yet also—since I had to use my eyes on the balcony, it was a great exercise in quietly watching things.' By the time the isolation came to an end, Sansom adds, 'I'd got used to being alone, I'm not sure I really wanted to get out into the world again.' Vernon Scannell's isolation came as the result of war wounds, and then desertion from the army. Thomas Hinde was isolated from the world by his service in a submarine, and from his companion sailors by his personality. John Bowen's first book was, in his own eyes, his ' "loneliness" book'. Michael Baldwin begins his reminiscences with the game he used to play at being lonely. Julian Mitchell recalls the time when he emerged out of misery and discovered, he says, that 'What was making me happy was that I was putting my loneliness to use.' David Storey, driven, while living at home, to spending long periods alone, felt he 'was inhabiting a place so inaccessible as virtually to be non-existent'. Sylvia Plath recalls that when she was a young child she learned that her mother was about to give birth. The information struck her hard. She says,

As from a star I saw, coldly and soberly, the *separateness* of everything. I felt the wall of my skin: I am I. That stone is a stone. My beautiful fusion with the things of this world was over.

So much confirmation of the creative effect, which I assume, of loneliness, makes me uncomfortable. The truth cannot be that simple; but I find it hard to give up even excessive evidence. It should be registered, and then somewhat doubted.

To return to the general problem of scientists and artists, it should not be thought that their relation to their work was easy. If scientists, they might be cool and objective with people, but never with their own scientific ideas. The systematic rationality of science was used by some of them to ward off frightening impulses. This observation is in keeping with the instances discovered by psychoanalysts in which pure mathematics shield a man from insanity. In such instances, the man identifies himself subjectively with his abstract thoughts, yet the thoughts have objective value; and while, with pure mathematics, he cuts himself off from the physical and social world, his social value restores him to it indirectly. Briefly, creative men are likely to be at once more sick, more troubled psychologically, and more healthy, more resourceful in surmounting inner difficulties, than other people.

Often, a scientist or artist is fulfilling a parental ideal. If he dislikes the parent whose ideal he has assimilated, he will turn this dislike against his own work. Such was the case of one unfortunate scientist who was unable to respect his own genuine accomplishments because he disliked the father with whom he identified himself. Rather like him, there was an artist who always painted helpless sufferers, allowing himself, in this way, to create the suffering and to sympathize with its victims. Another artist could paint only in black and white; colours frightened him with their open expression of aggressiveness. A third used his art to exorcise the fantasies that haunted him, so that he could return to an old peace.[3]

This, briefly, is what I have found as an objective background. Having paid our respects to the more objective studies, we may turn to particular, subjectively chosen examples of scientists, writers, and artists. For the first category, I have chosen two physicists, Schrödinger and Einstein, and a psychologist, Carl Jung, who will serve as a transition from the scientist to the artist.

Schrödinger tells us that when, at the age of thirty-one, he was offered his first position lecturing on theoretical physics, he still expected to devote himself mainly to philosophy. He was imbued, he says, with the writings of Spinoza, Schopenhauer, Richard Semon, and Richard Avenarius. I have no independent knowledge of Semon, but the rest of the group is surely symptomatic. Spinoza is a rationalist and determinist with a mystical yearning to identify his own thought with the infinite, eternal intellect of the universe. Mach and Avenarius hoped to persuade their readers that nothing could be known apart from our sensations, which they regarded as neither purely physical nor psychical. This insight, they thought, would eliminate metaphysical distinctions and end the futile attempt to penetrate behind appearances. The stranger in this company is Schopenhauer, the outright mystic.

A few months before he became absorbed in inventing the revolutionary idea of wave mechanics, Schrödinger wrote an essay, 'Seek for the Road', in which he justified mysticism. It is easy, he said, to eliminate the whole of metaphysics, but if we were to do so, we should take the soul out of both art and science. We must, on the one hand, restrain metaphysics from influencing the individual sciences, and, on the other, preserve it as the only possible basis of our knowledge. Appearances, which must be kept pure, are no more than appearances. The plurality we perceive is not real. The knowledge, the feeling, the choice, that each of us calls his own cannot have sprung suddenly out of nothingness. These are essentially eternal and numerically one in all sentient beings. The life we are living is that of the whole. One's self is not, as is said, linked to its ancestors; it is, quite strictly, the same one substance as they.

Schrödinger supports these conclusions, which he recognizes as those of the Vedanta, that is, of Shankara's school, by reasoning in Vedantic style about the nature of consciousness. The cells and organs of his body, he says, are a multitude. How, out of them, or out of the multitude of his brain-cells, could the unity of his Self have been constituted? As Shankara said, the only perfectly certain piece of knowledge we can attain is that we experience consciousness always and everywhere in the singular. The directly experienced unity of consciousness or Self is not subject to the categories of number or of whole and part.

At this point Schrödinger connects Mach and Avenarius with the Vedanta. They show us, he says, that consciousness is the same as the external world. Consciousness and external world are equally of the nature of sensations; they are in perfect commerce with one another and form the same essential community in all men. From

Mach and Avenarius we are able to conclude that there is only one world, and it makes little difference if we speak of it as one external or one internal world, one consciousness. As Schrödinger said later, the hypothesis of a really external, plural world is just as irrational as that of universal identity. The doctrine of identity makes it hard to explain why there seem to be different people and things, but this is a minor defect compared with its higher ethical content and deep religious consolation.

Schrödinger retained this position all his life. I do not think he added any essential arguments to it. He was sure that we were outside of the material world that science constructs for us. 'We are not in it,' he said, 'we are outside. We are only spectators. The reason why we believe that we are in it, that we belong to the picture, is that our bodies are in the picture. Our bodies belong to it. Not only my body, but also those of my friends, also of my dog and cat and horse, and of all the other people and animals. And this is my only means of communicating with them.'

This must sound rather enigmatic. The beginning is familiar to me from the Vedanta; the end I can interpret psychologically, but I can make no logical or, should I say, despite Schrödinger, empirical sense out of it. It must be a reason only in the sense of a feeling.

I do not know either Schrödinger or his theories well enough to connect his mysticism with them except very generally. Very generally, one might say that Schrödinger completed the analogy in which particle waves were to particle orbits as light waves had been found to be to light rays. This microcosmic-macrocosmic analogy he might then take as an instance of the principle that the variety of the world was a deceptive emanation of its uniformity. Furthermore, 'particles' have an only relative location—everything is to some degree everywhere, everything affects everything else. When Schrödinger tells us that 'acausality, wave mechanics indeterminacy relation, complementarity, an expanding universe, etc. do not have as much connection as is currently supposed with a philosophical view of the world', he means, I take it, that current scientific views cannot be integrated into a philosophy because they are its opposite. Whatever his conscious position, I am sure that there must have been a psychological relationship in Schrö-dinger's mind between the two trains of thought that dominated it, between his scientific theories and his mysticism. Both are highly abstract, that is, both arrive at a world very different from that of ordinary perception. The one train of thought involves plurality, the other, the mystical, refuses it; but both withdraw attention from our bodies and dogs and cats, and centre it, in the one case, on an 'energy-smear' or a vibrating 'psi-essence', and, in the other, on Brahman or Atman, which is 'being-awareness-bliss'. In his thought, electrons are transcended by a continuous vibrating 'cloud', just as individuals of any kind are transcended by an ineffable, blissful continuity.

Schödinger was an eloquent but lonely man. No more than three of his ninety papers were written in collaboration with another author. Indirectly, he tells us that he was schizoid, a nature not surprising in a theoretical physicist. He was not his body, he felt, though he could communicate with others only through the body that he was not, as if, I suppose, two disembodied minds could communicate only through the illusion of a material telephone. He could not bear to think that reality might be different from his awareness of himself. Perhaps the clearest clue he gives us is his equation of Machism and mysticism, for both make the universe out to be all of one pure and simple kind.[4]

Einstein seems to me to have been a more rational kind of mystic, confining his mysticism to emotions and ideals. As a child, he was withdrawn. He did not speak, we are told, until he was three years old, and he always remained sure that most thinking was wordless and, beyond wordlessness, unconscious. He liked to assemble shapes out of children's blocks and 'shapes cut out with a jigsaw'. Soon he developed a feeling of the difference between what things looked like and what, behind them, made them react as they did. He never forgot the time when, at the age of four or five, he was shown a compass and felt that 'something deeply hidden had to be behind things'.

As a schoolboy, Einstein persisted in learning only what interested him, Euclid's geometry, for example, which transported him with pleasure. Aloof, bookish, and painfully solitary, he regarded the teachers who tried to force him to learn what they, rather than he wanted as attacking his sincerity and self-confidence. In spite of the irreligiousness of his Jewish parents, he himself was deeply religious, until, at the age of twelve, the popular scientific books he read convinced him that the stories in the Bible could not be true just as they stood. 'The consequence was a positively fanatical free-thinking coupled with the impression that youth is intentionally deceived by the state through lies; it was a crushing impression. Suspicion against every kind of authority grew out of this experience.' But the strivings of most men seemed empty to him, and he soon noticed that the men he admired had found their inner freedom and security in a life of contemplation.

Contemplative men are, I suppose, generally lonely and find their company mainly in themselves. Einstein always felt himself to be remote from other people. He himself testifies so, while his elder son recalls how Einstein would suddenly estrange himself. According to his son, 'He would not let himself go. He would turn off his emotion like a tap.' At times, he would simply not see or hear the person confronting him, but live within his own fantasies. No doubt this self-immersion was allied with his 'wonderful purity at once childlike and profoundly stubborn'.

Einstein's miniature 'Self-Portrait' emphasizes mystery, isolation, determination by one's own nature, and the eventual rewards of solitude:

Of what is significant in one's own existence one is hardly aware, and it certainly should not bother the other fellow. What does a fish know about the water in which he swims all his life?

The bitter and the sweet come from the outside, the hard from within, from one's own efforts. For the most part I do the thing which my own nature drives me to do. It is embarrassing to earn so much respect and love for it. Arrows of hate have been shot at me too; but they never hit me, because somehow they belonged to another world with which I have no connection whatsoever.

I live in that solitude which is painful in youth, but delicious in the years of maturity.

I think there is another, earlier emotional self-portrait in the tribute he paid in 1918 to his friend, Max Planck. Perhaps because this portrait is earlier, the scientist Einstein speaks of seems rather more vulnerable to pain, less firmly established in the hate-free world:

I believe with Schopenhauer that one of the strongest motives that leads me to art and science is escape from life with its painful crudity and hopeless dreariness, from the fetters of one's own ever shifting desires. A finely tempered nature longs to escape from personal life into the world of impersonal perception and thought. . . . With this negative motive there goes a positive one. Man tries to make for himself in the fashion that suits him best a simplified and intelligible picture of the world; he then tries to some extent to substitute this cosmos of his for the world of experience, and thus to overcome it. This is what the painter, the poet, the speculative philosopher, and the natural scientist do, each in his own fashion. Each makes this cosmos and its construction the pivot of his emotional life, in order to find in this way the peace and security which he cannot find in the narrow whirlpool of his personal experience. The longing to behold this preestablished harmony is the source of the inexhaustible patience with which Planck has devoted himself, as we see, to the most general problems of our science. . . . The state of mind which enables a man to do work of this kind is akin to that of the religious worshipper or the lover.

Like Planck's, Einstein's appetite for learning and thinking was insatiable. During his later years, he would withdraw completely into his attic room, sometimes for three days at a stretch—just like Spinoza, to whom Einstein rightly felt very close. Spinoza did not want possessions, nor did Einstein. 'Every possession', said Einstein, 'is a stone around the leg. . . . There is nothing I could not dispense with at any moment.'

Simplicity seemed allied with constancy—the world was really more constant than its shifting surface—and constancy of the simple sort with a minimum of constraints and so with freedom. This was the more true if the simplicity or the invariant was that discovered by oneself, out of one's own desires and expressed in a language that had become native to oneself. The three great papers Einstein wrote in 1905 did away with asymmetries in theory by showing that they stemmed from too narrow a view of things. To paraphrase Einstein, the ability of God to choose the sort of world he made could be shown by the degree of simplicity and invariance on which He constructed it. The world, as he hoped and then discovered, did not really have to wear socks and fancy clothes.

To Einstein, the world was plausible only if continuous. A scientific essay he wrote at the age of about fifteen shows him already devoted to the continuum. Shankara-like, he regarded the discreteness of particles as an illusion. Although he himself helped to establish quantum physics, he said to one friend, Leopold Infeld, 'I may have started it, but I always regarded these ideas as temporary,' and to another, Michel Besso, 'The quantum does what it should, but it does not exist.'

Long after most physicists had given up absolute determinism, Einstein insisted that he, personally, *could* not doubt it, and that it ought to be believed in. How could Einstein have thought otherwise when he had always felt that he, the man, could not really decide anything? He was sure that factors he could not control determined everything, including the whole of his life and reasoning. His nature, which drove him to do what he did, was itself, he felt, driven.*

Einstein's last years were given over to the establishment of a unified field theory, which would describe both the gravitational and electromagnetic fields in one set of equations. He believed in what he called 'cosmic religion', the religion of the vanity of human desires and aims and the nobility and marvellous order of nature. He was impressed by individual existence as a sort of prison and wanted to experience the universe as a single significant whole. He had, he said, the mystical emotion, the pleasure of the experience of the inexplicable intellectual penetrability of the universe. He united

---

* Although what I say about Einstein's determinism is based on his own remarks, he seems, at least when older, to have arrived at a more subtle position. The physicist, Wolfgang Pauli, who discussed the matter with Einstein in 1954, reported that 'in particular, Einstein does not consider the concept of "determinism" to be as fundamental as it is frequently held to be (as he told me emphatically many times). . . . He *disputes* that he uses as a criterion for the admissibility of a theory the question: "Is it rigorously deterministic?" Einstein's point of departure is "realistic" rather than "deterministic", which means that his philosophical prejudice is a different one.' (*The Born-Einstein Letters*, translated by Irene Born, Macmillan, London, 1971, p. 221 (letter 115).)

in himself, as he acknowleged, possible opposites, such as rationalism and empiricism, between which he wavered.

Everything Einstein thought and did took the form of an answer to death. His answer was the mystic's. He was concerned, he said, with eternity and with the continuity of mankind. He added, movingly, 'It does not matter to me where a single life starts and stops.'[5]

Physicists may by nature be unwilling or unable to reveal much about themselves. Jung, the psychologist, reveals himself even disturbingly. This is not because he engages, like some modern novelists, in scatology, but because he shows, clearly and in detail, how close he lived to the borderline of schizophrenia.

When Jung was a child of about seven, he would identify himself with different objects. He was particularly concerned with a stone he found on a slope. He would sit on the stone and think, 'I am sitting on top of this stone and it is underneath.' But the stone, he thought, was also an 'It' and could think, 'I am lying here on this slope and he is sitting on top of me.' Then the question arose, 'Am I the one who is sitting on the stone, or am I the stone on which he is sitting?' A Taoist might have accepted the question as an answer, but to Jung the answer remained unclear and accompanied by a feeling of fascinating darkness.

Jung tended to divide himself into at least two distinct persons. One of them he thought of as ordinary and not very intelligent, but clean and decent. The other was remote from the world of men, and close, instead, to the night, to dreams, and to whatever 'God', Jung felt, worked in him directly. The second self, the 'Other', knew God as both personal and suprapersonal. This self lived in a temple-like cosmos in which he forgot himself and looked down upon creation simultaneously with God. 'Nobody', writes Jung, 'could rob me of the conviction that it was enjoined upon me to do what God wanted and not what I wanted.' His talks with the 'Other' were his most profound experiences, on the one hand, as he says, a bloody struggle, but on the other, the supreme ecstasy.

Sitting inside the tower he had constructed at Bollingen, Jung sensed himself to be united with everything, but especially with the silent, centuries-old family to which he belonged. He felt spread out into all things, omni-linked. In his own words:

At times I feel as if I am spread out over the landscape and inside things, and am myself living in every tree, in the plashing of the waves, in the clouds and the animals that come and go, in the procession of the seasons. There is nothing in the Tower that has not grown into its own form over the decades, nothing with which I am not linked. Here everything has its own history, and mind; here is space for the spaceless kingdom of the world's and the psyche's hinterland.

In a retrospective, old man's mood, Jung said that he was not wise, that he did nothing, but that he could see, because for him, unlike most persons, the dividing walls between himself and nature were transparent. Loneliness does not come, he said, from having no people about one, but from being unable to communicate the things that seem important to oneself. Even his own relation to himself had not been easy. 'I have had much trouble in getting along with my ideas,' he summed up. 'There was a daimon in me, and in the end its presence proved decisive.' The daimon was that of creation.

What feeling remains towards the end of life?

I am disappointed and not disappointed. I am disappointed with people and disappointed with myself. I have learned amazing things from people, and have accomplished more than I expected of myself. . . . I am astonished, disappointed, pleased with myself. I am distressed, depressed, rapturous. I am all these things at once, and cannot add up the sum . . . I have no definite convictions—not about anything, really. I know only that I was born and exist, and it seems to me that I have been carried along. I exist on the foundation of something that I do not know. In spite of all uncertainties, I feel a solidity underlying all existence and a continuity in my mode of being. . . . Life is—or has—meaning and meaninglessness. I cherish the hope that meaning will preponderate and win the battle.

In this last passage there is no conversation between Jung One and Jung Two, but every question is answered with 'Yes' and with 'No', and everything is sure and doubtful at once. If One and Two and 'Yes' and 'No' are to survive as a single person, some alchemical union must be created between them. As Jung was once describing his different selves to himself, a voice arose in him and told him that he was engaged not in science but in art. Jung answered the new member of his self-contained family, "No, it is not art! On the contrary, it is nature.' But the voice was not wholly wrong. Not only is Jung always in search of deeply-felt images, focal points of his own and everyone's life, but his writing constantly expresses the poetic, mystic strain between separation—within his mind, between his mind and body, between himself and others, between himself and everything—and unity.[6]

This search and this expressiveness make Jung resemble, in a quite general way, the two artist-intellectuals, Valéry and Sartre, who furnish the next examples.

Valéry's struggle over his own unity is the main theme of his writing. One stormy night, after a disappointment in love, he went through a crisis of self-division that he was afraid would end in madness. At least from then on, he felt the profound difference between the 'myself' in him and the 'me'. This was a sense, like Jung's, of the distinct potentialities he contained. Everything tended to break into fragments. Perceived time was a chaos of isolated instants. It could be given order only to the extent that he, the writer, invented a direction for it; but by freeing himself from perceived time so as to conceive it better, he was left in the end with his isolated intellect, and then he could be reborn each moment, he felt, for each moment. We must be reminded by Valéry of the Buddhist Saint who occupies the pure moment. 'I am,' Valéry said, 'is this not extraordinary? To keep afloat above death as a stone might float in space? It is incredible.'

Sometimes Valéry sees his writing as the expression of a struggle between a repetitive spontaneity and a difficult conscious originality; at other times he takes it to express the struggle between the treacherous, instinctive woman in himself and the lucid and intellectual but blind man. He was searching for a friendship with himself. At one time in his life he hoped to find it round about, by an ideal friendship with another man. He thought that, when perfected, friendship would transfigure him, open a superior level of existence to him, begin his metamorphosis towards the divine. He offered Gide their 'perfect confusion into a single person'. At another time he advised himself to substitute life in another living being for the mystic's life in God.[7]

Jean-Paul Sartre's early life is described in his autobiography,

Words. While still young, he found life too hard and became intoxicated with the thought of death. However, he was terrified of death, and so he undertook to write as an excuse for being alive. He discovered that in literature the Giver can change himself into his own Gift, changing in this way from an accidentally existing man into a timeless generosity 'other than myself, other than others, other than everything'. He imagined himself transformed into his works and deposited in the Bibliothèque Nationale, 25 volumes comprised of 18,000 pages of text and 300 illustrations, including a portrait of the author. He saw himself in his leather and cardboard bones and parchment flesh, swaggering easily across the reams of his paper. Reborn so from nullity into completeness, he would speak at last with the peremptory force of matter. Now no one would be able to forget or ignore him. His own consciousness would be fragmented, but he would be assimilated into that of everyone else, would become a universal and singular language spoken by everyone. To be and not to be would then be the same. Imagining this Buddhistic condition, Sartre writes,

For anyone who knows how to live me, I am his most intimate disquiet, but if he wants to touch me, I efface myself and disappear; I no longer exist anywhere, at last I *am*! I am everywhere: the parasite of humanity, my good deeds torment it and force it constantly to revive my absence.

To be present in the constant renewal of one's absence is a good definition of the Buddhist's Nirvana.

Sartre tried to save himself by writing, with words. He confused things, he now says, with their names. He emerged out of this stage at the age of thirty, when, in *La Nausée*, he exposed himself. He was Roquentin, the novel's hero. If we leave Sartre's autobiography and turn to the novel, what do we find? An anxious and depressed man alienated from reality. He loves to touch things; but one day the crumpled newspaper in his hand seems to join his hand and become part of his body. This nauseates him; but his consciousness of the sensation allows him to remain separate from it. When existence touches him too closely, it seems to penetrate him everywhere, by his eyes, nose, and mouth, and suffocate him. And yet he wants to experience strong sensations and to reassure himself that the world is not all unreal. Sometimes he identifies himself not with his sensations but with his thoughts. But he is unable to complete the identification. He is afraid. He feels his thoughts arising behind him, behind his head, and growing immensely within him. 'My thought is me,' he feels.

That is why I can't stop . . . I exist by what I think . . . and I can't prevent myself from thinking. At this very moment—this is terrible—if I exist, *it is because* I hate existing. It is I, *it is I* who pull myself away from the nothing to which I aspire: hatred and disgust for existence are just so many ways of *making me* exist, of thrusting me into existence. Thoughts are born behind me like a feeling of giddiness, I can feel their being born behind my head.

Roquentin-Sartre finds that he is both an 'I' and a 'he', and the I and the he accompany one another and both suspect that they are mad. Their hand lies open on the table like a crab lying dead on its back.* The face reflected at Roquentin by the mirror does not seem to belong to him.

Apart from the talent with which they are expressed, and even this does not distinguish them absolutely, these experiences might occur in the memoirs of anyone on or over the verge of schizophrenia, or enduring the 'black night' that precedes a mystical revelation. In the novel, Roquentin decides to give up the biography he has been writing and to *create* a novel, by means of which he might be able to recall his life without repugnance. Sartre tells us that in writing *La Nausée* he was enabled to be cheerful about our wretched lot and be happy because he took anxiety as the proof of his safety. He still writes, he says with an air of helplessness. 'What else can I do? . . . You can get rid of a neurosis but you can never be cured of yourself.' Confidently, however, he adds, 'I have changed.'

That Sartre has changed is easy to believe. But it is no discourtesy to point out, much as he does, that the change is not complete. Like his earlier books, his *Critique of Dialectical Reason* was written to protect him by means of the furious work it required. He was troubled by Algeria, by the defeat of the left, and especially by

* A similar detached-hand image is found in Rilke's *Notebooks of Malte Laurid Brigge* and in Malraux's *The Royal Way*.

De Gaulle's rise to power; and also, circularly and paradoxically, by 'the fear of spoiling a work that was enormously important to him' and by the method he used of 'thinking against himself', But not alone is Sartre's writing in the *Critique* still a form of self-protection, but it still shows his old appetite to touch, fathom, assimilate, and transform the world, to transform it into himself-not-quite-himself. He takes everything to be truly significant because it relates to the whole, which is neither opaque nor transparent. Like a Plotinus or Proclus, Sartre discovers that every word or concept contains the whole of language within it. The word is objective, it designates what it is meant to, but it refers to a deeper, non-verbal 'comprehension', which is existence itself, always in process.

I do not want to try to explain these words about words. This would take us too exclusively into Sartre. Strange as it may seem, however, their psychic atmosphere is Neoplatonic. And there is something like Neoplatonism, or even Vedanta, in him when he speaks of 'rational non-knowledge', meaning the knowledge that cannot be put into words but which is at the heart of the knowledge that can be. 'A discipline in which the questioner, the question, and the questioned are one' sounds for all the world like a Vedantic discipline, and the 'singularized universals' he searches for are not unlike the Atman that is Brahman, meaning, the very awareness, proper to the individual, that is also the universal reality. Our reality, he says, is the irreducible internalization of the exterior and exteriorization of the internal. I should regard this as an incomplete but penetrating definition of mysticism. His 'total totalization' may have an ugly sound, but it evokes the mystic's infinite appetite very well.

I think that we should allow Sartre to define himself, and agree, as he wishes, that he is no longer a mystic. But his vocabulary of 'totalization', 'transcendence', and the like, reminds us of his child-hood dreams; and the history he envisions, great, comprehending, dialectical, totally total, is not altogether different from the 18,000 pages of text he once dreamed of, that speak 'a universal and singular language' and dominate everyone by Sartre's simultaneous presence and absence. Nor is it quite different from Roquentin's union with and separation from that which he touches and that which he thinks.

Sartre's problem or tension has remained that of keeping things together, of being great and small, universal and singular at the same time. He thinks that history arrives at such a union. He calls the historic process the 'constituting dialectic'; but the dialectic by which he constitutes himself is the process by which he writes and, in writing, creates.[8]

My last illustrations are Van Gogh, Rodin, and Rilke.

Like Sartre, Van Gogh often disliked himself. He subjected himself to both psychic and physical punishment. While a theological student, he would sleep on the floor, and also flagellate himself. When he was told by the parents of Kornelia, the young woman he loved, that she refused to see him again, he put his finger into the flame of a lamp and threatened to keep it there until she returned. It may have been as a further self-punishment that he took up with a forlorn prostitute. As he said to his brother, 'I demand sympathy with a kind of hunger and thirst, and if I don't find that sympathy I show myself indifferent and pour more oil into the flame myself.'

Van Gogh's paintings are consciously symbolic. For instance, he regarded the horizon, separating earth from sky, as the separation between that which man could and could not know. There, above the line, was 'the other side of life, where one might perhaps understand the existence of pain which, looked at from here, occupies so much of the horizon'. In his self-portrait with a bandaged ear, the horizon-line is exactly at the level of his eyes, as if he were on the verge of seeing over life and into death.

Van Gogh painted his need for love. Explaining himself through Whitman, he said that Whitman 'sees in the future, and even in the present, a world of health, of carnal love, great and frank—of friendship—of work, with the great starry firmament, something which in short one can call only God and eternity, placed again above this world'. Van Gogh's *Starry Night*, especially in its later version, bodies forth such feelings as if fulfilled. Its cypresses are sharp, straight, and tall, its stars are bright and huge, the bulge of the sun coincides with the hollow of the moon, and one cloud is fitted into another.

In his colours, Van Gogh tried to achieve, so he said, a balance with 'pairs enhancing and completing each other like man and woman'. He dreamed of an ideal community of painters and wanted to be 'a link in the chain of artists'. His ideal was union through love. 'To live,' he said, 'to work, to love are really one. . . . The more I think about it the more I feel that there is nothing more really artistic than to love people.'[9]

Rodin's self-enlargement was love in a narrower, more direct sense. Like Roquentin, he assimilated through touch, but only with pleasure. This is especially clear in a description he gave of his modelling and drawing. As he explained to a friend:

For my work of modelling I have not only to possess a very complete *knowledge* of the human form, but also a deep *feeling* for every aspect of it. I have, as it were, to *incorporate* the lines of the human body, and they must become permeated with the secrets of myself, deeply seated in my instincts. I must become permeated with the secrets of its contours, all the masses that it presents to the eye. I must feel them at the end of my fingers. All this must flow naturally from my eye to my hand. . . . Now look! What is this drawing? Not once in describing the shape of the mass did I shift my eyes from the model. Why? Because I wanted to be sure that nothing evaded my grasp of it. The moment I drop my eyes that flow stops. That is why my drawings are only my way of testing myself. They are my ways of proving to myself how far this incorporation of the subtle secrets of the human form has taken place within me. I try to see the figure as a mass, as volume. It is this voluminousness that I try to understand. This is why . . . I sometimes wash a tint over my drawings. This completes the impression of massiveness, and helps me to ascertain how far I have succeeded in grasping the movement as a mass. . . . My object is to test to what extent my hands already feel what my eyes see.

Rodin resembles Renoir in that he handles the forms of his art like the bodies of the women he loved. He believed that he 'entered into the truth' by means of 'the hugging execution of the contours'. He sculptured hands with endless passion. Rilke, who acted as his secretary, said of these:

There are among the works of Rodin hands, single, small hands which, without belonging to a body, are alive. Hands that rise, irritated and in wrath; hands whose five bristling fingers seem to bark like the five jaws of a dog of Hell. Hands that walk, sleeping hands, and hands that are awakening; criminal hands, tainted with hereditary disease; hands that are tired and will do no more, and have lain down in some corner like sick animals that know no one can help them. But hands are a complicated organism, a delta into which many divergent streams of life rush together in order to pour themselves into the great storm of action.

Rodin's handling of his sculptures was lifelike in more than one sense. In life, his sexual appetites were insatiable, and rich women who had sat for him hinted proudly that there had been at least the suggestion of an affair.* But Rodin's art was more a marriage than a casual liaison. In it he could create and recreate the consciousness of including and being included at once, of living in one and in more than one skin and mind. Sculpture gave him an intimacy through muscular tension and touch; but, like a Descartes of sculpture, he had to keep proving to himself that he was touching a sufficient reality, something moving and massive, curved subtly, sensual, and penetrable. Given this need to touch, discover, and take in, without end, it was natural for him to paraphrase Spinoza and say, in more conventionally mystical words, that he was striving to gain knowledge of the union which the thinking soul has with the whole of Nature, and to help others attain to this knowledge along with him.[10]

In his book on Rodin, Rilke argued that sculpture helps us because it turns human yearnings and fears into external things. He praised Rodin for his adult mastery of experience, though he himself wished to be a masterly artist but childlike man. He was more sceptical of the flesh than Rodin, or yearned more to go beyond it. He was happy when his married friends separated. The great lovers, he thought, were women who had lost the hope of fulfilment in the body and had risen to an 'intransitive', lonely love. The intention of sex must be infinite, and the aim of coming together only an increase in loneliness. Rilke broached all this to Rodin. He gave the example of the Portuguese nun, Marianna Alcoforado, but to no effect. 'I speak to

---

* 'It is said that Fra Lippo Lippi was so lustful that he would give anything to enjoy a woman he wanted if he thought he could have his way; and if he couldn't buy what he wanted, then he would cool his passion by painting her portrait and reasoning with himself.' (G. Vasari, *The Lives of the Artists*, trans. G. Bull, Penguin Books, 1966, p. 216.)

him', he said, 'of all her rapture transformed, and the woman's will *beyond* gratification; he does not believe it.' Years later, his feeling, that love, like art, should go against nature, was confirmed when he saw that the seventy-year-old Rodin had become an old satyr, mastered by his obsession 'as though all his infinite work had not existed'.

For Rilke, art has a simultaneous personal and cosmic function. Early in his career he imagined the artist-god who would take the external world into himself:

There will be nothing outside him; for trees and mountains, clouds and waves will be but symbols of the realities he will find *within* himself. Everything has flowed together in him. . . . The very ground beneath his feet is too much. He will roll it up like a prayer-carpet. He will just *be*.

Late in his career, in the *Duino Elegies*, Rilke imagined an angel, perfectly unified, with no split between thought and action, will and ability, or actual and ideal. Sometimes lovers, he wrote, almost transcend the distinction between subject and object, sometimes children do transcend it, and in the womb it is always transcended. He was still lonely. He wrote:

I have no window on human beings, definitely. They yield themselves to me only in so far as they are able to make themselves heard within myself, and, during these last years, they have been communicating with me almost entirely through two figures, on which I base my conjectures about human beings in general.

Lou Andreas-Salomé, one of these two figures, was the person best fitted to describe him, for she had loved and lived with him, had remained, with a break, close to him, respected his poetry greatly, and had acquired the sharp, relatively objective eyes of the psychoanalyst. Speaking both in the past and present tenses, she saw him so:

A lyric poet, he nevertheless concentrated his powers early in life and unsparingly sheared off all dilettantism and vacillation, but became totally disorganized in his personal life. . . . A typical hysteric, the victim of his physical condition, abandoning himself in his devotion, owned by nobody, not knowing to whom he belongs, until he comes as one delivered into the homeland of creativity. . . . Rainer's dream: to be 'a thing among things', at peace and finally integrated. . . . Consequently Rainer stands

free among men, driven almost out of himself, capable of playing any
role, happy in acting, reciting, being loved, and at the same time a passionate solitary because he can also do all these things alone by himself.

The very fact that he no longer comes apart into two beings, too alien
from each other to suffer from each other, is enough to make him suffer
from everything that is still not quite organized and realized in himself
and yet is part of him and no longer a split-off personality. Simultaneously
the distorted and aberrant elements in him seem now to make more for
hysteria than ever before. The inner centre of his personality is no longer
split in two, but is maturing and growing in spite of everything. It remains
his body's task to express his difficulties. And not only paroxysmally
as in the past or in isolated traits, but as a whole, his body is much more
disposed to illness.

In the same years in which Rilke began his *Duino Elegies*, when
his tormenting passivity reversed itself into the euphoria of creation,
he 'got to the other side of Nature' in a mystical experience. It was
not the only one he had undergone. Much later, he sent an extract
from his notebook to Lou Andreas-Salomé, and in it described a
mystical experience, no doubt the one which has just been referred
to. It seemed to him to have grown out of similar past moments:

Later, he thought he could recall certain moments in which the power
of this one was already contained, as in a seed. He remembered the hour
in that other southern garden (Capri), when, both outside and within
him, the cry of a bird was correspondingly present, did not, so to speak,
break upon the barriers of his body, but gathered inner and outer together
into one uninterrupted space, in which, mysteriously protected, only one
single spot of purest, deepest consciousness remained. That time he had
shut his eyes, so as not to be confused in so generous an experience by
the contour of his body, and the infinite passed into him so intimately
from every side, that he could believe he felt the light reposing of the
already appearing stars within his breast.[11]

Enough illustrations have been given, I think. Now the conclusions
can be drawn. I hope it will be obvious that they are not simply my
private opinion, but that they emerge out of the experience of
creative men. What I say must be very far from the whole truth,
but I cannot shake off the conviction that it is a necessary part of it.

Mystics, artists, and scientists have a genuine likeness. The
voluntary mystic, with whom I am chiefly concerned here, practises

an art like music, though only he can hear what he has composed. To the degree that he is systematic, he also practises a kind of science, for he is a psychoanalyst in reverse, using psychic mechanisms with equal skill, but to a generally opposite purpose.

Compared with the mystic's internal work of art, the artist's is evidently external; compared with the scientist's work, that of mystic and artist is unrational; but all three, mystic, artist, and scientist, transform a painful variety into an extraordinarily pleasant unity. The old truism that art is unity in variety can be extended to every form of creation, and the unity regarded as the pleasure, to give it a weak name, of variety subdued, or disintegration mastered.

So, by discipline and meditation, the mystic reaches what he thinks is reality, and which is at the least a superlative, hard-earned moment of unity. Since it is this inner state that is important to him, he is not troubled by his inability to exhibit or communicate it. On the contrary, he wants his state to be beyond communication. His dumbness in principle is his reward in practice.

As in the case of the mystic, the discipline and meditation of the artist or scientist lead him to what he thinks is reality. But his accomplishment is just to externalize and communicate, and his purely inner state, much as he may value it, appears incidental. In psychological terminology, the mystic's accomplishment is narcissistic, the creator's social. It is obvious that we recognize the creator's social value by paying him. It is equally true, though less obvious, that he feels that he is offering a gift at large, which others will accept gratefully, though only, perhaps, after a time. Of course, something similar can be said of a mystic who trains others to become like himself.

Particularly in China and India, there has been a difficult but attractive ideal of the man who is, at once, a mystic, an artist, and a scientist in the sense of knowing all there is to know. As a variant of the Indian ideal, that of the aristocratic Javanese unites the aesthetic and the mystical, both of which are superlatively civilized to him, or, in his terminology, *alus*. What is this, exactly?

Alus means pure, refined, polished, polite, exquisite, etherial, subtle, civilized, smooth. A man who speaks flawless high-Javanese is *alus*, as is the high-Javanese itself. A piece of cloth with intricate, subtle designs painted on to it is *alus*. So is a smooth stone, a dog with his hair petted down, a far-fetched joke, or a clever poetic conceit. God is, of course, *alus* (as are all invisible spirits), and so is the mystical experience of Him. One's own soul and character are *alus* in so far as one emotionally comprehends the ultimate structure of existence; and one's behaviour and actions are *alus* in so far as they are regulated by the delicate intricacies of the complex court-derived etiquette. The person who wishes to be *alus* must order both his inner, emotional life, and his external actions. Ordering one's inner life is known to be far more difficult, and to be, in fact, the mystic's identity of the inner and the outer. The ordering of the outward life leaves one free to turn to the ordering of the inward. The cultivated man needs to give form both to the naturally jagged physical gestures which make up his external behaviour and to the fluctuating states of feeling which comprise his inner experience. A truly *alus* man is polite all the way through.[12]

To go back to more exclusive ideals, we see that the mystic and the creator begin their lives alike, in isolation and inner danger, and learn alike how imaginative effort can rescue and reward them. Methods, tools, and results vary, but the parallelism remains fairly constant. There are mystics and creators who wait for inspiration and tend to be haphazard and spontaneous, as, for example, the classical Taoist, or a certain peculiarly spontaneous type of Chinese or Japanese artist. Others work towards their goal systematically, but use only psychic tools. They are the purely meditative or thoughtful creators, such as the Schrödingers, Einsteins, and, quite differently, the Valérys and Sartres, and, again differently, the mystics who hardly care for special bodily disciplines. Such men stand in contrast to those who create also by means of their bodies, who are manipulative inventors, musicians, painters, dancers, acrobats, whirling dervishes, or Yogins. Rodin would fit into this group. Rilke would, too, if, as Lou Andreas-Salomé said, there was a curious reciprocity of psychic union and somatic disturbance in him—his body was, so to speak, the chariot that bore the weight of his psyche's triumph. And even Valéry, whom I have included in the previous, non-physical group, needed the physical act of writing.*

* The stress here is on *physical*. Of the need as such, Sartre says, 'If I go a day without writing, the *scar* burns me; if I write too easily, it also burns me.' (*Works*, Part II, B. Frechtman's translation.)

The explicit intellectuality of the mystics and the other creators varies. Some are logicians or mathematicians, or mystical or anti-mystical philosophers. Some, whether poets, painters, dancers, or mystics, deny the intellect as completely as they can. Of the men we have explicitly discussed as creators, perhaps Jung was the most concerned to show that intellectual accomplishments are, by nature, relatively superficial.

The explicit use of sexuality varies. Some, the erotic mystics, and the Rodins, Renoirs, and Van Goghs, identify creation with sexual love. Because of the identification, they may decide, as did Van Gogh, that one is engaged in at the cost of the other. Either, they may say, one is physically or creatively virile, but not both. This attitude is reminiscent of the Tantrism in which the sexual impulse is aroused but thwarted and redirected for mystical purposes, which require the union of 'sun' and 'moon' to be consummated in the mystic's own head. Yet mystics, including the approximately Tantric ones of Kashmir, and the poetic Sufis, often prefer to arrive at mystical experience with the help of art. From their standpoint, they create art in order to be.

At times, sexuality and creation are thought to be simply antagonistic to one another. The mystical or creative experience is felt to be good and Godlike, and any appetite, but especially sex, to be evil and satanical. As we know, this feeling is fairly usual among mystics and has been experienced by such an artist as Leonardo da Vinci and such a writer as Valéry. It would not be surprising if it were shared by schizoid or compulsive scientists.

Creation, then, whether internal or external, mystical, scientific, or artistic, expresses the need for unity. The inner person needs to be united with himself and with his body, and the single person with others and with real and ideal communities. We have definite enough bodily shapes and egoistic enough desires, and yet, in the act of creation, we open and extend ourselves. Even if we deny mysticism or stress its self-love, art, its unifying external analogue, includes us in other states, men, and things. Modern art, especially, violates all conventional reserve and engulfs us in the raw experience of the artist. If it cannot offer faith, it offers and even demands union. The demand is more or less mystical.

Plato once said that we had universal heads, meaning that our heads were round in imitation of the round universe. Valéry suggested that the universe might be head-shaped. Jung carved himself as a two-inch man and hid his little self where no one could find or harm him. Jayavarman VII had himself carved as Buddha and set on a throne in the middle of the smiling temple in the middle of the capital city in the middle of the universe. Reality is like a set of Chinese boxes, the small within the large within the larger, perhaps without end, and the similar within the similar, but with a boundary set between them. We, standing in the middle, but feeling quite small, find it impossible to imagine that the rest of the universe is either like or unlike us. We feel, though doubtfully, that reality must resemble our consciousness, our emotions, or our abstractions. The mystic overcomes his doubts by finding the reality, as consciousness, within himself, and he tries to persuade us that it is located there. The artist constructs a new external reality and tries to persuade us emotionally that it is universal. And the scientist, with his mathematical head, logical tongue, and empirical fingers, proves to us that reality is made in the image of the symbols he has drawn out of it mysteriously. Our effort to understand is uncomfortable and possibly dangerous, but what, without it, could we ever accomplish? We may as well put on the Buddha's smile. It fits a human face very well.

7

Mystical Techniques

To the extent that mysticism is art or science, it cannot be effectively grasped without its techniques. These are numerous and detailed, and though they are usually transmitted in person, an enormous handbook could be compiled of those that have been put into writing. I have not the least ambition to compile such a handbook. I should like to do no more than give an idea of the kinds of techniques and their effects, with a few examples detailed enough to take us beyond mere generalization. And before the subject is ended, I should like to suggest unmystical explanations for the effectiveness of the techniques.

As a rule, mystical techniques are used in combination with one another and in the context of an elaborately controlled life. It will simplify our attempt to understand if we describe the techniques in isolation from one another and forget for the while how an apprentice mystic readies himself to use them.

A fairly simple classification of mystical techniques, into, as it happens, eight different kinds, might be as follows:

(1) Techniques of concentration, which are equally techniques for excluding unwanted perceptions or thoughts;

(2) mainly bodily techniques, by which I mean cleansing techniques, postural techniques, and breathing techniques;

(3) association techniques, to make certain perceptions and thoughts always displeasing, and others, which are approved of, always pleasing;

(4) techniques to arouse spontaneity, that is, to startle the novice into mystic insight;

(5) techniques to arouse ecstasy;

(6) explicitly sexual techniques;
(7) techniques of projection, by which the novice identifies himself
     with himself as he thinks he really is;
(8) psychophysical dramas.

The first, concentration techniques can be illustrated from Buddhist practice. Buddhists, for example, advocate staring at 'devices' such as circles of earth-coloured clay, blue flowers, or light. Their object is to transform the gross, physical circle into an afterimage, and the afterimage into a dematerialized, brilliantly pervasive trance-inducing reality.

For the practice of the earth-coloured device, one is supposed to get light red clay, like that found in the bed of the Ganges. One should find an isolated spot, a cave or a hut of leaves, and there make a frame to which a support of cloth or the like is attached. On the support a spot 'of the size of a winnowing basket or of a dish' is drawn in clean light red clay. The spot should be as smooth as a drumhead, and the man who is to stare at it should seat himself comfortably and not too far away. He must think of how wretched mere pleasures are, he must reflect on the Buddha, and he must say to himself, 'By this method I shall become a partaker of the sweet blessings of isolation.'

Now the practitioner must open his eyes partially and evenly, as if he were looking at his face in a mirror. If he opens his eyes too wide, they ache, the circle appears too plainly, and the afterimage will not develop; and if he opens his eyes too little, the circle is obscured, his thoughts are sluggish, and the afterimage also fails to develop. 'He must contemplate the circle, sometimes with his eyes open, sometimes with them shut; and thus for a hundred times, or for a thousand times, or even more, he must do until the securing of the mental reflex (that is, the afterimage). When in his meditation the circle appears equally visible, whether his eyes are open or shut, that is the securing of the mental reflex. When this occurs, he must no longer remain seated in that spot, but must return and seat himself in his lodging-place, and there go on with his meditation.

In order, however, to avoid being delayed by the necessity of washing his feet, he must endeavour to have on hand some single-soled sandals and a walking-stick. Then, if his feeble concentration is destroyed by some untoward event, he should slip his feet into his sandals, take his walking-stick, and go back to that place, and after obtaining the mental reflex, return and develop it, seated at his ease, and mull it over again and again, and engrain it into his mind.

Now, a new mental reflex, the afterimage of the afterimage, must be developed. This no longer exhibits the imperfections of the original circle, but 'like a polished conch-shell, or like the disc of the moon issuing from the clouds, or like cranes in the clouds', appears with a thousandfold greater clarity. But because it is not a material circle, of the kind the eye sees, it has neither colour nor shape. 'It is only a reflex existing in the perception of the person practising concentration. From the instant, however, it appears, the hindrances are checked, the corruptions become assuaged, and the mind concentrates itself . . .'[1]

Concentration-techniques are not only visual, but also vocal. Like members of other cultures, the Hindus and Buddhists repeat holy formulas for their magical and mystical effects. Their theorists believe that the holy words are themselves the eternal truth and, even more, the eternal substance. Thus the Trika philosophers of Kashmir regard the brilliant consciousness which is, they think, the fundamental reality of the universe, as a vibration; and this vibration, they think, is the seminal absolute word or idea on which all the relative words or ideas depend. They believe that the adept is able, by his concentration on holy words, to grow conscious that he is the same as this phonemic substance of all things, his own shining self-identity.

Theories such as these are hardly grasped by ordinary Hindus and Buddhists. But the repetition of holy formulas is widespread among them.

The monk and priest murmurs or thinks it without any particular occasion many times a day or whenever they commence any activity; the pious rickshaw-puller mumbles his *mantra*, which in northern India is '*Ram Ram*' when he lifts and transports loads. The same *mantra* may then be used by the initiates as part of the daily ritual. The ideal achievement is . . . the incessant repetition of the *mantra*; this is more frequent than one would think, not limited to the professionally religious, and practised by men and women on the land as in metropolitan Calcutta, Madras, and Delhi, even in 1964.[2]

Buddhists of the Pure Land sect believe in salvation by faith in Amitabha Buddha, whose name they repeat over and over, either to themselves, under their breath, or aloud.

Followers of this school usually set a fixed number of repetitions a day, from 50,000 to 500,000 or more, and wherever they may happen to be, they mentally call the Buddha's name without interruption. This enables them to put an end to all other thoughts and to purify their minds without difficulty. . . . Devotees usually vow to save all living things after their own self-enlightenment and when their vows unite with those of Amitabha, the combined power of their devotion will enable them to experience an all-embracing state of purity and cleanness . . . There are many adherents of this school who succeed in purifying their minds with the aid of this practice and who know in advance the exact time of their death. There are numerous cases of old people who bathed, put on their best clothes, sat cross-legged and passed away peacefully. To preserve stillness of mind they did not tell their families that they were about to die, lest their last moments be disturbed by weeping.[3]

The Sufis practise what they call 'remembrance', *dhikr*, the repetition of holy words to the point of annihilation in God. The beginner's words are usually, 'There is no god but Allah', *La ilah illa Allah*. The more advanced may prefer *Allah* alone. Beyond this, in tribute to God's ineffability or to his various attributes, there are 'He', 'Truth', 'The Living', 'The Subsisting', and so on. A single syllable or a sound 'not sustained by a letter' may be enough for a God-intoxicated man.

According to one description, the reciter should sit cross-legged, head between his knees, arms around his legs, and eyes closed. 'There is no', the denial, should be said with a rising head, 'god' should be said when the mouth reaches the level of the heart, and 'Allah', more forcefully, opposite the heart. Directions for breathing and for the number of repetitions are often given.

Some of the emotion of remembrance comes through in this description:

Let the seeker sever all the ties of this world and empty it from his heart. Let him cut away all anxiety for family, wealth, children, home; for knowledge, rule, ambition. Let him reduce his heart to a state in which the existence of anything and its non-existence are the same to him. Then let him sit alone in some corner, limiting his religious duties to what are absolutely incumbent, and not occupying himself either with the reciting of the *Quran* or considering its meaning or with books of religious tradition or anything of the like. And let him see to it that nothing save God most High enters his mind. Then as he sits alone in solitude, let him not cease saying continuously with his tongue, '*Allah*, *Allah*', keeping his thought on it. At last he will reach a state when the motion of his tongue will cease, and it will seem as though the word flowed from it. Let him persevere in this until all trace of motion is removed from his tongue, and he finds his heart persevering in the thought. Let him still persevere until the form of the word, its letters and shape, is removed from his heart, and there remains the idea alone, as though clinging to the heart, inseparable from it. So far all is dependent on his will and choice; his continuance, too, in this state and his warding off the whispering of Satan are also thus dependent; but to bring the Mercy of God does not stand in his will or choice. He has now laid himself bare to the breathings of that mercy, and nothing now remains but to await what God will open to him, as God has done after this manner to prophets and saints. If he follows the above course, he may be sure that the light of the real will shine out in his heart. At first unstable, like a flash of lightning, it turns and returns; though sometimes it hangs back. And if it returns, sometimes it abides and sometimes it is momentary. And if it abides, sometimes its abiding is long, and sometimes short.

As the character of the remembrance changes, the phenomena that may accompany it change. Trumpets and cymbals, like those that announce a Sultan, are heard 'within the circumference of the head'. Then, as if in response to the micro-cosmic completeness of man, one hears water, wind, a fierce fire, mills, horses, wind-blown leaves. Colours and objects appear, and at the annihilating height there are constant clear, very hot flames; and there are lights that rise and fall.[4]

The cleansing, postural, and breathing techniques occur together in Yoga, and I shall therefore describe them in relation to it, especially to the classical kind associated with the name of Patanjali.

The objective of classical Yoga is immobility in all respects, which is supposed to part pure, immobile intelligence, the true person, from the body to which it is so painfully attached. The Yogin-to-be must begin his separation from the body he misidentifies as himself by refraining from all sins, for these attach him the more firmly to his body and its perturbations. He must also purify himself physically, and see even his well-cleaned body as disgusting and too often in contact with the impure, and so more disgusting bodies of others. He assumes steady postures, such as the lotus-posture, the hero-posture, and the staff-posture, which eventually make his body stable, motionless, relaxed, and completely unagitated. He breathes more slowly, to reduce the fluctuation by which we take in and expel air. The incredible ideal seems to be to stop breathing altogether. Above all, the Yogin, seated in steady relaxation and breathing slowly and imperceptibly, immobilizes his mind. This he does by fixing it on some object until it unites with it and stops its frantic, painful movements. He changes the objects, as has been said, for finer, less material ones, and his concentration, one with its object, dematerializes itself. As this occurs, he acquires, he thinks, super-normal powers, which are so many temptations he must resist, and supernormal perception. Finally he reaches the supra-conscious concentration which is isolated and purely self-identical and immobile.

Cleansings, postures, and breathing techniques are more empha-sized in Hatha Yoga, which has little philosophy, and which con-centrates on overcoming old age and death. The stomach is cleansed by means of a long cloth, which is swallowed, left in the stomach for a while, and then pulled out—the Yogin must be careful not to swallow all of it. The intestines are cleansed by sucking in and expelling water through the rectum, and the nasal passages by means of water and of a thread which is inserted into them. These and other cleansings are supposed to purify and confer good health.

The postures are often quite difficult to assume in the begining. But it is 'when efforts cease' that 'the posture is completed' and one pays no more attention to one's body. A standard text of Hatha Yoga lists thirty-two postures. It gives, for example, this description of one of the most common:

Place the right foot on the left thigh and similarly the left one on the right thigh, also cross the hands behind the back and firmly catch the great toes of the feet so crossed (the right hand on the great toe and the left hand on the left). Place the chin on the chest and fix the gaze on the tip of the nose.

As the discipline of breathing is cultivated, the Yogin, it is said, sleeps and excretes less. But he perspires and, with progress, feels his body tremble, with further progress, hops, involuntarily, 'like a frog', and, at last, is said to levitate. According to Patanjali, he measures his breathing by 'instants' and 'moments', the instant being 'the time required for the act of winking', and the moment, 'the time limited by snapping the thumb and forefinger after having three times rubbed one's own knee-pan with the hand. The time for this latter is equal to that defined by the action of inhalation and exhalation of a man in good health.' The Yogin tries to harmonize and to prolong each of the three moments of breathing, which are, inhalation, retention of air, and exhalation. As a result of this harmonizing, the Yogin is said to feel himself to be present in his own body, exalted, and great.

Taoists searching for long life tried a variety of means, including breathing techniques. They thought that if they could stop breathing for the length of 1,000 usual breaths they would approach immortality, a conclusion that may be accepted even by the sceptical. They tried 'embryonic breathing', and since the price for an enormously prolonged life must be high, it is not surprising that it was difficult, as the following directions show:

Shut in the breath until it becomes intolerable. Darken the heart so that it does not think, let the breath go where it will and, when the breath is intolerable, open the mouth and let it out; when the breath has just escaped, respiration is rapid; harmonize the breaths; after seven or eight breaths, it rapidly becomes quieter. Then begin to melt the breath again in the same way. If one has time left over, stop after ten meltings. . . . Melting the breath cannot be done every day.

So the Taoist teaches himself to live on his internal breath and, like the Yogin, his saliva, so that he may become proof against drowning, burning, and disease. He wishes to be careless and passive as an embryo, and sealed, like an embryo against danger.[5]

Association techniques are very simple. For instance, a Buddhist monk who wants to convince himself that food, the appetite for which keeps him subjected to life, is really repulsive, meditates on how it is eaten and says to himself:

Crushed by the teeth and smeared with saliva the crushed food becomes a mixture from which all visual beauty and good odour have disappeared, and it reaches a state of extreme repulsivenes, like a dog's vomit in a dog's trough. And although it is in such a state, one has to swallow it down, though at least it has passed out of the range of sight.

Thankful as he is for the small favour that has removed the food from his sight, the monk continues relentlessly and imagines, among other things, what the food resembles while still undigested, in the place 'which is like an unwashed cesspool, pitch dark, traversed by winds which are scented with various rotten smells, excessively malodorous and loathsome'.

Compassion, on the other hand, is to be promoted by equally extreme efforts of the imagination. The monk

. . . should direct his compassion on a man whom he sees to be pitiable, deformed, in extreme distress, ill-fated, ill-favoured, and wretched, with mutilated hands and feet, with a begging bowl in front of him, sitting in a rest-house for the poor, with plenty of vermin oozing from his limbs, and uttering moans of distress. And the disciple should think, 'Alas, this man has fallen on evil days? Good were it if he were freed from this suffering!'

If no one like that is met with, compassion should be aroused for an evil-doer. . . . Just so the monk, who practises the meditation on compassion, may feel compassion even for a happy person, and think: 'Even though this poor fellow at present is happy and well-provided, and enjoys his possessions, he will nevertheless, in the absence of any wholesome deeds . . . soon experience not a little pain and sadness in the states of woe.

This exercise in compassion should then be repeated in appropriate ways for a beloved person, a person to whom one is indifferent, and an enemy.[6]

The deliberate cultivation of spontaneity for creative and mystical purposes is characteristic of China and Japan. The Taoist classics constantly advise one not to be systematic, studious, or calculating, but to yield to nature, including one's own, move in the rhythms of nature, wear the rustic's simplicity and hats of straw, and walk in the meditative mountains. In Chinese talk, there might be an almost Surrealistic yielding to impulse and association, a 'pure', whimsical, narcissistic, subtly dialectical intercourse. In art, there might be the 'crazy' calligrapher emitting his brushed words like the swirling rapids of a river, he no doubt befuddled with alcohol just enough to give his script a final, amazing, scarcely human touch of wildness. The spontaneous poet or painter was, if not this calligrapher himself, his brother in spontaneity.

In India, too, systematic and spontaneous experience, or gradual and sudden enlightenment, came to be distinguished. Of course it was hard for chastened, learned monks to concede that anyone might at any time suddenly intuit the mystic truth. Some of them compromised by confining the possibility of sudden enlightenment to those who, like themselves, had undergone the right discipline. The issue caused a venomous debate in eighth-century Tibet between the exponents of the 'sudden' Chinese method and the 'gradualist' Indian one.

All Chinese thought, including the Confucian, exhibits the polarity of the disciplined and the spontaneous. But Ch'an, that is, Zen Buddhism, exhibits it most dramatically, with its austere discipline on the one hand, and its methods for spontaneous realization on the other. Allowing neither custom nor study to be the arbiters, the Zen master may suddenly slap the learner, to make him angry, to make him more anxious, to change him as words are unable to. And the learner, sweating, tense, caught perhaps in the Great Doubt that Hakuin described, strains to resolve his irrational riddle, but really to raise his divisive tensions to so great a pitch that their harmonization, if it comes, will give him peace for a while. As in psychoanalysis, though less directly, he has aroused his inner demons in order to confront and defeat them. The Zen riddle, the *koan*, and the tactics of the Zen master have been described so often that I forbear to give details. But I must add that a learner unable to withstand such a training may grow psychotic.[7]

To arouse ecstasy, many techniques are used, apart from the sexual. The examples may again be drawn from the Sufis, more exactly, from their collective *dhikrs*. Rumi's fraternity, it may be recalled, uses the whirling dance—some whirling saints are said to go on for days. Other fraternities use drums. Whether the eating of glowing embers or live snakes, which is also practised, arouses ecstasy, I do not know, but I suspect that it may do so with its mingled fear and faith in the midst of the crowd's enthusiasm. In any case, there is the 'remembrance' itself, one of which is described as follows:

The members of the fraternity rise and hold hands in a circle. For some eight minutes they chant, 'The Living', the Arabic sound of which is reduced to the two syllables *cha-ha*. The first sound is prolonged and exhaled, the second inhaled, and both chanted rapidly, about sixty times a minute. At the sheikh's command, the men change their chant. The second syllable, sounded like *hai*, is now prolonged and exhaled, while the rate of the chant is slower, both syllables being repeated about forty times a minute. The sheikh participates in the chant from time to time, but also approaches one man or another and stares at him intently. He signals, and the circle returns to the first chant, signals again, it returns to the second, signals again, and it returns to the first, and again, and it returns to the second. The men now seem to be in a deeply hypnotic state. The sheikh approaches them more often, moving ecstatically before and behind them.

The exaltation mounts. When it seems at its paroxysm, the sheikh lets out a cry, at the same time vibrating his index and middle fingers 'with an incredible and inimitable rapidity'. He kneels in the midst of the circle, while his disciples prostrate themselves 'in a star around the Master, their foreheads touching the ground; they are almost all in trance. The Master makes them come out of it by saying *Allahu akbar* (God most great), and by clapping his hands three times.'[8]

There are many explicitly sexual techniques. Those of Taoism and the similar ones of Tantric Buddhism and Hinduism are particularly interesting. All three exploit sexual union to create mystic union, and all three assume that a man, to succeed, must retain his semen, his physical and spiritual life, by means of which he may as it were conceive himself anew within himself.

For reasons I am unable to estimate, there are certain more-than-technical differences between Buddhist and Hindu Tantrism. The most striking is the different role assigned to the male and the female. In Buddhism, the woman partner represents the tranquil Void; in

Hinduism, she represents primal energy. In Buddhism, the man is energy, skill, or compassionate activity; in Hinduism, he is the undifferentiating absolute to be awakened by feminine energy. Furthermore, the Buddhist adept of Tantra almost always insists that semen must not be emitted at all, for he has learned that 'there is no greater sin than discharge', and that discharge leads to sorrow, the loss of the 'vital element', and death. He retains his semen by mechanical pressure that forces it into the bladder (technically *coitus obstructus*), or by, it seems, control of the muscles of the penis. The Hindu adept of Tantrism, on the other hand, is more likely to emit his semen, though only at the proper moment, and to draw it back through his penis by a Hathayogic technique; and then his woman partner is supposed to reabsorb her vital fluid. There are other differences between the Buddhist and Hindu doctrines, but these are not nearly as impressive, at least to outsiders, as their likeness.

According to Tantric doctrines, the vital breaths or energies of the body circulate through a multitude of channels. The most important of the channels are three in number, one to the left of the spinal column, carrying feminine energy, one to the right, carrying masculine energy, and one in the centre, carrying both energies, when, that is, a mystic inner marriage becomes possible.

The adept's purpose is to force his leftward, feminine energy, and his rightward, masculine energy, into the bottom of the middle channel, for it is along this channel that lie the sleeping forces he must yet awaken. In Hindu belief, the lowest centre, the root-centre, of force lies near the genital organs. It has the shape of a four-petalled lotus. It is red and inscribed in golden letters. Inside it is a yellow square marked with the earth symbol. Inside the square is a triangle, its point down, marked with the female symbol. Inside the triangle is the phallus, its head bright as a jewel. And coiled around the phallus eight times is the dazzling but dormant goddess, the serpentine force whose mouth blocks the phallic entrance. The man seeking mystic experience must awaken her and with his breath draw her higher, as a needle draws a thread up. To do this, he turns his tongue, which has been cut partly loose from the floor of his mouth, backwards into his throat, so that he cannot breathe. The longer he immobilizes his breath, the better the chance, he thinks, that, with the help of 'immobilized' thought and semen, he will draw the serpentine force to the end of the central channel. There, at the top of his head, is the upside-down thousand-petalled lotus, each petal with one of the thousand combinations of Sanskrit letters. Inside the lotus is the full moon, and inside the moon the triangle within which his marriage of left and right is consummated. This is the exact point of transcendence, for it is here that his materiality and pain are exchanged for nowhere's bliss.[9]

Techniques of identification and projection are used by mystics everywhere. We may suggest the variety of examples by recalling the Taoist's projection of the child or embryo he thinks he is becoming, the Sufi's projection of the ideal teacher who is, in a way, none other than himself, and the Tantric disciple's identification with the universe he has ceremonially imagined into being.

The ideal of the Taoist, which has been expressed in other ways, is also childlikeness, for the child is as supple, he says, as life itself. He says:

> One who possesses virtue in abundance is comparable to a new born babe.
> Poisonous insects will not sting it;
> Ferocious animals will not pounce on it;
> Predatory birds will not swoop down on it.
> Its bones are weak and its sinews supple yet its hold is firm.
> It does not know of the union of male and female yet its
>   male member will stir:
> This is because its virility is at its height.
> It howls all day yet does not become hoarse;
> This is because its harmony is at its height.[10]

The ideal of the baby as the supple hero, with his real or imagined ease and invulnerability, led Taoists to 'embryonic breathing' and other practices, including 'return of the semen'. Their purpose was to transform themselves into embryos. The details of this transformation need not be gone into; but it should be kept in mind that the Taoist believed that he could grow himself anew and, when the embryo in him was completed, could, I suppose, slough off his old self as a snake its old skin.

The Sufis projected their ideal selves into their 'Saints'. Perhaps the more conservative did not follow Rumi in believing that men literally identical with God walked the earth among them. But they agreed that a seeker might relate himself to God through his sheikh, and that his love for his ideal image in the sheikh's person might lead him to his mystic goal.

We can see such a projection being created in the biography of Molla-Shah, a seventeenth-century Sufi. His biographer and pupil Tawakkul Beg, tells how Molla-Shah made him 'open the knot' of his heart:

He made me sit before him, my senses being as though intoxicated, and ordered me to reproduce his own image within myself; and, after having bandaged my eyes, he asked me to concentrate all my mental faculties on my heart. I obeyed, and in an instant, by the divine favour and by the spiritual assistance of the shaykh, my heart opened. I saw, then, that there was something like an overturned cup within me. This having been set upright, a sensation of unbounded happiness filled my being. I said to my master, 'This cell, where I am seated before you—I see a faithful reproduction of it within me and it appears to me as though another Tawakkul Beg were seated before another Molla-Shah.' He replied, 'Very good! The first apparition which appears to thee is the image of the master. Thy companions (the other novices) have been prevented by other mystical exercises; but, as far as regards myself, this is not the first time that I have met such a case.' He then ordered me to uncover my eyes; and I saw him, then, with the physical organ of vision, seated before me. He then made me bind my eyes again, and I perceived him with my spiritual sight, seated similarly before me. Full of astonishment, I cried out, 'O Master! whether I look with my physical organs or with my spiritual sight, always it is you that I see.'[11]

The ritual of Tantrism is largely based upon projection. The *mandalas* it makes use of are complex representations of the universe, designed to teach a disciple that he can emit and be this universe, for its ontological structure is his own. Ring on ring of reality and image on image of truth surround the microcosmic-macrocosmic centre. The ring of fire excludes the profane and burns away

ignorance, the ring of diamond casts the illumination of pure consciousness the ring of leaves is rebirth, the fierce guardians of the
inner palace hold off enemies, the terrifying gods are one's fears to be
overcome, and the palace is the transcendency that may be entered.

For a ceremony of initiation, such a *mandala* is marked off on the
ground with differently coloured strings. As the ceremony progresses, the initiate is entered by and becomes the god of wrath.
He sings and dances wrath, it subsides, and he is entered by and
becomes calm gods. Blindfolded, he throws a flower into the
mandala to discover which god contained in it is about to give him
especial aid. He enters the *mandala* and meditates the gods who are
in his heart. They grow from his heart and fill all space, then subside
into his heart, for they are he, who creates and destroys the universe
and, knowing this, intuits its voidness. Everything, he learns, is
projection, projection is consciousness, and consciousness, which is
nothing in particular, must be void, though, as everything that can
possibly be, it must be void in a superlatively full way.[12]

Mystical training, when long and complicated, has the nature of
a psychophysical drama. It is slow, setbacks interrupt it, and during
its progress mind and body injure and aid one another. When the
ascension is ended, the mystic looks back and discerns the plot of
the drama he has enacted. This is all usual. Tantrism, however,
with its extravagance and projective intensity creates such dramas to
conscious dramatic effect. If I may speak frivolously, it is an operatic
mysticism.

To show this, I should like to return to the mystic, Naropa, at
the time he abandoned Nalanda and his students there. He abandoned them, his biography tells us, because of a vision that came
upon him of an ugly old crone. The vision talked with him, and
when he said, uncomprehendingly, that he understood not only the
words but also the sense of the sacred books, it, or she, began to
weep and tremble. The crone, we may guess, was ugly because he
was internally ugly. She was female and old because the intuitive
is older and deeper than cold, male reason; and she was godly
because she was everything beyond his individual self. She was,
speaking Tantrically or projectively, none other than himself.

Naropa set out in search of his destined teacher in mysticism. The teacher showed himself in eleven further visions, but the still self-divided Naropa was blind to him. In despair, Naropa was about to commit suicide, when the teacher, Tilopa by name, came to him. The destructive training was ended, and twelve years and twelve lessons in unity and voidness began.

The episodes of Naropa's drama ought not to be summarized and cannot all be repeated here. I shall cite a fragment and let it stand for the whole.

Naropa had finished the ninth stage in his training and was awaiting the tenth, of Eternal Delight. As before each stage, his teacher, Tilopa sat silent and motionless for a year. As before, Naropa then made a *mandala*, paid reverence with folded hands, and asked for instruction. 'Tilopa said: "Get a girl". When Naropa associated with a girl who was healthy and very faithful, for some time he felt pleased, but afterwards he did not listen to what the girl said, nor she to him. He became lean, his skin grew rough, and he took service with a smith. When he was suffering from this unaccustomed change, Tilopa came and asked: "Naropa, are you happy?" Naropa answered:

> "I suffer by being constantly engaged
> With my self-dividedness in an apparent dual world."

Tilopa said:

> "Naropa, you should strive
> For Samsara and Nirvana's unity.
> Look into the mirror of your mind, which is delight eternal,
> The mysterious home of the Dakini (the ugly old crone)." '

Tilopa then taught Naropa the Tantric discipline of sexual intercourse. He recommended that the girl be a Brahmin, have the right 'overt, covert, and mystic' qualities in her actions, and be, when drunk with sexual desire, shameless and unrestrained with her ritual partner. He taught him to be the kind of man who tries 'to experience the meaning of his own or his partner's being. The first', he said, 'is experienced by stimulating one's sexual power and vitality, not allowing it to decrease; the second by absorbing the partner's equivalent, so producing a constant feeling of bliss and nothingness.'

This teaching alludes, of course, to some Tantric technique. Whatever it was, Naropa made use of it. 'When a few days had passed Tilopa came and said: "Naropa, how is it that you who have renounced the world according to the teaching of the Buddha, as a Bhikshu (monk) are living with a girl? This is not a proper thing, punish yourself." Naropa said: "This is not my fault, but that of this," and he hit his erect penis with a stone. When through excessive pain he was near death, Tilopa asked: "Naropa, is something wrong with you?" And Naropa answered:

> "I suffer from having hit my penis
> In answer to desire which is the root of evil."

Tilopa said:

> "Listen to my words, listen. . . .
> You should beat yourself, Naropa,
> To realize that pain and pleasure are the same.
> Look into the mirror of your mind where values are as one,
> The mysterious home of the Dakini."

'He then touched him with his hand so that he could at least urinate again, gave him the name Naropa, and instructed him in the sixfold sameness of value.'

In brief, 'this instruction is that all the entities of the world of appearance are but the motion of original awareness. . . . In brief, just like a feather drifting in the wind, one roams among things without becoming attached to them.'

Afterwards, and just as dramatically, Tilopa gave Naropa his eleventh and twelfth lessons. His teaching completed, Tilopa became invisible. Naropa's greatness had now become so exemplary that his protector-god once showed himself to him and said, 'Washing away the stains of emotional instability with the nectar of speech, which is not normal speech, from the pure stream of instruction, Naropa speaks, but not with normal words.' Naropa had become altogether non-dual, prepared, at the semblance of his death, to enter the indestructible union of being-as-such with being-oneself, of mother with child, of light with light.[13]

The eight mystical techniques that have been described are embedded in dogmatic systems, are embellished with fancies, and are meant to but cannot confer perfect peace, immortality, or any final goal of mysticism but the mystical experience itself; but the evidence is, I think, that they all are effective. If they had no practical value, they would have been abandoned long ago.

Granted that this is true, we may try to gain some prosaic understanding of their effect. It would be interesting to make a detailed psychological commentary on each of them, to go, for example, into each of the methods of Yogic cleansing and identify the changes in feeling, and especially the relief from guilt, that accompany them. It would also be interesting, though beyond my competence, to go into physiological matters, such as the carbon-dioxide intoxication that results from holding the breath a long time and that gives visual hallucinations and a feeling of euphoria.* Even if I had the competence, however, neither the scale on which I can discuss mystical techniques nor my own inclinations allow me to be so thorough. I think it best, then, to take up a few subjects that may aid in the understanding of all the techniques. These subjects are, the effect of traditional drugs, the effect of sensory deprivation, the effect of relative motionlessness (with a note on concentration), and the newly obvious abilities to exercise some conscious control over functions that used to be thought quite autonomous.

I use the words, 'traditional drugs', to confine myself to those which have been used for a long time for religious or mystical purposes. Such drugs, as everyone now knows, cause dramatic

---

* On the other hand, continued rapid or deep breathing may cause an epileptic attack. 'Hyperventilation' can even be used to diagnose the susceptibility to petit mal epilepsy:
'This diagnostic procedure, when carried out properly, will precipitate a clinical petit mal spell in practically all patients with this form of epilepsy.'
Furthermore, 'Sensory-precipitation epilepsy (also called *reflex epilepsy*) may occur in response to tactile, visual, or startle stimuli, as well as with more specific situations such as reading, listening to music, or photic stimulation, including watching television.' This suggests a possible outcome of Kashmiri, *Trika* techniques. (S. Livingston, Epilepsy in Infancy, Childhood, and Adolescence', in B. B. Wolman, *Manual of Child Psychopathology*, McGraw-Hill, N.Y., 1972, pp. 241–2.)

changes in perception. It is not unusual to read that someone who takes them feels an 'awareness of a totality and awareness of nothing', or finds himself to be in 'a pure state of being'.[14] The change in the sense of certainty is often striking. A user of marijuana often gets the feeling that he is on the verge of a supreme insight. He may become dogmatic, as if he had a 'free-floating' conviction, prepared to attach itself with violence to any handy idea. He half believes in almost any notion, possible or not.[15]

Of the traditional religious drugs, the one most used in the cultures from which I have drawn my examples seems to be marijuana, Indian hemp, which is, in other forms, hashish, bhang, or the like. Bhang, for instance, is deliberately taken in India for its help in meditation.

We have referred to India so often that it is particularly worthwhile to cite an experience of the anthropologist, Colin Turnbull. Turnbull went to India as a postgraduate student of Sanskrit and Vedic philosophy. He wanted to be 'both scientist and Hindu'. He tried bhang, and the effect on him, he writes, was this:

I was very aware that the real 'I' was floating around somewhere, completely dissociated from the body on the ground. I remember thinking that I would not leave my body parked anywhere else other than at the Ashram; I knew it would be safe there.

From that moment of surrender I forgot all about the body. It was not only that the body had no feelings, it was rather that I just had no use for it any longer. I felt completely free. There was no longer anything remarkable about the sensation, certainly nothing frightening. I had no inclination to do one thing rather than another. It was rather that I had no desires at all, but was content to drift along wherever I might be led . . . I was no longer there. These were real clouds, but I was in them only a short while. I rose above them, and as far as I can recall there was a distinct feeling of elevation, or soaring. Then I was above their woolly surface, and saw the peaks of the Himalaya shining through, white against a dark blue sky. . . . Then I returned through the same dark clouds to Banares.[16]

The description fits Hindu mystical ideas very well, but it must be remembered that its author had already been well stocked with them. A man stocked with Chinese ideas would still probably have flown, but in a different style and to a different place.

The likeness of drug-states to mystical ones should not give us the illusion of understanding the latter, for we do not understand the former. But the comparison broadens the problem for us and makes it more accessible, at least in theory, to physiological and psychological research. We are, after all, complex, delicately adjusted organisms. It is not very hard to derange such organisms, to make them into Tinguely-machines, which give out impressive noises and have gloriously spinning wheels, but which go nowhere in particular and do nothing useful. From the biological standpoint, it is just our normal functioning that is the great accomplishment. We have been constructed, over hundreds of thousands of years, with extraordinary precision, to act the parts of ordinary selfish and social human beings. Yet, to learn just how we are constructed, we must observe ourselves when we are, so to speak, out of repair. Scientists therefore make use of derangement as deliberately as mystics, and learn some of the same lessons, though in the end, I believe, less superficially.

The kind of derangement I am particularly referring to is provoked by isolation and by stillness. The Polar explorer buried under the snow in a hut grows apathetic and hallucinates. But he also experiences a feeling of oneness with the universe, and he floats psychically through featureless space. The unchanging whiteness of the snow and the unending rhythm of their paddles put Eskimos into a dangerous state of trance. Like them, detached and submerged in a featureless medium, aeroplane pilots may feel themselves unreal and 'broken off' from everything. Prisoners, too, when in solitary confinement, become entranced in sameness.[17]

Perhaps related to such sameness-entrancement, there are experiments in concentration, in the case I am thinking of, on a blue vase, in the mystic-sounding attempt 'to see the vase as it exists in itself, without any connections to other things'. The results of this experiment were that 'most if not all subjects experienced perceptual changes relating to the vase, modifications of the state of concentration and a general feeling that the sessions were pleasurable and valuable. Quite commonly the vase became more vivid or luminous; a loss of the third dimension was often noted. Some subjects felt a loss of ego boundaries, confusion of subject-object thought as though they and the vase were merging. Such experiences occurred spontaneously and unexpectedly and were sometimes frightening.' The experimenter explained these effects as the results of what he called 'de-automatization', 'perceptual expansion', and 'reality-transfer'. By these terms he meant that the subjects had their minds focused again on the minute and intermediate steps in perception, which regained the freshness of childhood. Perception was so fixed and vivid that it expanded and lost its usual limits, and the sensation or feeling of reality became displaced to the sight of the vase, in and for itself, excluding everything in the usual context of perception and action.[18]

The many observations on the effects of isolation, stillness, and sameness have been assimilated in recent decades into the theory that, speaking very roughly, sameness and stillness destroy our capacity to perceive and think. The theory has been confirmed by experiments in sensory deprivation.

In a typical series of such experiments, the subject is paid to do nothing but lie on a bed in a small closed cubicle. He gets food when he asks for it, goes to the toilet when he wants to, and that is all the external change that is allowed him. Over his eyes he wears lenses that admit light but no pattern, over his ears, sponge rubber, and over his hands gloves, while cardboard cuffs extend over and beyond his fingers. The situation is hard to bear. Objects begin to look fuzzy and two-dimensional, colours look abnormally saturated, and there are headaches, fatigue, and feelings of confusion. The subject may set himself an intellectual problem, but it is hard to concentrate, his mind wanders, and he lapses into daydreams. He may experience 'blank periods', during which he is unable to think of anything at all—the analogy with mystic goals of 'isolation', 'nothingness', and the 'void' is obvious.*

At times, sensory deprivation and mystical exercises have very close results. We read that one experimental subject felt 'that his

---

* The situation of the subject is like that of a species of mystic, the Tibetan Ku-sa-li. In Tibetan, this word names 'a man who has three thoughts. Apart from thinking about eating and drinking, defecation and urination, and sleeping, he has given up all other occupations and is absorbed in meditative concentration. . . . In India, however, there are two types, a superior and an inferior one.' (H. V. Guenther, *The Life and Teaching of Naropa*, Oxford U.P., 1963, p. 34, note.)

mind was like a ball of cottonwool floating in the air above him'. We may then remember that the advanced Yogin is said to become as light as cotton-fibre and walk on spider-threads and sunbeams, and thereafter to fly through the air at will. We read that two experimental subjects saw a second body or person in their cubicles, and that one of the subjects could not tell which of the bodies was his own, for they overlapped in space. Such an experience might well inspire the promise made to the Yogin that his 'mind-stuff' will penetrate the bodies of others. The traditional commentary says, 'The Yogin by withdrawing mind-stuff from his own body deposits it in other bodies. The organs also fly after the mind-stuff thus deposited.' The content of the experimental and Yogic hallucinations offers still another analogy. Experimental subjects saw dots and patterns of light, and these merged into sharp-coloured scenes and hallucinations of 'everything from a peaceful rural scene to naked women diving and swimming in a woodland pool to prehistoric animals plunging through tropical forest'. The Yogin's final hallucinatory equivalent is the traditional 'golden King of mountains, Sumeru', with peaks of silver gems, lapis lazuli, crystal, and gold. He is invited to the godly Wishing Trees and to the use of beautiful, brazen nymphs, which he, though he hallucinates them, is told to refuse.*[19]

* 'Hallucinates them' is meant pejoratively, yet is not so far from the view of some intelligent practitioners of Yoga. When Father Denys Rutledge, a Benedictine monk, went in search of a Yogin who was clearly approaching the realization of Yogic ideals and powers, he found no one in India who claimed to be or to be personally acquainted with such a man. At the Yoga Vedanta Forest University, near Rishikesh, he was told, 'We in the ashram know of no one who has these *siddhis* (supernormal powers).' It was added, however, that 'they must be possible because we have conceived them'. In the Himalayas, a scholarly Buddhist lama, of German origin, said that he himself had experienced none of the *siddhis*. Of one of them, Yogic flying, he said that in a state of profound contemplation (not amounting to trance but a considerable degree of abstraction from external sights and sounds) one may experience a sensation of flying, *as though* the soul had soared aloft, taken wing and were present somewhere else. . . . He himself knew of no case of *bodily* travel of such a kind,' he said, smiling with slight irony. 'If the soul is many thousands of miles away,' he added, 'does it really matter very much whether the body has accompanied it or remains where it was, particularly if the body is, in any case, maya or illusion?' The Hindus interviewed by Rutledge claimed that the whole man, body and soul, was involved, but the Buddhist lama would only assess possibilities. In a profound enough state of abstraction, he

The postural stillness of the mystics also has its experiential counterparts. The conclusion is that we cannot learn to perceive, nor even continue to perceive well, if we remain too still. Unless we keep moving ourselves, we are unable to produce the clues we need to see and hear accurately. Without the muscles of our torsos, arms, and legs, we could hardly either perceive or think.[20]

Yet if we accept the conclusions of the experiments in sameness and stillness, a difficult question remains. Why are such uniformities so unpleasant and psychically dangerous to experimental subjects and so welcome to mystics? The answer must involve tradition, with its sanctions, ideals, and long elaboration of habits. But experiments also suggest that sensory deprivation is helpful to some schizophrenics and depressed persons.[21] If this is true, the men who choose themselves as subjects of their own experiments in mystic uniformity may be those, schizoid or depressive by nature, who sense that they will profit from them.

As is very natural, experimenters in both Japan and India have studied the physiological condition of, respectively, monks in Zen meditation and Yogins in Yogic meditation. The electroencephalograph has shown the Zen monks to sustain an alpha-wave state. That is, the train of their brain waves is like that of a person who has closed his eyes and, having stopped thinking of anything in particular, is on the verge of sleep. The Yogins, when they approach 'ecstasy', shifted from alpha waves to those that characterize the state of active dreaming or of intense waking concentrations. The experimenters say:

The evidence enables us to conclude that Yogic meditation, and the ecstasy to which it leads, represent a state of intense concentration of attention . . . The modifications recorded during very deep meditation and *samadhi* are much more dramatic than those known up till now (from scientific observation), which leads us to suppose that western subjects are far from being able to attain the Yogic state of mental concentration.

said, one loses consciousness of the body. 'On returning to oneself one may find oneself in exactly the same position as before, it is true; to another person it might seem that one had never left the place; but if it all happened in a flash, would one be missed, any more than a single blank on a reel of cinema film would be noticed?' (Dom Denys Rutledge, *In Search of a Yogi*, Farrar, Strauss & Co., N.Y., 1962, pp. 264, 228.)

The modification of the cardiac rhythm are clear and almost perfectly parallel to those of the EEG: definite acceleration during profound meditation and especially during ecstasy; a clearer slowing down after the end of the ecstatic period.

Further observations revealed a Yogin who could slow his heart down at will and another who, in meditation, consumed oxygen at only half the rate theoretically necessary to keep him alive.

It was perhaps such observations that stimulated the experiments in which ordinary subjects, with no special ideology and with no further instruction other than to try to remain in the 'alpha' state as recorded on the encephalograph, succeeded in sustaining the state and sometimes even in controlling the frequency of the alpha waves. About half of those who learned to sustain this 'tranquil, calm, and alert' state reported it to be very pleasant. It was later discovered that persons who were used to Zen or Yogic meditation learned to control their alpha waves much more easily than did ordinary subjects.

Another set of experiments, which has proved hard to repeat, has led to the belief that the visceral responses of the 'autonomic' nervous system can be controlled by voluntary learning. Given reinforcing rewards, dogs or rats learned to increase or decrease their heart rate, blood pressure, intestinal contractions, diameter of blood vessels, and rate of urine formation. These experiments of course suggested analogous ones with human beings. Necessarily less drastic than with animals, the experiments have had results that were less clear cut. It seems that not only psychosomatic diseases but also psychological states and even personality can be consciously learned.[22]

This is all I propose to say now about mystical techniques. I should like, however, to redress a deliberate fault in my discussion. The techniques have been too isolated from their ideologies and too cut from their natural sequence. I should therefore like to see one mystical method whole, if not with the anthropologist's intimate detail, at least with its parts considered together and its ideology clearly visible. I propose to attempt this with classic Yoga, and by means of a comparison of Freud and Patanjali.

8

Freud's Psychoanalysis and Patanjali's Yoga

We know who Freud is. The Patanjali to whom the *Yoga Sutras* are attributed remains, in contrast, completely obscure. It is barely possible that he is the grammarian, Patanjali, who lived in the second century A.D.[1] If he is, he cannot have written more than about a quarter of the work that bears his name; it was evidently the fourth century A.D. when some final editor composed the *Sutras* as they now stand. A modern reader sees that they are composite, advocating several Yogic methods, each of which rests on different philosophical and psychological assumptions. The Hindus, however, have always regarded this work as unitary, and I shall accordingly simplify matters by making no distinction between its methods or between the text itself and the classical commentary on it, which is no later than about A.D. 650. A traditional supercommentary will also be drawn on occasionally.

The Yoga of the *Yoga Sutras* and Freud's psychoanalysis are as far apart as the ages and cultures in which they originated, and their aims are opposite. Yet if their aims are really opposite, they are likely to be constructed in comparable ways. Their principles may be compared by way of two essays Freud wrote in 1915, one called, 'Instincts and their Vicissitudes', and the other, 'Repression'.

Freud wishes to clarify the idea of 'instinct' or 'drive'. To do this, he says, we must understand its impetus, its aims, its object, and its source. Its impetus is the degree of its force, its motor element, for every instinct is a kind of activity. Its aim, by definition and by nature, is satisfaction, and in order to arrive at this satisfaction it must abolish the stimulus by which it was aroused. The object of the instinct is, simply, whatever is best fitted to give it satisfaction. The instinct may be loosely or closely attached to its object; if the latter, it is said to be 'fixated' on it. As for the source of the instinct, it is some bodily process, whether centred in a particular organ or elsewhere.

Each instinct, according to Freud, belongs to one of the two primary types, the self-preservative, or the sexual. Confining ourselves, with him, to the sexual, we may note the major vicissitudes that instincts undergo. One of them is reversal into an opposite, as when sadism turns into masochism, or love into hate. An instinct may also be deflected back at its object. Sadism, for example, may turn against the subject's own ego and be transformed into masochism. Furthermore, repression may seem to extinguish an instinct, and sublimation may give it a more respectable form.

As we continue to think with Freud, we discover that our mental life is governed by three polarities—that of subject or ego against object or external world; that of pleasure against pain; and that of activity against passivity. These polarities are relatively direct in the infant. In the adult, however, they conflict and fuse and so create ambivalence and the possibility of falling from the difficult balance of adulthood into the primitivity of the child, who is always latent within us.

Instinctual repression humanizes us, but painfully. When our consciousness, says Freud, resists an instinct, as it often must, it causes a particular distortion or amnesia. But though repressed, the instinct becomes visible by its charge of 'affect', which often takes the form of anxiety. Repression of the instinct causes 'substitute-formations' and symptoms, in which the repressed returns and exhibits itself. All the different mechanisms of repression have in common a withdrawal of psychic energy, the directed kind that Freud calls 'cathexis'. In relation to the sexual instincts, the withdrawal is, of course, of the more particularly sexual energy, 'libido'.

In *Beyond the Pleasure Principle*, Freud adds that all organic instincts are acquired in the course of history, are conservative, and tend to go back to an earlier condition, just as spawning fish go back to the earlier homes of their species. The germ cell of a living animal, he says, repeats in its development the structures of all the forms from which the animal is descended.

The final goal of all organic striving can be stated too. It would be counter to the conservative nature of instinct if the goal of life were a state never hitherto reached. It must rather be an ancient starting point, which the living being left long ago, and to which it harks back. . . . 'The goal of all life is death.'

Freud assumes that among the traces of the distant past there are also those of social relations, preserved symbolically, for example, in the form of totemism. Totemism, he claims, contains within itself the germs of religion, morality, and social organization, and it re-enacts a substitute for the murder of the primeval chief by his own children. The impulse to this murder is experienced by each of us in his own early life.[2]

When Freud comes to ask how we can help ourselves to overcome our psychic difficulties, he shows little optimism. He supposes that social, and especially civilized life, demands renunciations that are extremely difficult for us to bear. The individual may, to be sure, try psychoanalysis. This does give hope for the future, but generally at the cost of the renunciation of immediate pleasures. With the analyst's help, and by virtue of a peculiar kind of alertness in a mind relaxed from ordinary purposive thinking, the patient grows increasingly aware of his instincts and affects, and this awareness, by some obscure combination of insight and affect, may allow him to satisfy himself more stably and with less pain.

Though I cannot now pursue the comparison to its end, it is not hard to identify quite Freud-like concepts in the *Yoga Sutras*. First, as in Freud, it is assumed that we are governed by instincts or drives, to whose objects we become fixated. Over and over again, the *Yoga Sutras* repeat that the ordinary human being is passionately and painfully fixated on objects. Among instincts, it is the self-preservative which is singled out as the most important. The text says, 'The will-to-live, sweeping on by force of its nature, exists in this form even in the wise.' And the commentary adds, 'In all living beings this craving for one's self ceaselessly rises, "May I not cease to live! May I live on!" '[3] Among polarities, those of true self and external world, pleasure and pain, and activity and passivity, are taken to be central, and they are related to sexuality, especially in its broad sense. For example, impulses are grouped under 'passion', defined as 'that which dwells upon pleasure', including greed, 'thirst', and desire; and under 'aversion', defined as 'that which dwells upon pain', including repulsion, wrath, and anger.[4]

The *Yoga Sutras* assume that we have a fundamentally painful 'thirst for either seen or revealed objects', the seen ones including women, food, drink, and power, and the revealed ones, heaven or the like superlative states. The concept of repression appears as the concept of amnesia for a past that never ceases to affect us deeply. Some of the energies precipitated, so to speak, by the past lie dormant until awakened by the right stimuli, which cause the repressed—in a not really Freudian sense—to return. In basic agreement with Freud, it is assumed that life is made possible only by aggression. 'From right-living', the aphoristic sentences read, 'results pleasure; from wrong-living, pain; from pleasure, passion; from pain, aversion; and from this, struggle. Quivering in central-organ or in vocal-organ or in body with this struggle, he (any man) either helps or injures another.'[5] Stated more extremely, life is aggression, for 'enjoyment is impossible unless one has killed some living creature'. Life is also always fundamentally anxious, marked by what the text calls 'the painfulness of anxiousness'. It says, 'Everyone has the experience of anxiousness', which is 'permeated by aversion and dependent upon animate and inanimate instruments'.[6]

Not only do the *Yoga Sutras* regard the interplay of conscious and unconscious, or reason and emotion, and of pleasure and pain, as constituting the nature of our unhappy lives, but they see the past as Freud does. That is, they, too, accept the belief in the biological and psychological effects of the distant past, retained by an enormous life-memory that includes all species-memories within itself. In one of their sections, the *Yoga Sutras* are based on the view that there is a single cosmic mind, out of which we, the individuals, are made.[7] And throughout the *Sutras* there is reliance upon the principle of transmigration, which causes memory to extend backwards without end. It is pointed out that even the youngest child can feel that life tends towards death, and the reason is that the child has already endured the pangs of death innumerable times and therefore remembers them, though unconsciously. 'The fear of the child is based on the memory of pain and aversion because it is a fear like any of our fears.'[8] All instincts and unlearned reactions are explained as the results of experience in previous lives.

When 'Patanjali' comes to explain what we can do to help ourselves, he seems to assume that not many of us can be saved. He goes to some trouble to prove that the world will always remain populated by the unredeemed. Otherwise, according to the laws of his own philosophical physics, a kind of law of entropy would split the phenomenal world into its two fundamentally different substances, the one, imperceptible, primal 'matter', and the other, pure, isolated consciousness. But the individual with the necessary aptitude and the willingness to renounce pleasure can be rescued from pain by means of Yoga. To prevent domination by troubling thoughts, he must reach himself to think effective counter-thoughts, to burn away the 'seeds' of life-and-death-enhancing subsconscious impressions, and to substitute benign for baneful psychic tendencies, the benign of the 'sublimated' type that can sublime themselves away and so vanish. With the help of his master in Yoga, his guru, and by means of a peculiar concentration in a mind relaxed from ordinary object-oriented thought, a mind mostly shut to the world outside and open to itself, the supra-worldly, the candidate for redemption becomes increasingly aware of his affects, instincts, and unconscious aims. If he perseveres, he may succeed in cutting his fixations to objects and reaching a motionless insight and an objectless trance.

The analogies I have made between Freud and Patanjali might well be explored more exactly. I will assume that they are accurate and sufficient for our immediate purposes, and will turn to an explanation of Yoga through psychoanalytic concepts, which, as a somewhat faithful Westerner, I take to be more illuminating than an explanation of psychoanalysis through Yogic concepts.

It may seem at first that the *Yoga Sutras* teach a deliberate and systematic use of pathological mechanisms; but further reflection makes it clear that a pathological explanation would be misleading.

The Yoga taught in the *Yoga Sutras* rests on self-observation. This is essentially a withdrawal of emotion, or, more technically, of libido, from the external world to one's own, internal one.

Ordinarily, such self-observation takes place in a purely spontaneous way. It is a sign of anxiety, which signals, in turn, the presence or at least suspicion of psychic pain. It is the effect of real or feared depletion of the ego, that is, of a profound feeling of weakness, inability, worthlessness, or depression. But the *Yoga Sutras* do not assume that self-observation will come about spontaneously, or that, if it does, it will be adequate. For the sake of the self-observation they teach, they try to arouse the memory of pain and mobilize anxiety. They stress that 'that which is to be escaped is pain yet to come'.[9] Naturally, they regard the self-observation as healing when properly carried out. In the cultural context of India, this faith does not require the candidate to begin with more than the ambition to achieve perhaps the highest goal recognized by society. I suppose that the degree of his accomplishment is determined by the degree and kind of his suffering, by the force of his instincts and his ability to deflect or weaken their cathective power, by his identification with his guru, by the social prestige he acquires, by his success in libidinizing his perceptual processes, and by the release, in Yogic meditation, of powerful and yet not too disturbing fantasies. The general satisfaction he may obtain ought not to be questioned. From the standpoint of psychoanalysis, however, no matter how keen his insights or elaborate his methods, his goals remain primitive.

Yoga wants its passionlessness to cut the tie to the object. It describes our psychic life as a river whose 'stream towards objects is dammed by passionlessness'. What is this passionlessness? 'The consciousness of being master on the part of one who has rid himself of thirst for either seen or (religiously) revealed objects.'[10] This state seems to require the Yogin to retreat, as the analyst would say, narcissistically. We may imagine the guru saying to his pupil, 'You feel that objects will make you happy. But they can give you only pain. You may not realize this because you are not yet sensitive enough to the pain you are suffering. The thirst for objects is blind and fateful. It brings with it the endless "fruit" of transmigration. Abandon the object, rid yourself of anxiety. If the world then takes on the appearance of an illusion, if you recognize that the lusting, suffering ego is not really yourself, this insight will bring you closer to the final goal, which is the trance of isolation.'

In other words, the guru teaches that even the stage of narcissistic retreat that causes deep depletion of the ego and deep fear, the stage of feelings of illusion that suggest schizophrenic estrangement or death, should be cultivated and regarded as good. Now this particular kind of guru does not think that the world is literally an illusion. He believes in primal matter and its flickering, world-making effects. To him, the illusion lies in the feeling that the true self is identical with the empirical ego and its sensations, perceptions, memories, lusts, and fate. The empirical ego should be recognized as only an unnecessary supplement to the true one. After this insight, the cathexis between true self and empirical ego vanishes. Like a king bee flying from his hive, the 'mind-stuff' flies away from the world of objects. Like the subject bees, the senses follow after. 'The withdrawal of the senses is as it were the imitation of the mind-stuff itself on the part of the sense-organs by disjoining themselves from their objects.'[11]

As we know, many of the practices of Yoga are meant to alter the nature of perception, in order to make the Yogin finally independent of objects, that is, of his libidinal attachment to them. Therefore the Yogin sits in long 'one-pointed' concentration on selected objects or particular organs or parts of his body. By means of a three-level concentration he exercises 'constraint' upon these organs or bodily parts. His aim, I think, is similar to the unconscious one behind hysterical blockages of sensation, such as the blindness, narrowing of vision, or deafness caused by a refusal and a desire to see or hear something dangerously attractive.* The Yogin trains himself to

* Some of the phenomena thought to verify the mystical effect of Yogic exercises may themselves be of hysterical origin. For instance, a twentieth-century Chinese mystic describes how his meditation, which caused him to vibrate internally, cured him of 'old ailments such as nervousness, palpitation, lumbago, headache, buzzing in the ears, dizziness, coughing and spitting blood'. He tells us that, to develop his vitality, he abstained from sexual desires, to invigorate his breath, from speech, and to raise his spirits, from gazing. He took daily notes of his progress. After a time, his internal vibration became intense and stopped between his eyebrows, then returned to the 'central spot', between navel and pit of the stomach, where it had begun. The vibration travelled through his body. 'It pulsed up and down, causing the penis to erect.... One night ... the vibration caused my arms to revolve backwards and forwards quickly like a wheel with the same number of turns each way. Then it reached my legs so that the left one bent while the right one straightened and vice versa. These movements could not be

alter the psychic distance, quality, and intensity of the sense-object, to change it from malign to benign, or from attractive to neutral, and then to shut it out of his consciousness. By making such an effort of concentration, alteration, and suppression, he has so libidinized the sense or bodily area or function he is 'constraining', has so deprived perception of its normal thing-structure and thing-power, that his fantasies, provided that they remain vague enough, are allowed to fill his consciousness. The particular organic abilities he acquires may be athletic, but may also be like hysterical hyperfunctions, or like the child's plasticity, the greater responsiveness of the whole body to affect.

And so the Yogin diminishes his external sensation and perception, or their libidinal importance, in order to be able to concentrate on his internal sensation and perception. He shifts his interest from the external object to the process by which it is ordinarily grasped, and makes sensation and perception their own object. Then, having isolated himself from the world outside, he weakens his sense of isolation by creating an internal world-analogue. To further his destruction and creation, he trains himself to believe that the external world is unstable, and only appears to be steady, real, or good. He says to himself, 'The recognition of the permanent, of the pure, of pleasure, and of a self in what is impermanent, impure and not-self' is only the falsehood conveyed by a blinded consciousness. 'The earth or the sky with its moon and stars may seem to be perpetual, and a girl may seem to have the crescent moon's beauty; but they are impermanent, painful, and a hindrance to insight.[12] To compensate for this psychic destruction of stability and value, the Yogin maintains his inner world more stably, giving it the feeling of reality. To gain stability, he expels and retains air according to the rhythm he imposes. To gain stability, he concentrates on the particular senses. 'These sense-activities when arisen bring the mind-stuff into a relation of stability and dispel doubt and become

explained by orthodox science and were involuntary. After that my head (seemed to) swell and the upper part of my body stretch so that I (seemed) to be over ten feet tall.' He felt he says, as if only the lower half of his body remained, and 'with the disappearance of both body and mind, I experienced unusual bliss'. (Yin Shih Tsu, quoted in C. Luk, *The Secrets of Chinese Meditation*, Rider & Co., London, 1964, pp. 177–8, 194–6 (quotations from 178, 196).)

a way of approach to concentrated insight.' The Yogin's 'mind-stuff comes to a sense of balance with regard to the feeling-of-personality and becomes waveless like the Great Sea'. Eventually, it is said, the 'mind-stuff' becomes indistinguishable from the object-to-be-known as it is in itself, without the distance and distortion caused by ordinary perception and by the categories of thought and the conventions of language.[13] Not only does the Yogin reach an objective-feeling stability, but he identifies himself with, or becomes internally, the secret substance of the external world.

The result of such withdrawals, concentrations, destructions, and creations, is a feeling of enormous power. Prolonged stoppage of breath intoxicates the Yogin, and by the stoppage he also mimes death and victory over it—it is he who is the Lord of breathing and who determines how and when it is to be carried on, and who will eventually dispense with it. The Yogin believes that he can or will be able to grasp objects with perfect intuition, will know everything inside and outside of himself, enter other men, as we have said, with his own mind, sense the minutest things with superlative sensory power, shrink himself to an atom and dive into the earth, fly through the air with the speed of thought, and possess all beauty, grace, and power.[14]

But the *Yoga Sutras* reinstate reality through the medium of conscience. They warn the Yogin that such powers, though they are within his grasp, will block the way to final release if he uses them. There is an especially strong warning against the gods who try to seduce the still incomplete Yogin, one who has reached only the second Honeyed State. They propose rest for him, because his exertions have made him weary, elixir against old age, Wishing-Trees, the Stream-of-heaven, perfect sageness, the incomparable and willing nymphs we have already met, supernal hearing, and a diamond-like body.

These are great temptations. But the Yogin is told to answer sharply,

I have found the lamp of Yoga which makes an end to the obscurations of the hindrances. How then could it be that I who have seen its light could be led astray by these mere things of sense, a mere mirage, and make of myself fuel for that same fire of the round-of-rebirths as it flares up again. Fare ye well! Sensual things are dreams, and to be craved by vile folk![15]

In other words, the Yogin, if he accepts the advice of the *Yoga Sutras,* enjoys the feeling of powers which he does not have to prove by performance. He remains intelligent enough not to test his omnipotence in practice. In psychoanalytic terms, he has regressed to the child's omnipotence, he has introjected the world, in order to concentrate all pleasures in himself. But his self-love and internally-guarded omnipotence remain this side of sanity.

We see that the goal of Yoga is depersonalization. Yet, though the term must sound strange to an analyst, it is a happy depersonalization. It must sound strange because depersonalization usually follows a sudden wounding loss. It is a feeling that the world and even one's inner self are apart from oneself, have come painfully unjoined. One perceives things and people, but they are shadows, robbed of their libidinal reality. The Yogin, however, does not sense his like state to be painful. He comes to it gradually, with, it must be emphasized, the approval of society, of his teacher, and of his own conscience. He redirects his instincts towards inner processes; he lowers his instinctual pressures as much as possible. The fantasies he enjoys are of the kind he has been told he would enjoy, or they are so unstructured that they cannot, in any case, frighten him. He has learned to cope with his open and concealed anxieties.

What then can we say in evaluation? No reasoning will necessarily overcome one's subjective preference for either Yogic or psychoanalytic ideal. If we confine ourselves to India, not only may Yoga have helped the individual, but it may have given him satisfactions greater than any he might have acquired in other ways. Not only may the Yogin have learned to withstand very difficult external conditions, but also typically Indian psychic pressures, which intensify sexual guilts, cause hysterical rapidity and intensity of emotional change, and, often, *painful* depersonalization.[16] Being Western, I cannot help feeling that the accomplishment of the Yogin, even the one who practises the most philosophical and contemplative type of Yoga, the kind which has been described here, is too selfish and too nourished on fantasies. The serious Yogin has substantial insight and great discipline, but he uses insight and discipline to remain self-enclosed. Freud's well-known contrast of the basic forces of Eros and Thanatos is congenial to Indian thought, but while Freud chooses Eros, the Yogin chooses Thanatos, or timelessness, isolation, and quiescence, which we call simply death.

9

Psychotic Mysticism

Normality is a tricky concept, and I am glad to avoid defining it. Yet I am sure that the mysticism we have been discussing has, for the most part, been normal in its own environments. But something in mysticism is not merely environmental, because it expresses the centredness of all human beings in themselves, expresses their shifting personal boundaries, and expresses their attempts to renew and unify themselves. To a degree, then, mysticism is normal everywhere. But it also merges into psychosis. There have been many psychotic mystics and mystical psychotics, assuming that these categories can really be distinguished from one another. It seems to me, then, that mysticism takes abnormal, that is, psychotic forms everywhere.

It is not difficult to enumerate the qualities of mysticism that, at their extreme, are psychotic. The sense of drastic separation from everything, even one's body and self, is definable as psychotic. The loss of oneself in fusion with other people and things is characteristic of psychosis, and so are the fear and guilt that acquire a hallucinatory presence, as they did in the devil that terrified St. Teresa with his flaming, shadowless body and menacing voice, or in the *maras* of Buddhist tradition that 'appear as worms and grubs that sting' the meditator's head, 'tickle him under the arms, clutch at him, make a disturbing noise or appear as beasts or in other strange forms to annoy him'.[1] Even apart from hallucinations, we ought not to hesitate to classify such influential mystics as Swedenborg or Böhme among the paranoids, though they may, like many other psychotics, have said penetrating things and had powerful fantasies.

These likenesses or identities call for some description of the relevant psychotic traits. I shall take the traits to be the psychotic experience of time, mode of speech, hallucination, certainty, bliss, depersonalization and loss of identity, and sense of unreality.

The sense of time varies not only from psychotic person to person, but from psychotic state to state. When in a manic state, one may feel Godlike and invulnerable to death. 'Death will never occur again,' says the person in manic elation, 'I will be happy forever, forever.' In a depressed state, however, especially when it is psychotic, time may appear to stand still. Its variety can no longer be experienced, it is all the same hopelessness, all frozen cold and hard. Close, and yet not identical with this time is the schizophrenic's possible isolation in moments, his previous world, with its past, having foundered. He says, 'If I speak or do something, I don't feel that I am speaking or doing something at the same time; that is terrible for me. I am living and actually not living.' Or he says, 'There is no longer any past for me; people appear so strange; it is as if I could not see any reality, as if I were in a theatre. . . . Everything floats before my eyes, but leaves no impression.'[2]

The emptiness of time can be paralleled by a certain emptiness of speech. That is, speech may cease to have any public meaning, for the differences between speaker, person spoken to, words spoken with, and subject spoken of may vanish and only a subjective thing-like word or word-like thing be left. Words that are things and make up subjective worlds are controlled by him who speaks them. Thus, in one case, the letters of the French alphabet were felt to be each a different part of the speaker's body, and he guarded the parts against infection by pronouncing the letters in the right way and order. The emptiness of speech, as I have named it, is really its transformation into an idiosyncratic magical being, which is created by utterance to guard, to avenge, and to grant and be fulfilment.[3]

Psychotic hallucination can be illustrated by the well-known case of the paranoidal judge, Daniel Paul Schreber, who was discussed by Freud and who wrote revealing memoirs of his 'nervous illness'. Schreber believed that he was in 'nerve contact' with God. He thought that nerve-filaments led from God to his own brain and from there to all other souls, transmitting both voices and poisons. Not only did Schreber hear the apparently transmitted voices and feel the poisons, but he saw them, in the form of rays, with his 'mind's eye':

With my mind's eye I *see* the rays which are both the carriers of the voices and of the poison of corpses to be unloaded on my body, as long drawn out filaments approaching my head from some vast distant spot on the horizon. I can see them *only* with my mind's eye when my eyes are closed by miracles or when I close them voluntarily, that is to say when they are then reflected on my inner nervous system as long filaments stretching towards my head, sometimes withdrawing from it.

By the same kind of transmission Schreber had, he believed, direct vision of God's omnipotence. 'The radiant picture of his rays', he says,

became visible to my inner eye, while I was lying in bed not sleeping but awake—that is to say he was reflected on my inner nervous system. Simultaneously I heard his voice; but it was not a soft whisper—as the talk of the voices always was before and after that time—it resounded in a mighty bass as if directly in front of my bedroom windows.

Schreber also believed that he would be transformed into a woman, and that this would be a preparation for the renewal of mankind, that the weather was 'to a certain extent' dependent on his actions and thoughts, and that he was the human being around which literally everything in the universe turned.

I assume that no sane person would contest that Schreber was psychotic; but Schreber himself, who was not sane, did. He drew up a plea to be released from the hospital in which he was kept In this plea he contested the judgment of the famous psychiatrist, Kraeplin. He said:

The total content of the present work will hardly show anything *in my case* which justifies speaking of 'the inability of the patient to use earlier experiences to correct thoroughly and accurately his new ideas' . . . or of 'faulty judgment', which Kraeplin says 'invariably accompanies delusions'. I trust I have proved that I am not 'controlled by fixed and previously formed ideas', but that I also possess in full measure the 'capacity to evaluate critically the content of consciousness with the help of judgment and deduction'.

Schreber then went on to oppose that shallow rationalism of the eighteenth-century Enlightenment that had long been under attack, and defended his own experience with the mystic's argument of the third eye. In his words:

Human beings who are fortunate enough to enjoy healthy nerves cannot (as a rule anyway) have 'illusions', 'hallucinations', 'visions', or whatever expression one wants to use for these phenomena; it would certainly therefore be desirable if all human beings remained free from such experiences; they would then subjectively feel very much better. But this does not imply that the events resulting from a diseased nervous system are altogether unfounded in objective reality or have to be regarded as nervous excitations lacking all external cause. I can therefore not share Kraeplin's astonishment which he expresses repeatedly . . . that the 'voices', etc., seem to have a far greater power of conviction for hallucinated patients than 'anything said by those around them'. A person with sound nerves is, so to speak, *mentally* blind compared with him who receives supernatural impressions by virtue of his diseased nerves; he is therefore as little likely to persuade the visionary of the unreality of his visions as a person who can see will be persuaded by a really blind person that there are not colours, that blue is not blue, red not red, etc.[4]

Not only may the psychotic be sure of the correctness of his experience, but he may have a heightened sense of reality that turns into bliss. 'First', says one, recalling his manic attacks, 'comes the general sense of well-being . . . which . . . remains as a sort of permanent background. . . . Closely allied is . . . the second main feature . . . well described . . . as a "heightened sense of reality".' This consists 'of a considerable number of related sensations, the net result of which is that the outer world makes a much more vivid and intense impression than usual. . . . The first thing I note is the peculiar appearances of the lights—the ordinary electric lights in the ward. They are not exactly brighter, but deeper, more intense, perhaps a trifle more ruddy than usual.'

Another patient, recalling his attacks, mingles belief in the insights they reveal with a sense of their irrationality:

The point seems to be, so far as I can grasp it, that during an exhilaration the mind penetrates infinitely more deeply into all things, and receives flashes of almost divine light and wisdom, which open to it, momentarily, regions of thought hitherto difficult or impossible of penetration. But, except in the milder forms of the exhilaration, the mind's own restlessness, and impatient activity, interfere, for the time being at least, with the just application and the rational and appropriate, not to say the sane, use of what it has thus acquired. . . . Naturally the more exhilarated I become the more difficult it is for me to reason to myself and to admit the insanity of my projects and hence to be willing to renounce or break away from them.[5]

As against mania, which is usually exhilarating and even blissful, depersonalization is never anything but painful. The person seems to be observing himself from the outside. 'He', the body and mind he is observing, are unfamiliar automata, and the external world, too, looks strange, blurred, perhaps, or fogged or flat or at once minute and enormous or at once terribly separate and extremely identical. In psychotic depersonalization, men feel shadow-like, that is, dead. They vacillate between different components of themselves and become literally dizzy. They become confused and do not know how they are composed. 'Do I have a face?' one of them asked, and continued, 'It's my face. I have a face. Is this my face? There is only one face, one nurse, one hospital.' Another said, 'What I was and what you were I often could not tell. . . . You and I. . . . It's all the same, isn't it?' And another seemed to herself to break apart. She said:

I run into myself. I break me into pieces. I am like a spray. I lose my centre of gravity. I have no weight. I am quite mechanical. I have gone to pieces. I am like a marionette. I lack something to hold me together. I am not on earth; I am somewhere else; I am in between. I am rigid, I cannot cry . . . I am completely in pieces, there is no ground under the feet when you are not on earth. I feel the ground very rarely. . . . Everything pulls me apart, therefore I do not like the saying, 'to jump out of one's skin'. The skin is the only possible means of keeping the different pieces together. There is no connection between the different parts of my body. Sometimes the roof of my skull flies away. When it does not come back, I stand on my head immediately and it tears me to pieces.

Another form of self-loss may threaten the psychotic, or near-psychotic, engulfment in other things. A schizophrenic woman recalls:

I was about twelve, and I had to walk to my father's shop through a large park, which was a long, dreary walk. I suppose, too, that I was rather scared. I didn't like it, especially when it was getting dark. I started to play a game to help pass the time. You know how as a child you count the stones or stand on the crosses on the pavement—well, I hit on this way of passing the time. It struck me that if I stared long enough at the environment that I would blend with it and disappear just as if the place was empty and I had disappeared. It is as if you get yourself to feel that you don't know who you are or where you are. To blend into the scenery so to speak. Then, you are scared of it because it begins to come on without encouragement. I would just be walking along and felt that I had blended with the landscape. Then I would get frightened and repeat my name over and over again to bring me back to life, so to speak.

The schizophrenic's engulfment in others or conglomeration with them is terribly painful. 'Gradually', one of them said, 'I am no longer able to distinguish how much of myself is in me and how much is already in others. I am a conglomeration, a monstrosity, modelled anew each day.'' A similar pain is expressed in the words, 'I have lived with these other people for so long and we have eaten and drunk together. Now they are all part of me and I am part of them. I'm frightened—I only want to be myself.'[6]

Running through all these accounts there is, of course, the sense of unreality. Depersonalized, de-realized, the world assumes the unreality the mystic attributes to it. To the mystic, this unreality is an insight, to the psychotic it is an unavoidable torture. 'Renée', a Swiss girl who underwent a remarkable cure, recalls the devastating crises in which everything turned unreal.

One day, while I was in the principal's office, suddenly the room became enormous, illuminated by a dreadful electric light that cast false shadows. Everything was exact, smooth, artificial, extremely tense; the chairs and tables seemed models placed here and there. Pupils and teachers were puppets revolving, without cause, without objective. I recognized nothing, nobody. It was as though reality, attenuated, had slipped away from all these things and these people. Profound dread overwhelmed me, and as though lost, I looked around desperately for help. I heard people talking but I did not grasp the meaning of words. The voices were metallic, without warmth or colour. From time to time, a word detached itself from the rest. It repeated itself over and over in my head, absurd, as though cut off by a knife.[7]

The psychotic pain we have been concerned with can be grasped as the pain of a great loss and an attempted restitution. The loss is of time, speech, external world, others, self, and so of reality in general. The restitution is made by way of a malignly creative retreat into oneself. In this retreat, the love, hate, and concern that are lavished as a rule upon the world of things and people are lavished upon some aspect of oneself. Lacking the usual gratifications, the psychotic tries to replace them with self-gratification.

When the psychotic makes restitution to himself by concern with his own body, he may give in to the infant's simple, lulling motions, he may twist his body with some symbolic appropriateness, or he may fix himself in a posture that has a special meaning to him; and he may tap, hum, or mutter. When the psychotic is more concerned with his perceptions, he may contemplate anything, even a spot or stain, and see pleasure into it, or hallucinate sights, sounds, or smells, or, more elaborately, whole bizarre universes. Or he may be concerned with his ideas, and then create idea-fantasies and bizarre pseudo-philosophical systems. He may also, like some Taoists or Zen monks, execute a hostile mockery of the world by his disordered gestures, strident cries, and strangely appropriate laughter.[8]

These restitutions all prove insufficient. Sometimes there is a happier one, of sanity itself. This return of a lost sanity is best described by those who have felt it in themselves. Renée may be our witness here. When the psychoanalyst who had helped to cure her asked what difference there was between her present sanity and her earlier pre-psychotic condition, Renée answered:

I no longer live in a dream. I no longer take pleasure in a life of unreality, I am no longer in autism. I recognize you as in individuality: I accept that you can be tired, discouraged or happy, whereas before, you were 'disguised', 'angry', or 'mother'. Now I want to live; I take care of myself when I feel sick, and I no longer want to die. I know myself; I have some narcissistic desires and I take care of my body, it exists. Before, I had wanted to succeed so as not to suffer any more, not to have 'voices' and to have mother all to myself. Now, I still want to succeed, but I know that it does not mean perfect joy; it is the ability to make sacrifices, and being happy at the same time; it is to know reality.

I also recognize others a little.

I am still not oriented in space, but I no longer make mistakes in setting down objects; before I didn't bother with the limits of tables. And then, too, I am interested in time; I know the difference between day and night and I know that an hour is short in contrast to the whole day. I feel perspective in drawing.

The analyst asked Renée what was essential in all this, and Renée answered:

It is the fact that I no longer desire death, that I have no delirium, nor any autism. It just does not compare with the age of thirteen or fourteen when I wanted to build a machine to destroy the world. I am no longer lost in dreams, and above all, I recognize you, I see you in a normal way.[9]

Eleven Quintessences of the Mystic State

One thing and another and another have come up. What is the point of it all? That mysticism is selfish, superstitious, mad, inescapable, and salutary? Surely, the mystic aims straighter at the point, the infinitely dense and contractable truth, 'more minute than the minute, greater than the great'. He aims with such confidence; but is there really one point to aim at? In any case, I have only a complex impression and a final attitude, which I must try to convey by renewing what has already been said, and by making the last of the series of enumerations on the framework of which this book has been constructed.

As I began, I end in the belief that mysticism is not completely opaque to reason. It seems to me about as intelligible as love or economics, and sometimes no less important. It has been so varied that we should learn to stop speaking of it always in the singular. The experience of a mystic may be as peculiar to him as the work of art is to an individual artist. But even if we neglect the sheer individuality of mystical experiences and classify them by their recurrent styles, we may find that we cannot make illuminating generalizations about all of them at once. My use of the singular, 'mystic' or 'mysticism', is therefore rough and for the sake, mainly, of brevity. There will always be exceptions to the judgments I make. But I have been less concerned to take account of exceptions than to remain open to possibilities. Instead of ending with a sharp definition of mysticism, I prefer the set of its interlocking characteristics, each of which I call a 'quintessence' because it might serve as a complete though narrow explanation.

Since the characteristics I have found interlock, they are not always clearly distinct from one another; but I think that when they are grasped together, they evoke mysticism, as it has in fact existed, with reasonable completeness. As for the number of quintessential characteristics, eleven, I cannot justify it with either mystical or unmystical reasons. It is simply the number I have happened on. There is a tradition that this number signifies excess and, as exceeding the ten of the Ten Commandments, sin as well. Maybe, then, the number signifies that I am about to sin against mysticism, for it is true that I have approached it with some coolness and, at times, animosity.

The quintessences I have found are these: sameness; separation; uniqueness; inclusion; familiar strangeness; depletion; aggression; conscience; mirror-reversal; humour; reality. Reality, as the critical characteristic, is put last. To a mystic, it may seem to be the only one worth emphasizing, but he is inclined, after all, to dismiss many of the more interesting features of experience, his own no less than ours.

The first quintessence is sameness. Even the mystic confesses that things look different from one another, but their difference, he says, is illusory. There are not really, he says, any stones, butterflies, raindrops, cats, trees, dollars, houses, Hindus, Jews, persons called Luigi, Hayyim, Margot, or even you or I; or, rather, they are all the same one thing, which is different from all their differences. Fundamentally, stones are butterflies, butterflies are raindrops, raindrops are cats, and so on. In the words of the solemn, contentiously individual philosopher, Fichte, 'Being is absolutely single; there are not several Beings but only one Being.'[1]

The more intellectual mystics do not merely deny that things can be different, but, as we know, try to prove that they cannot be. As we approach our conclusion, we may recall the intellectual techniques they have elaborated.

One such technique, which we have found in Plato's descendant, Proclus, is to identify the real with the utterly single, and the utterly single with the utterly good. Another, that of Plato and Shankara, makes the analogy between the world we appear to sense and a sensory illusion, a shadow, Plato says, cast by an image and mistaken for a living man, or a rope, Shankara says, mistaken in the twilight for a snake. The illusion is as if superimposed upon the indescribably real.

Another technique, Eastern and Western, is meant to demonstrate that everything is consciousness. It stresses that we cannot separate the perceiver from that which he perceives. It reminds us that consciousness creates dreams, and requires us to see that we also dream the dream, of the world, that does not appear to be one. There is only consciousness, an unblinking light that gives perceptible forms to the apparently separate objects that enter the circle of its illumination. But it is they that, so to speak, enter and leave, blinking on and off as they do, while it remains in unshadowed brightness, dwelling on itself alone.

Still another technique, we may recall, is to demonstrate the relativity of everything we ordinarily sense or think of. This technique, most effectively developed by the Buddhist 'logicians', starts from the assumption that everything real must be independent, must have, as they say, its 'own-being'. Nothing such can be found in ordinary experience because the real is 'signless' and 'empty'. By what means is this wordless truth to be grasped? By the dialectical demonstration of the relativity of all that is taken to be true, the dialectical structure showing itself to be 'like a framework which leads upwards from the ground' towards the 'empty' truth which neither affirms nor denies anything. To this truth, speech, the art of particularizing and affirming and denying, cannot, by its very nature, be true. And so 'the wise man discerns the rise and fall of speech, or song, or noise, or any sound. They are but momentary and empty; all speech is similar to an echo.' Finally, 'Bliss consists in the cessation of all thought, in the quiescence of plurality.'[2]

These conceptions have been paralleled in the West. Ludwig Wittgenstein may again serve as an example. In his *Tractatus Logico-Philosophicus*, Wittgenstein contends that whatever has value in itself must be necessary, uncreated, indestructible, and immutable; but everything that is in this our world is contingent, that is, relative. Speaking as a possible crypto-Buddhist, he tells us that 'if there is a value which is of value, it must be outside of all happening and being-so. For all happening and being-so is accidental. What makes it non-accidental cannot be *in* the world, for otherwise this would again be accidental. It must be outside the world', or, in Buddhist terminology, signless.

What then, according to Wittgenstein, is the use of the philosophy he has been proposing? 'My statements', he answers,

elucidate by leading anyone who understands them to recognize them eventually as nonsense—after he has climbed up them—by them, on them, over them. (He must as it were throw away the ladder, after he has ascended it.) He must overcome these statements: then he will see the world rightly.

Finally, he says, there is nothing to be said. One hears the sigh of the controversialist grown weary and introverted at last:

Whereof one cannot speak, thereof one must be silent.[3]

Invented chiefly in India, such polemical techniques were ground to the sharpest cutting edges. The instance of Naropa will recall the mystical champions of their sects whose logic turned the heads of kings and ruled the fortunes of great monasteries. Only a few years ago, the mystical philosophers or theologians of Tibet were still being trained for argument-to-argument combat, in which the cut and thrust of logic was heightened by scowls, bullying postures, and an artistically intimidating voice. I must own that it seems fitting to me to conduct a philosophic congress in the style of a shadow-boxing tournament.

So much for the intellectual techniques. But since the achievement of sameness cannot be entrusted to them alone, they are accompanied or superseded by perceptual, bodily, and emotional ones, not to speak of the projections and explicit dramas.

The exclusively perceptual techniques, we know, train the mystic to turn his senses into himself. He may no longer persist in his careless visual flirtation with every attractive object that meets the eye. He sits stolid in his Yogic posture and stares at a chosen object and its afterimage until the afterimage is enlarged to a pervasive brilliance that concentrates him to oneness. Or he stares, if that is the right word, at an immaterial object, uniting with it, he thinks, and becoming equally immaterial or non-objective at last.

Much of the bodily training is designed, as we recall, to teach one to breathe in predetermined rhythms and to assume the different Yogic postures. Rhythmic breathing, compounded or not with magical utterances, engulfs the mystic in a long series of attentive inhalations, retentions of breath, and exhalations; the posture he assumes ties his body into a self-contained knot; and breathing and posture together guard his senses from shifting about in their ordinary way. And because he does not wish to keep his feet on the ground, the stony, plastic foundation of our material lives, the mystic tucks them between his thighs and so is the better able to enter a state of sameness. Wishing to remain neither distant nor close to anything other than his own self, he grasps nothing but his own body. His hands need not preserve a changing balance by swinging out or holding on to something else; they do not stretch out and find either something or nothing; they do not signal remoteness or contact, except with himself. And if someone else is with him, he is likely to use him (or her) to arouse him to couple as if with himself, allowing him to keep himself, including his precious seed, intact and self-enclosed.

As for the emotional techniques, they are used, we have said, to startle or awaken the mystic into ecstasy, but perhaps more often to encourage revulsion against material things, including the mystic's own bodily self. The Buddhist, the same one who is taught to be disgusted with food, is also taught to meditate on the 'thirty-two' parts of his body, from the hairs of his head to his tears, sweat, spittle, snot, joint-fluid, and urine. He fixes in his mind some one of the parts, and then thinks, slowly and carefully, of its repulsive colours, shapes, smells, origin, and locality. But while particular things are associated in such ways with all possible negative emotions, that which is not particular, which is too much the same even to particularize sharply, is associated with a state of being that may be called calmly ecstatic.

So the substance of every particular thing is withdrawn from it. Every thing, everything identifiable, that is, that consciousness may be aware of, is shown to be intellectually null, perceptually absent, and emotionally repellent. One's attention shifts from its ordinary objects to the processes by which one knows them. One tries to see, not a sight, but one's seeing, to hear, not a sound, but one's hearing, to desire, not a pleasure, but only one's desire. This is not the end, however. Further concentration robs the modalities of consciousness of their differences. Instead of seeing one's seeing, hearing one's hearing, and desiring one's desiring, one is left, one thinks and hopes, with a totally undifferentiated consciousness. Everything is so much the same that nothing is left to perceive.

On hearing that it is possible to arrive at such a state, the mystic's disciple is said to ask:

'What is the meaning of "nothing to perceive"?'

He asks, and his master answers:

'Being able to behold men, women and all the various sorts of appearances while remaining as free from love or aversion as if they were actually not seen at all—that is what is meant by "nothing to perceive".'

The disciple asks:

'That which occurs when we are confronted by all sorts of shapes and forms is called perception. Can we speak of perception taking place when nothing confronts us?'

The answer is:

'Yes.'

The disciple then asks:

'When something confronts us, it follows that we perceive it, but how can there be perception when we are confronted by nothing at all?'

And the master then answers:

'We are talking of that perception which is independent of there being an object or not. How can that be? The nature of perception being eternal, we go on perceiving whether objects are present or not. Thereby we come to understand that, whereas objects naturally appear and disappear, the nature of perception does neither of those things.'[4]

The second quintessence is separation. The sameness we have been speaking of is arrived at by the separation of reality from that which, according to the mystic, obscures it. The normal touchstones of reality are perception, emotion, and intellect, and these remain touchstones to the mystic as well. He does not so much refuse them as separate them from the external world. Whereas he used to look out through his windows and go out through his door, he now pulls his windowshades down and locks his door. His lights he keeps on and his eyes open, but they are inverted into himself.

Think of the kind of separation the mystic makes between the world we see and the reality he takes to be hidden in or under it. To unmystical eyes, the world is alive with motion; even when things are relatively still, the person who is looking at them moves; and even if he is relatively still, at least his eyes move as they take them in. The world is saturated with different colours, which inhere in or are, speaking visually, the different things we see; and the world and the things that make it up look and feel three-dimensional. Whatever still's the world's motion, lowers the saturation of its colours or confuses their placement, or weakens the sense of its three-dimensionality, also makes it appear less real. When the eye sees only the same textureless colour wherever it looks, the colour seems to saturate space and not a surface a particular distance away. Exact uniformity of colour makes distances vanish. Further, when, under laboratory conditions, the same image is projected continuously on the same retinal spot, the image flickers and disappears. We see as and because we move, and exact motionlessness makes us blind.

What we learn in our psychological laboratories, the mystic knows from tradition or personal experience. Feeling himself a prisoner in the moving, colourful, solid world, he escapes by halting, greying, and dissolving it. He sits as still as he can. He stills his eyes. The residue of motion, for there always is a little, seems to be that of consciousness rather than objects. Once, so an old story goes, some Chinese monks were arguing about the fluttering of a pennant. One of them said that the wind was the cause of the motion, another that motion was an illusion, and still another that the flapping was the result of a certain combination of cause and condition. But their master, Huineng, regarded as the founder of Zen Buddhism, interrupted them and said, 'It is neither wind nor pennant but your own mind which flaps.'[5] Of course, the flapping of the mind too, can be stilled, but flapping must first be separated from objects and located in the mind before the mind can undertake to still it, that is, to still itself.

As with motion, so with colour and three-dimensionality. The right prolonged staring separates colour from objects and transforms it into unlocalized space-colour. The residue of three-dimensionality is located in the mystic's own ocular strain and his own internal expansiveness. Like motion, space comes to exist only within himself. No longer 'blinded with an eye' or 'deaf with the drumming of an ear', he has separated reality from the outside and moved it within. Before, the world had an uncounted number of more-or-less independent centres; now, it has one centre, which is his own.

When the mystic liberates himself from the blindness his eyes, he supposes, subject him to, he becomes like a little child, 'like a baby that has not yet learned to smile', for he finds no particular persons at whom to smile. Baby-like, he is muddled and comfortable.

He says, 'My mind is that of a fool—how blank! Vulgar people are clear. I alone am drowsy. Vulgar people are alert. I alone am muddled. Calm like the sea; like a high wind that never ceases. The multitude all have a purpose. I alone am foolish and uncouth. I alone am different from others and value being fed by the mother.[6]

A child of this sort is separated or independent in the sense that it struggles against nothing; that is, it is wholly dependent on, integrated into, and immersed in something greater. It is separated from our world because inseparable from its own. This mystic child is less like the ordinary one, which slowly accomplishes its independence, than like the little blind child, who for a long time cannot master and perhaps not even conceive objects, for they appear and reappear to him suddenly and discontinuously. Left to himself, he is less a 'me' or an 'other' than a seeing child. He rocks, he waves his hands, he postures, he sinks into the external lethargy which accompanies his own internal experiencing of himself. Unlike the seeing child, who falls in love with externality, he, the blind one, falls in love with internality. Toukaram, the seventeenth-century Indian poet, was a voluntarily 'blinded' mystic, but he was expressing the involuntarily blind, separated and yet undifferentiated child when he said:

> I am by nature blind
> in my featureless face.
> Movement is motionless to me.
> Of men, I see nothing.
> I remain in this place
> where 'I' and 'mine' have fallen.
> All the visible is invisible to me.
>
> Detached from the nullity,
> my happiness is a sleep
> on the summit of a the mountain
> where I get without giving a thing.[7]

Separation of the senses and the self from the ordinary, external world, is parallel to another kind of separation, of ideals or values. To an antagonist, the mystic may seem to retreat from the world because he is too weak to cope with its demands. But the mystic is more likely to regard himself as a stubborn idealist who is discovering how to attain the ideal. He wants to rise from shifting to permanent values, from his limited self to mystical tradition and to the reality in which truth, beauty, and goodness are one. By a species of separation or extraction, he gets from his heroes to their heroism, and from valuable things and actions to value in itself. He reasons in Platonic style: whatever we desire, we desire because of its value; value alone, then, is truly valuable; and perhaps from value itself, the valuable within it, its essence, can be extracted. The mystic holds experience in his hand like a fruit or nut. The fruit he peels, the nut he cracks, and he throws away the particularity, the peel or husk, of the particular, and enjoys its flesh, which we have been calling its sameness. He lives in the community of those who have 'penetrated to the kernel'. He says, once again in the guise of Toukaram:

The husk of the coconut is hard, its flesh, a delicacy. Why examine the outside when the pure is inside? . . . The husk of the sugar cane is black; what exquisite sap inside! . . . The taste is the reward, says Touka; what does the appearance matter?[8]

The third quintessence is uniqueness. What has preceded, 'sameness' and 'separation', make it clear that the mystic state must, by its own standard, be unique; but this uniqueness has the air of a forced analogy. To say that there is only one reality and to say that reality is unique is merely tautological. Ordinarily, when we consider something to be unique, we are at least unconsciously comparing it with something that is not unique. Now we may choose to consider nature 'unique', meaning that it is the sum total of all that exists, and that, as is self-evident, there is only one such sum-total. The mystic's uniqueness, however, is no sum-total, but the undifferentiated perfection apart from which there is nothing either unique or similar. Its uniqueness cannot be sensed or conceived, strictly speaking, in relation to anything else, for nothing else exists. This uniqueness is the absolute superlative to which there are no comparatives or degrees. As long as it is understood to be superlative, it makes no difference if it is considered to be the maximum, which is all-encompassing, or the minimum, which is all-penetrating and perfectly concentrated. The identity of the maximum and minimum is emphasized by mathematically-tinged Neo-Platonists. Nicholas of Cusa writes characteristically:

The absolute maximum is in act the most perfect, since it is in act all that it can be. Being all that it can be, it is, for the same reason, as great as it can be and as small as it can be. By definition the minimum is that which cannot be less that it is; and since that is also true of the maximum, it is evident that the minimum is identified with the maximum.[9]

In mathematics, as one sees, this Neoplatonism tends towards the infinite and the infinitesimal. At least on the surface, Buddhism tends more towards the infinitesimal, tries, that is, to shatter the unity and continuity of everything, including the self. Therefore the Buddhist 'logician's' Saint exists in the unique, uncaused, self-sufficient point-instant. Detached from the categories of human thought and from space, time, and cause, he is free from all anxiety. In his careless immersion in the instant, he resembles the hedonist; but this is a metaphysical, mystical, and not a hedonist instant. For the Saint, history has ended, and, with it, obligation, reward, punishment, sorrow, and hope. Doctrinal differences apart, he seems not unlike the Meister Eckhart who says that the Now-moment of Adam's creation, the Now-moment of the end of human history, and the Now-moment in which he is speaking are one in God, in whom there is only one Now. 'Look!' he exclaims, 'The person who lives in the light of God is conscious neither of time past nor of time to come but only of one eternity.... Therefore he gets nothing new out of future events, nor from chance, for he lives in the Now-moment that is, unfailingly, "in verdure newly clad".'[10]

The fourth quintessence is inclusion. Everything in mysticism, all the quintessences that have preceded and are to follow, require it. The mystic wants his borders to have infinite elasticity. He thinks he 'should consider the differentiation of the skin of the body as a wall'. Then, he thinks, he should perceive everything within the wall as a void, an internal void. Little by little, the limiting wall should be effaced, the inner void join the outer, and one should become omni-penetrant, all-inclusive consciousness.[11]

This infinite elasticity or omnipenetrance can be conferred by any overpowering emotion, positive or negative, and apathy as well. The mystic therefore welcomes extremes. More calculatingly, he pierces some part of his body with a pointed instrument and concentrates on the exact place of the pain, until all else disappears from the field of consciousness.[12] The principle is to paint the world all in the same colour, make it vibrate all in the same sound, suffuse it all with the same state of being. We know this principle from our ordinary experience, our ordinary optimism, pessimism, or depression, though they do not usually overwhelm us enough to expand us to mystic proportions.

We might recall one emotion out of what I take to be our common past. Recall fear and how pervasive it can be, especially towards the beginning of our lives. An infant, who might be any one of us, lies still in bed. Its parents are gone. There is no one to call to. The infant shifts back and forth from sleep to waking. While it dreams, it hardly distinguishes dream from reality, and the frequent and some-times long transitions from sleeping to waking have much the quality of a dream, as in the strange but empirically possible case of a man who sleeps with his eyes open. Just because there is no escape, any slight noise or motion may frighten the infant. Its apprehension envelops the room, the room itself grows apprehensive. The infant tries, by wishing, to keep it still, empty of any new movement, object, or person, for whatever changes or moves within it is moving within the infant. The fear of the room is no different from the fear for oneself, one's own stillness is that of the room, the self and the room are identical. Even when enlarged to the proportions of the room, the child continues to feel small, because its smallness is simply its fear, and its room-size is simply its enlarged sensitivity to fear.

In the life of the mystic, fear and the other unpleasant emotions are not generally characteristic of his mystical experience as such, but precede and perhaps underlie it. Mystical experience, or something sufficiently like it, may be the rejection of physical reality as the result of great fear, as when inmates of concentration camps or fliers in combat begin to sense that what they are undergoing is not really happening to them. Whatever the reasons, the feeling of inclusion may also be peaceful or ecstatic. Lieh Tzu's tends to be peaceful and expressed without excitement. He says:

My body is in accord with my mind, my mind with my energies, my spirit with Nothing. Whenever the minutest existing thing or the faintest sound affects me, whether it is far away between the eight borderlands, or close at hand between my eyebrows and eyelashes, I am bound to know it. However, I do not know whether I perceived it with the seven holes in my head and my four limbs, or knew it through my belly and internal organs. It is simply self-knowledge.[13]

The Upanishadic teacher drifts less and is more still within being. Yet he tells his disciple that the whole real city of Brahma is his heart, or is in his heart. In his heart, he tells him, is a small lotus flower, and inside that a small but great space. 'As far as this world-space extends,' he says, 'the space within the heart extends. It contains within it both heaven and earth, both fire and wind, both sun and moon, lightning and stars, both what one possesses here and what one does not possess; everything here is contained within it.' The teacher may be asked, the text says, that 'if this city of Brahma contains everything here, all beings as well as all desires, when old age overtakes it and it perishes, what is left? The teacher is told to answer, 'That (the superlative space) does not grow old with one's old age; it is not slain with one's murder. That (and not the body) is the real city of Brahma. In it desires are contained. That is the Self, free from evil, ageless, deathless, sorrowless, hungerless, thirstless, whose desire is the Real, whose conception is the Real.'[14]

The mystic, we see, is superlatively large; and his largeness is the same as his overwhelming feeling of peace, safety, knowledge, power, joy, or love, for his largeness is the greatest possible enhancement of the sense of self and the transformation of alien and painful outerness to at least peaceful innerness.

According to the story of the Indian god, Krishna, when he was a little, human-seeming boy, he once opened his mouth, and his quite human mother saw the whole universe, or, rather, the whole infinite set of universes, in his gullet. Krishna is the romantic proto-type of the mystic, whose nature it is to internalize all universes and monopolize all loves.

The fifth quintessence is familiar strangeness or strange familiarity. This, too, is a feeling that we all experience to some degree. Something familiar suddenly appears odd, or something new evokes an obscure familiarity. The illusion of false recognition or *déja vu* is well known. The opposite one of *jamais vu* is less often mentioned, but no less interesting. A man testifies, for instance, that he was walking along some familiar streets when, all at once, the sensation of strangeness came down on him:

I looked ahead, to the right and to the left, and then turned and looked back, but in no direction could I see anything I had ever seen before. I walked back to the street I had last crossed and looked up and down but could see no familiar object. I then retraced my steps to the place where I had last crossed and looked about with the same result. . . . There was nothing familiar, in fact nothing I could recognize as having seen it before.[15]

When this feeling comes by itself, it is unwelcome. The mystic, however, often suggests that it should be cultivated. Like other mystics, Chuang Tzu wants us to regard our own bodies as alien to us. He says:

Your own body is not your possession. . . . It is the shape lent to you by heaven and earth. Your life is not your possession; it is harmony between your forces, granted for a time by heaven and earth. . . . You are the breath of heaven and earth which goes to and fro; how can you ever possess it?[16]

Although I do not know its cause, I imagine that the involuntary infection of the familiar with strangeness is the result of a fear too strong to tolerate openly. If this is true, the strangeness is a variant of the unreality experienced by men in intolerable danger. When, therefore, the strangeness is felt together with the familiarity, when, that is, the need to escape does not succeed in abolishing consciousness of the danger, the whole may be felt as an unresolved and inescapable anguish. To the French poet, Henri Michaux, both space and time are quasi-mystic realities painfully tensed between what would be, if taken to exist, opposite poles. Space, he says, lies 'between centre and absence . . . between the indefinite and the infinite', and he adds, 'Space, you cannot conceive that horrible internality-externality which is true space.' And as for time, he feels it on him, with him, in him, and by him, and yet preying upon him. He touches and seduces himself with time, he says, but he also hits himself with it.[17]

When we succeed in estranging something because it is too difficult to bear, we try to replace it with an equivalent. If the friend I have known for so long betrays me and thereby proves that he is a stranger, I am more likely to meet a stranger to whom I take an instant, intuitive liking, and whom I therefore feel I have always known. I need an always-known friend, even if I have to find him on the spur of the moment. The paranoiac, estranged from the common world, replaces it by another, more to his nature. The mystic estranged from his family may discover that his true family consists of his disciples. Estranged from disciples, he may turn to mankind, and estranged from mankind, he may find his true friends among the animals. Estranged from everything living, he may commune with the landscape. Estranged from everything particular, even the landscape, he may be able to love only the universe at large. If the universe appears too gross to love, he may love the spiritual reality upon which it rests; and if love itself appears too gross, his communion must become confined beyond even love. Eventually, he can remain familiar only with 'emptiness', which is obviously and utterly strange.

The fact is that an utter commitment to either familiarity or strangeness forces the other to appear, though transformed. The real point-instants in which the Buddhist Saint lodges himself are impervious to one another, and Eckhart's Now-moment is always self-identical. But the difficulty the mystic experiences in becoming a saint and entering a Buddhist or Christian Now implies that he is especially sensitive to his estrangement from the total familiarity he prefers. His experience is such that he often finds it natural to conceive it as a union of opposites. 'Nothing without contrariety', he says, 'can become manifest to itself; for it has nothing to resist it, it goes continually of itself outwards, and returns not again into itself.' And once there is a contrary, he says, each contrary quality 'occasions the other to bring itself into desire or will to fight against the other, and to dominate it. . . . Hence struggle and anxiety, also contrary, will take their rise in the soul, so that the whole soul is thereby instituted to enter into a breaking of the senses, and of the self-will of the senses, as of the natural centre, and, passing out of the pain of rebellion and strife, out of anxiety, to desire to sink into the eternal rest, as into God, from whence it sprang.'[18]

When the mystic immerses himself in the superlative identity of contradictories, he may feel himself identical with it; and yet how can he be identical with an identity of contradictories if he does not continue to sense the contradicton between them? Even if he feels no more than his immensity, he must feel it strange that he, who once felt himself to be so limited, now has become immense. Instead of simply unselfconscious immersion in that with which he is identical, the mystic remains conscious of his union and moved to express it, because it appears extraordinary, to him. The image of love is useful to him, not only because his mystic emotion may be love, but also because love requires duality to begin with, and the pleasure of love's 'identity' rests on consciousness of the lovers' difference. In Toukaram's words:

> You, you take form,
> I, I am reborn endlessly:
> both to the pursuit of the union.
> My joy, your body,
> Your delights, my presence

I give you appearance,
You make me infinite.

We two, a single body.
A new being is born,
The You-I, the I-You.

Between us no difference any longer,
I-You, You-Touka.[19]

The mystic becomes the I-You and the You-I, but he cannot collapse the two pronouns or states, the one of familiarity and the other of strangeness, into one another.

The simultaneity of the familiar and the strange is affirmed with particular directness by the aged Carl Jung, who quotes the same passage from Lao Tzu that we have quoted, not many pages ago, in a different translation:

When Lao Tzu says: 'All are clear, I alone am clouded,' he is expressing what I now feel in advanced old age. . . . The more uncertain I have felt about myself, the more there has grown up in me a feeling of kinship with all things. In fact it seems to me as if that alienation which so long separated me from the world has now become transferred into my own inner world, and has revealed to me an unexpected familiarity with myself.[20]

We now come to the sixth quintessence, which is depletion. This is an unusual word for mysticism. I have chosen it because it has been used in psychiatric literature, but I do not intend it in a genuinely technical sense. It is a helpful word because we cannot avoid thinking of the states of the self as states of more or less, or of higher or lower strain or pressure. Desires and fears build up internal pressure-equivalents. Since the pressure is not a literal one, except, to our knowledge, as translated into blood pressure, a person, unlike a boiler, does not burst when it gets too high. But a psychic structure may weaken or give way. The person may then commit a crime, or become neurotic or psychotic. He may also grow depressed, the depression being an extreme lowering of all internal, psychic pressures, or, perhaps, the neutralizing of one pressure by another. Like the many physiological responses that can grow dangerously strong, depression can itself be a disease; but it has a protective function. It guards against emotional explosions, against mania, against psychosis (of which it may also be a sign), and even against suicide. By depleting us, it allows us to abandon the object we desired too much, or to forget the too-threatening fear. But depletion, abandonment, and forgetfulness may be arrived at not only by means of depression, but also by creation and by mystical experience.

Sharing, as they do, the means of depletion, depression and mystic states are close alternatives. This may be the reason that mystics alternate black nights with mystic satisfactions. Both the depressed and the mystical use a negative vocabulary. They speak of withdrawal, absence, nothingness, and emptiness. They suffer or seek apathy. It is no accident that the Buddhists, who try to fragment the self and kill its desires, have chosen 'emptiness' as the ideal. The Buddhist who is trying to develop 'the base consisting of nothingness' should, he is told, refer to his previous consciousness again and again in the following way:

'There is not, there is not' or 'Void, void' or 'Secluded, secluded', and give his attention to it, review it, and strike at it with thought and applied thought.[21]

Naturally, negation and 'emptiness' suggest that the mystic ideal cannot be described; but I think that they also suggest that the mystic wants to be voided of desires, fears, hatreds, and all tensions. Because matter is solid and desire, fear, and hatred are tense, he chooses certain protective metaphors. Sometimes he thinks of space, an omnipresent, imperturbable nothingness, as Nirvana. On the analogy, perhaps, of the protective cave or hole, he imagines that reality has become one great protective emptiness. Samuel Beckett's Murphy has a mind that is a 'hollow sphere', and he wants to realize this hollow sphericalness in the world outside him. The more we want, the more we need; but we never get enough; and therefore the more we want, the more we need to want less. Therefore, when 'God most High said to Ba Yazid, 'What do you desire, Ba Yazid?' he answered, "I desire not to desire." '[22] Like the doctors who used to bleed their patients of disease, the mystic bleeds himself of desire.

The seventh quintessence is aggression. It comes in fitting sequence to the last image, of the mystic bleeding himself of desire. Though a mystic may be even superlatively self-effacing, it is a mistake to suppose that he can be as passive as he may look. His passivity or mildness is the result of a self-conquest, which is not possible without aggression. What is it that he obligates himself to conquer? First, to repeat, desire, which he sees as ignorant or sinful; then spatio-temporal existence, which is the condition for desire; and then multiplicity, in which existence in space and time shows itself. Multiplicity must be conquered because it is equivalent to distraction, competition, self-defeating effort, merely temporary satisfaction, ageing, and death. 'Three things there are,' says Meister Eckhart, 'that hinder one from hearing the eternal Word, The first is corporeality, the second number, and the third, time. If a person has overcome these three, he dwells in eternity, is alive spiritually, and remains in the unity, the desert of solitude, and there he hears the eternal Word.'[23]

The mildest aggression the mystic can inflict on the spatio-temporal world, including all his friends and relations, is to forget it. We find him doing this in the *Book of Lieh Tzu*, where a middle-aged man, Hua Tzu of Yang-li by name, is said to have enjoyed a remarkable success in forgetting. 'In the street he would forget to walk, at home he would forget to sit down. Today he would not remember yesterday, tomorrow he would not remember today.' His family was troubled but could find no one to help. Finally they discovered a scholarly anti-mystic, meaning, in this context, a Confucian, and he cured Hua Tzu. He stripped Hua Tzu of all his clothes until he remembered to look for them, starved him until he looked for food, and the like. In addition to this practical therapy, some other, unspecified methods were used, and Hua Tzu was awakened out of forgetfulness. He woke up furious, dismissed his wife, punished his sons, and drove the Confucian away with a spear. When arrested for his aggressions, he explained them and said:

Formerly, when I forgot, I was boundless; I did not notice whether heaven and earth existed or not. Now suddenly I remember; and all the disasters and recoveries, gains and losses, joys and sorrows, loves and hatreds of twenty or thirty years past rise up in a thousand tangled threads. I fear that all the disasters, joys and sorrows, loves and hates still to come will confound my heart just as much. Shall I never again find a moment of forgetfulness?[24]

In spite of his forgetting, Hua Tzu had not forgotten how to be a misogynist and warrior. How sharply he turned his spear against the invader of his solitude! Was his alacrity no more than a turning of aggressive fantasies into aggressive acts?

The question need not be taken seriously, because Hua Tzu may be the figment of a philosopher's mind. But mystics do try to forget the world, to destroy it as far as possible by excluding it from consciousness. Is it an exaggeration to call this effort psychic murder, or to call its converse, the destruction of the ego, psychic suicide? The metaphor of suicide is often used by mystics. Rumi says that the body is a sepulchre and ought not to be beautified. A person can become God's dust only by digging himself a grave in spiritual purity and by burying his egoism in God's Egoism.[25]

The metaphor of suicide is not forced here. It is necessary, the mystic thinks, to avoid sensual gratification. But unsatisfied desire is more painful and imperious than satisfied desire. The desire itself must be killed. To kill it is to commit partial suicide, the logical extreme of which is unqualified suicide. There are mystical traditions that recommend suicide, though only out of proper motives. Usually, these traditions reserve suicide for aged and saintly men. Tradition tries to prevent mystics from acting too impulsively.

I do not think that mystics must be cruel in the most usual sense, but they must be cruel to themselves. Success in mysticism, like success in business or war, requires aggressiveness—some cruelty, some maiming, some death. Thus in the standard Buddhist list of subjects for meditation, we find death too. The Buddhist is instructed to recall death from eight points of view, and, to begin with, as if a murderer were standing in front of him. 'One should recall,' the text says,

that death stands in front of us just like a murderer, who confronts us with his drawn sword raised to our neck, intending to cut off our head. And why? Because death comes together with birth and deprives us of life. . . . Like the murderer who has raised his sword to our neck, so it deprives us of life. And there is no chance that it will desist.

The Buddhist monk, the recipient of this advice, is being urged to identify himself repeatedly with his own murderer. That is, he must create the murderer in his own imagination and then submit himself, without protest, to the murderer's will.[26]

A similar psychic cruelty is shown by the Kashmiris, the Trika theorists, when they advise the would-be mystic to concentrate on 'his own fortress as if it were consumed by the fire of Time'. The advice is to touch the various members and organs of the body in succession and imagine that the fires of the destroyer-god are reducing the body to ashes. The flames are to burn away concepts, burn away body, and (in another meditation) burn away the world. Only flames and peace are to remain.[27]

Perhaps the aggressiveness that may lie latent in identification will stand out better if we look at some of its pathological forms. When Rodin sketched a person, he wanted to feel himself inside his skin. A terrible step further, and the Aztec priest flayed a prisoner and actually got inside his skin. But the pathological extreme is that of the schizophrenic who believes that he can hurt or kill others by hurting or killing himself. I have read of a schizophrenic boy who would cut himself, smile, and say, 'All the world bleeds when I'm cut, but I have more blood than they do and I'll live when they are all bled out. . . . But my parents and sister bleed most of all when I cut myself.' In a schizophrenic of this sort, suicide is both universal and particular murder.[28] The logic or magic of his act is mystical though the emotion, I should say, is not.

The eighth quintessence is conscience. The mystic wants to be absorbed into his ideal self. As we have said, he is likely to model this self on his teacher, and both he and his teacher are likely to draw on a tradition with its own heroes and values. Hindu tradition, like any other I can remember, opposes genuinely independent study. In the *Upanishads*, the very god, Indra, gets perfect learning only when he becomes the reverent and serviceable pupil of another god. The teacher, the *guru*, expresses the divinity of truth through himself, and so is himself divine. The *guru* of the Krishna cult is Krishna, or more, for the moment, than Krishna himself, because he guides the devotee to him.

Indian, or, rather, Buddhist devotion to the religious guide can be illustrated by the story of three monks who came to their elder. 'One of them said, "Venerable sir, I am ready to fall from a cliff the height of one hundred men, if it is said to be to your advantage." The second said, "Venerable sir, I am ready to grind away this body from the heels up without remainder on a flat stone, if it is said to be to your advantage." The third said, "Venerable sir, I am ready to die by stopping to breathe, if it is said to be to your advantage." ' The Elder was impressed by such devotion. He said, 'These monks are certainly capable of progress,' and, in fact, on following his advice, all three attained to Saintship.

In Yogic and Tantric tradition, the esoteric sense of the texts depends absolutely on the *guru*, through whom Reality dispenses understanding of itself. This is made dramatically clear in the following Tibetan instructions:

In meditation, one conceives one's Guru as the incarnate reality of Vajradhara, Lord over the five Buddha-families, who in turn is the symbol of the basic oneness of all constituents of reality. One has to imagine him sitting on a throne supported by eight lions symbolizing fearlessness and the conquest of all obnoxious powers, on a seat formed by lotus, moon, and sun, symbolizing respectively undefilement by evil, the dispersal of the darkness of spiritual ignorance, and the spread of light of transcendental awareness. Further, one has to conceive of one's Guru as being deep blue in colour as a symbol of the unchanging reality, holding in his crossed hands a sceptre and a bell, symbolizing the indivisibility of nothingness and compassion. . . . One allows this vision to dissolve in one's Guru, whose image fuses with oneself in another feeling of composure. . . . When all the external reference has subsided and one has reached a state of pure awareness one must become aware of oneself as Vajrayogini (Vajradhara's ecstatic spouse). . . . Directly over the crown of her head one has to imagine one's own Guru in the shape of Vajradhara, sitting on a richly adorned throne, and above him, one above the other, the line of Gurus who represent the tradition of this particular school.[29]

Whether or not the mystic's sense of good and evil is attractive to us, it is generally acute. He distinguishes between his own, absolute morality, and the conventional, relative morality. Sometimes, however, he shows a sympathetic awareness that he is like the men whom he might condemn. Out of such an awareness, Rumi says:

If you perceive a fault in your brother, the fault which you perceive in him is within yourself. . . . Get rid of that fault in you, for what distresses you in him distresses you in yourself.

Rumi goes on with an illustration:

An elephant was led to a well to drink. Perceiving himself in the water, he shied away. He supposed that he was shying away from another elephant, and he did not realize that it was from himself that he shied away.

All the evil qualities—oppression, hatred, envy, greed, mercilessness, pride—when they are within yourself, do not pain you. When you perceive them in another, then you shy away and are pained.[30]

But sometimes, as we have seen, the mystic reaches the conclusion that what he does does not matter; what matters is only the spirit in which he does it. He then resembles the artist who claims not to care how repulsive his subject may be as long as the expression of it is artistic. In this temper the mystic says, 'Purity and impurity are thought-constructions.' Therefore he does not distinguish, he says, 'between the self and the enemy, the wife and daughter, the mother and a public woman, cloth or animal skin, jewel or corn husk, urine and a good drink, cooked food and waste matter—past and present—happiness and sorrow—hell and heaven—vice and virtue.' And he adds, 'What binds the fool, liberates the wise.'[31]

In a spirit rather like this, the mystic may depend on no more than his spontaneous decisions. The same Rumi whose sympathetic modesty we have heard also says:

There is no absolute evil in the world: evil is relative. . . . God has said, 'Whoever belongs to Me, I belong to him: I am his eye and his hand and his heart.'

Everything loathsome becomes lovely when it leads you to your beloved.[32]

Such sentences might imply that a person in a mystic state, like a person in a manic one, is able to dissolve his conscience in his optimism or egoism. In any case, there comes a moment in which his self-approval is untainted by any shadow of lust, guilt, pain, time, or death. I do not know what immortality feels like, but this mystic guiltlessness must glow with its impossible radiance.

In the light of immortality, the mystic dreams the angelic lives or utopias of which his imagination is capable. The African dreams of the time when he had not yet been punished with death, or when he and god lived close together. But men, he remembers, were too difficult. 'In the beginning the creator lived among men; but men were quarrelsome. One day they had a big quarrel and Akongo left them to themselves. He went and hid in the forest and nobody has seen him since.' According to another African story, the creator offered to give to the man and the woman he had made whatever they wanted. However, 'they came to him so frequently that he said to himself: "If I stay near these people they will wear me out with their requests; I will make another living place for myself, far above them." '[33]

The Taoist philosopher dreams of the utopian country of the Yellow Emperor:

In this country there are no teachers and leaders; all things follow their natural course. The people have no cravings and lusts; all men follow their natural course. They are incapable of delighting in life or hating death, and therefore none of them dies before his time. They do not know how to prefer themselves to others, and so they neither love nor hate. . . . There is nothing at all which they grudge or regret, nothing which they dread or envy. They go into water without drowning, into fire without burning; hack them, flog them, there is no wound or pain; poke them, scratch them, there is no ache or itch. They ride in space as though walking the solid earth, sleep on the void as though on their beds; clouds and mists do not hinder their sight, thunder does not confuse their hearing, beauty and ugliness do not disturb their hearts, mountains and valleys do not trip their feet—for they make only journeys of the spirit.[34]

The mystical Confucian dreams not of anarchistic freedom and emotional neutrality, but of filial piety, brotherly respect, and organic unity:

Only when I love my father, the fathers of others, and the fathers of all can my humanity really form one body with my father, the fathers of others, and the fathers of all men. When it truly forms one body with them, then the clear character of filial piety will be manifested. Only when I love my brother, the brothers of others, and the brothers of all men can my humanity really form one body with my brother, the brothers of others, and the brothers of all men. When it truly forms one body with them, then the clear character of brotherly respect will be manifested. Everything from ruler, minister, husband, wife, and friends to mountains, rivers, spiritual beings, birds, animals, and plants should be truly loved in order to realize my humanity that forms one body with them, and then my clear character will be completely manifested, and I will really form one body with Heaven, Earth, and the myriad things.[35]

The twentieth-century physicist speaks in more prosaic rhythms but dreams much the same at least psychic unity:

The goal I propose for humanity is the creation of a universal consciousness. This must be voluntary on the part of mankind, and it will eventually require the participation, in the deepest sense, of all men. Indeed, in order to create a universal mind, all conscious beings in the universe, from the simplest to the most advanced, should participate. Thus this should really be considered a goal for all conscious creatures, rather than just for the human race.[36]

The ninth quintessence is mirror-reversal. Mysticism obviously reverses the usual sense of reality; but the reversal I mean, that of psychosis into mysticism, is more subtle, because the two, though often quite different, are likely, even then, to seem identical. They differ rather as do our appearances in the flesh from those in the mirror. When I say this, I am not referring to the mildly mystical exaltations into which anyone may drift now and then, but to a pronounced and dominating mysticism, which is, I think, a hair's-breadth away from psychosis. I think that if the writing of admitted mystics and admitted psychotics is compared line by line, image by image, conviction by conviction, they will often not be distinguishable. Both, as we have seen, can share the feeling of the immensity and incommunicability of their experience. Both can be totally happy. Both can feel that they contain the universe or are joined with it in a surpassing union. Both can be overwhelmed by the sudden conviction that they see the truth now bare. Both can believe that they have godly wisdom and benevolence. Both can use Jehovah's self-definition and say of themselves, 'I AM'.[37]

What then is the difference? Something, first, in the quality of their suffering. The mystic has suffered and will continue somehow to suffer. But the psychotic's suffering is greater, or, at the least, more destructive, and though he may begin in euphoria and return to it episodically, the suffering slowly or suddenly invades the whole of his experience.

It is easy to follow the invasion. Renée, still sane, suffered until she tried to escape into madness, but, once mad, found the suffering worse. A psychotic who 'felt indescribably well and uplifted' in her 'enchanted world' also felt herself 'assaulted by a dark power which conjured up strange animals, houses, landscapes, grotesque and frightful situations'.

It seems that the psychotic is able to reach every goal the mystic aims at, but, more often than not, feels indescribably miserable in the condition in which the mystic feels indescribably happy. Is it the goal to become one with a single, pure, state of being? The psychotic reaches it, but in suffering. 'I had not the slightest defence,' he recalls, 'whether within myself or without. The sensation grew, rolled upon me like a gigantic wave. I gasped, I struggled; there was a sickening, acute moment, then a welding. The emotion became *me*.' Is it the goal to desire nothing? The psychotic may desire nothing, but suffers all the more. 'To be neither unhappy nor happy,' he says, 'to desire nothing, is very discouraging. You cannot imagine this feeling of a shadow which, little by little, invades the whole of life, like the eclipse of the sun.' When his acts are 'entirely devoid of sensation and desire', the psychotic is, to himself, 'painfully mechanical'. Is it the goal, as among the Buddhists, to break the self into fragments? If so, the psychotic who attains this state of nominalism and dissociation hates it. Pointing to himself, he says, 'That is only my name, not me. . . . They knock me in so many pieces that I can't get hold of myself.' Is the mystic's secret of happiness his selflessness? He claims so, but the psychotic answers, 'The secret of wretchedness is selflessness.'[38]

Now we can make out the most obvious difference, where it exists, between mysticism and psychosis. The mystic feels that he must recover from the illness which is the ordinary, material world, with its real and separate people, its fears and desires, and its space and time. When he experiences recovery, he calls out, 'Reality!' He feels born into a new life. But the psychotic is ill with the mystic's cure. If he recovers, he is able to see that he was living in a state of illusion, when 'Untruth becomes Truth.' He may use an image like that of mirror-reversal and say, 'My memory during this (deluded) phase might be likened to a photographic film, seven hundred and ninety days long. Each impression seems to have been made in a negative way and then, in a fraction of a second, miraculously developed and made positive.' When Renée saw not infinite but ordinary space and not identical phantoms but individual men and women, she became indescribably happy. 'With the astonishment that one views a miracle,' she remembered, 'I devoured with my eyes everything that happened. "This is it, this is it," I kept repeating, and I was actually saying, "This is it—Reality." . . . Only those who have lost reality and lived for years in the land of cruel, inhuman Enlightenment can truly taste the joy in living and prize the transcendent significance of being part of humanity.'[39] The psychotic is reborn into ordinary life. Then he is able to tell us that insanity had once felt like the truth. He says, 'It has a horrid concrete reality. Real life becomes the dream. I do feel as if a stone has been rolled away. Sanity is a coming of life, a resurrection. I am born again.[40]

I cannot understand much more than this gross difference between mystic and psychotic, but it is an essential one. The clearest reason for it is, I take it, that psychosis is involuntary and inescapable, while the mystic state tends to be voluntary—given a suitable training, it can be entered and left almost at will. The mystic does not suffer his internal ecstasy, infinity, or truth, but creates it. His sanity is his control, for he is, when sane, sure at the very least that he can emerge from his mystic state. It can be his release only because it is not his prison.

The tenth quintessence is humour. It is true that one is hardly led to expect a mystic to be humorous. He brushes aside as trivial everything that will not help him to conquer his peace. He is perhaps as tensely serious, as burdened with difficult emotions, as a psychotic. But mysticism has many alliances with other methods of escape from suffering, and such an alliance, when struck, should have exceptional power and stability.

The best alliances are with creation, which we have spoken of, with love, and with humour. The love to which I am referring is, precisely, ordinary human sexual love. In Sufi poetry, the mystic loves God by way of a man, or, if the Sufi is only a poet, by way, sometimes, of a woman. Mysticism of this kind does not detach the mystic from his animal and social life. A strain that might have been schizophrenic is resolved because the poet joins what his conscience might have sundered, because he uses his mystic-human love to create poetry, and because his mystic intoxication, as usual among Sufis, is enjoyed in the company of others. It is true that this humanization of the mystical experience has its human consequences, and the Sufi who writes that the contemplation of a boy's beauty is like 'gazing at a ruddy apple or blossom' may be a pederast, just as the beauty-loving Zen monk may be one.[11]

The alliance of mysticism with humour is more surprising than that with love, because the usual tactics of humour and mysticism are opposed. The mystic insists that he must escape the external world because it is too painful, too delusive, and too strange to his essential self, while the humorous man turns the external world, including whatever is painful in it, into a source of pleasure. He laughs at his tormentors, his hunger, his awkwardness, and his failures. Finding life, with all its pains, so pleasant, he is sure of his strength in meeting it and has no need to escape. He is strong, for humour allows him a safe but effective rebellion against anything he does not wish to tolerate, and he is also a realist, for humour demands the comparison of pretensions with actuality.

The attractiveness of two of the Taoistic classics, the books of Chuang Tzu and of Lieh Tzu, stems from their compelling union of mysticism with poetic fantasy and kindly, almost earthbound humour. Here, for once, the mystic laughs even at himself. His mysticism is relaxed. He can acknowledge death and not engage in the frantic alchemy of so many of the later Taoists, who were trying unhumorously, to abolish death for themselves. Though mystical, this humour-as-relativism-as-Tao is schizoid and shrinking in a peculiarly sane and robust temper.

The sanity of Taoistic mysticism is conferred upon Zen Buddhism. In accord with the Buddhist principle that Samsara is Nirvana, that is, that one cannot really split oneself off from the empirical world, and like the Sufi poet, but perhaps more generally, the Zen mystic identifies the ideal with the empirical. Because he remains fairly ordinary in the ordinary round of things, he need not kill the world perceptually or kill his own impulses. On the contrary, he can express his aggressions directly, as the warrior-monks of Japan discovered. Their mysticism allowed them to kill literal men with real weapons, 'literal' and 'real' in the qualified Zen sense, to be sure. And one can only imagine the pleasure of the pious Zen monk in tearing up the scriptures of his own religion, or in placing them, with contemptuous symbolism, near the toilet.

Zen is rather determinedly nonsensical and half-veiledly sarcastic. The demi-veil is the metaphysical justification; the sarcasm is itself, as a Taoist and Zen theme will convey. What theme? Well, Chuang Tzu was once asked by Tung-kuo, 'This thing called Tao, the Way—where does it exist?' Chuang Tzu said, 'There's no place it doesn't exist.' 'Come,' said Tung-kuo, 'you must be more specific!' So Chuang Tzu answered that the Way was to be found in the panic grass. When Tung-kuo was surprised at the answer, Chuang Tzu said that it was also in the tiles and shards. Tung-kuo was still more surprised, and then Chuang Tzu said with finality (and was it with a smile?), 'It is in the piss and shit.'[42] Recalling this answer, the Zen master who was asked by a monk, 'What is the Buddha?' said only, 'A dried shit-stick,' that is, a piece of bamboo used to wipe oneself. Officially, this answer was meant to awaken the monk to the absolute 'beyond both purity and impurity'.[43] I should prefer to regard it as a triumphantly simultaneous assertion of rebelliousness and ortho-doxy. The Zen master—because, no doubt, a master—could be a transcendental rebel.

As we might expect, the engagement of Zen in the round of life, death, and rebirth, has its social causes and consequences. A modern commentator, who loves Zen, says in criticism of it:

The Zen sect has always been, like Athens, a state of 'free' men among slaves, living on them more or less, and with no desire to free them socially, politically, or financially. It has no view of society, no view of human progress, material or spiritual. It is always all things to all men, and will support any government, fascistic or communistic or democratic. Its organization is unchangeably feudalistic, though on special occasions it has an All Fools' day when an absolute equality is *de rigueur*. The opinion of Zen adepts on world affairs has invariably been a patriotic opportunism dressed in Buddhist platitudes.[44]

I cannot say to what extent this criticism is justified, but it suggests that institutionalized humour and transcendental rebelliousness have their social cost.

Still, at least from the distance, early Taoism does not lose its charm. It tenders the advice that might be given to any person who feels the need to become a mystic: become one, if necessary, but with an easy laugh. Don't be a mystic too hard, it says.

In the interests of laughter, I want to reinforce the advice with an Indian myth, which is indirectly relevant to mystical appetites. This myth is about the elephant-faced God, Ganesha, who was insatiable in every respect. One day, having eaten almost more than possible of the sacrificial cakes offered to him, he went out for a ride on the large rat that served as his mount. A snake crawled into their path, the rat shied away, and the god fell to the ground. His tight belly burst open and all his hard-eaten cakes rolled out. But the god retrieved each one of them, inserted them back into his belly, and wound the snake around himself to keep it closed.

It seems that you can eat your worlds and have them too.

The eleventh and last quintessence of mysticism, the crucial one, is reality. I cannot, of course, simply affirm it of mysticism. Nor do I, in discussing it here, have any serious metaphysical intentions. I want to do no more than indicate what seems to me a roughly sensible attitude. I myself dislike and prefer to explain away much of mysticism, but it is in some ways essential to us, and it is too natively human ever to die. I should therefore like to end with some comments on its 'reality' that are more nearly comments on its power to harm and help.

Whatever semantic improprieties are involved in the usage, we may prefer to say, with the mystics, that reality is unique. But everyone and perhaps everything deserves its fraction of uniqueness. Every stone and raindrop is unique. There is not only a men's world, but a cats' world, and a dogs' world; and a world for each cat, dog, man, and other sentient creature (I'd maintain this stubbornly for cats and men, with the others I've had little to do). To each one of each kind, the world is perceived in a different way.

But the world is not left simply different. Experience teaches us to discount some of our perceptions, stress others, and combine the effect of all of them into something which is none. We distinguish between phenomena, or things as they appear, and their causes, though the distinction is learned, deviously, from the phenomena themselves. This happens slowly. Our touch and taste are immediate, but our sight and hearing give us distant horizons—we see and hear because we are separated and distant, and the immediacy of touch and taste is overborne. In time, our sensory horizons are qualified by the non-sensory ones, or indirectly sensory ones, of past and future. We become more objective, though never very objective, and we become human selves. Our history runs so: first we eat, move, sleep, and dream, we taste, touch, strain; then we sense, but especially see and hear, far off, and we move about from place to place; we perceive lasting things and people, we think in the forms of lasting, transferable logic; and by denying the mother we have been and remain attached to, we become separate selves. I have not tried to keep exactly to the sequence, but to suggest how immediacy is slowly converted to partial distances and separate human selves. Slowly, over many years, we achieve whatever humanity, normality, and practical force we have.

Yet however we learn to understand our perceptions, we continue to live in them, they are our unending milieu, the ocean of our existence. This, the world as each of us perceives it to be, is often not explained, and never fully explained; but taken as primitively as possible, including everything that later judgment shows to be illusory, it cannot be an outright illusion. To think of it as an illusion, we must be able to distinguish it from the reality we have learned to make out; but this world, to begin with, is not exactly true yet, and not false. It is simply there—a hardly-structured, quality-suffused semi-projection of ourselves. It is blue, eatable, filthy, light-struck, gay, great, beautiful, painful. It is as we are and we are as it is, blue, gay, beautiful, and painful, for we are in symbiosis with it, like an infant with its mother. Our perception of this our own world may be relatively associative or dissociative, and may feel familiar or strange or both. All such feelings are equally true, not in the sense that our judgment has validated them, but in the sense that they express the deepest complicity of each of us with that which is not ourselves. In this way we are attached and detached. So, in this way, the Chinese mystic was attached to and detached from the universe by the motions of his arm extended into a writing brush, and so, as he walked in the mountains, by his heaving chest and wandering eyes, his pleasure located in the motions and incipient motions that united him with the whole of the moving existence he was intimately apart from. So, too, the Indian mystic deified orgasm and routed his emissions back into himself, or, when against desire, translated the suppression of orgasm into the bliss of universal consciousness conscious of its universal bliss.

Immediate experience too grows refined and tentacular. It becomes a refined mysticism; but mysticism does not understand itself, either by reason, or by intuition. In so far as it makes a common mistake, it is a plain one. It is not irrationality as such. There have been too many sane, intelligent, and scientifically creative mystics for irrationality as such to be singled out. The mistake is the insistence of the mystics, in practice if not in theory, that the self of each of them, his particular sense of his individual self, as it turns out to be, is all that can be real. Since they insist that everything is the same, they have no choice but to regard it as the same as that which they, each of them alone, experience. They must deny that others can be really other, even somewhat, than *they* are. Because artists externalize themselves, we can see and hear the differences between one man's vision and another's. We also see and hear such differences when the artists happen to be explicitly mystical. We have every unmystical reason to think that purely inner visions are as different as those that have been given external forms. When the mystic denies this, when he denies everyone else the possibility of irreducible otherness, he shows his own narcissism and cruelty. He claims to believe in 'the absence of the notion of selfhood'. He makes a goddess of this absence, and he is 'consubstantiated' in her.[45] But he means, unfortunately, the absence of the selfhood of others, or, at least, of others not in his tradition and without his mystical accomplishments. No one but he, the Master, the Guru, and, through him, sometimes, his Master or Guru, is allowed to judge.

The mystic turns Procrustes. Mysticism becomes the radical twin of the intellectual abstraction it decries—the twin in replacing sensed differences by identity, and the radical twin in persuading us of the illusoriness of the differences.

When the mystic's narcissim, cruelty, and exaggerated levelling of differences are pronounced enough, he is isolated within his own subjectivity; and if he is unable to emerge, he misperceives more and more seriously and, by a cruel revenge on himself, grows insane.

But mysticism is more than a primitive reality that turns, when extreme, into a cruel isolation. It is able to denounce 'the sort of men who think that is sufficient to sit in emaciated meditation', and to praise the effort to think or do anything well. It can declare, when in this vein, 'If a man is a householder and has a rich aspiration for discernment, and is wise and sincere in his daily work, what difference is there between that and the forest? And that is why it is said, "If the Way is deep down in the mind, it is not necessary to live on Mount Yoshino." '[46]

Mysticism, as Hakuin implies in these words, and as Rumi says, participates in every highly creative effort. I think that enough evidence has been brought that the feelings of certainty, penetration, truth, or universality, can, like any other feelings, mislead us. But though often misleading and always insufficient, such feelings are as essential to the growth of science as are abstract intelligence or factual information. That some mystic strain is necessary to the discovery of truth must make a difference in the way truth is understood. It is impossible to make an entire separation between this strain and between the beliefs one holds and what one regards as the truth. In other words, feelings concerning the truth must be allowed some latitude if further truth is to be discovered. Yet they cannot be allowed any latitude. Therefore, in judging mysticism I should lay the stress not on 'mystic' as against 'non-mystic', but on 'sane' as against 'insane'. I think that this difference in stress is not merely terminological.

Mysticism is not a primitive reality alone. It lives in Chuang Tzu, Socrates, Aristotle, Patanjali, Spinoza, and Wittgenstein; and it lives in the creativity of an Einstein, a Schrödinger, and a Dirac.

The mystical or proto-mystical strivings of human creation in general have been more important than the explicit doctrines that mystics have taught. Yet some mystical doctrines are, as has been said, oddly like the even more fantastic ones of contemporary physics. An electron can be conceived of as a tiny bullet or, in a more advanced way, as a state of excitation of a quantized field. A man can be conceived of as a complex material structure or, in a more advanced way, as a state of excitation of the mystic 'field.' And a field, for all its fluctuations and effects, is something that by our ordinary standards is no thing, nothing. But to science, the emptiness of space, like mystic emptiness has become an endlessly full reality. And it is a contemporary scientist who hypothesizes 'superspace', in which time does not exist and in which 'pregeometry' constructs material out of non-material, that is, out of nothing. Reality, he says, is non-dimensional, for dimensionality, like time and space, is subsequent and subordinate to the true reality which is the foam and bubbles of nothing.[47]

More detailed analogies can be drawn. In both Tantric and nuclear theory, the meeting of one kind of substance or matter ('moon', male, or particle) with its opposite ('sun', female, antiparticle) results in the conversion of the pair into a flash of insight or a flash of light (as the case may be), the annihilation of the pair, and either the mystic's emptiness or the physicist's empty space. The experimental techniques of mystic and physicist are notably different, and a mathematical mystic and a mathematical physicist may not understand one another very well. But sometimes there is an approximate parallelism in thought which strikes one as more than amusing. I suspect, as I have said before, that scientific theorizing of great originality never takes place except on a mystical-mythical base, which is none other than creative imagination. The creative scientist has to have two sharp eyes in order to find his way safely and economically. But, like the mystic, he needs a third eye, to make out a still unknown destination.

However basic or explosive the particles he finds, and however qualified their causality, the physicist himself remains immersed in the world of ordinary human action and perception. He finds the atomic world, so to speak, inside the ordinary one, to which he must always return. Like the physicist, the mystic or psychotic finds a world he takes to be basic, but it too remains biologically and socially immersed in the usual environment. As macroscopic eyes are the condition of microscopes, unmystical is the condition of mystical experience. This empirical order of precedence ought to be respected even by mystics. We may fly easily where the air is pure and thin, but we would be fool birds, as Kant said, if we thought that we could flap away still faster where there was no air at all.

A mystic, too, can be unreasonable. I think he is if he insists that we must, above all else, 'bear witness' to an experience that transcends science and every kind and quality of rational thought and ordinary empirical life. Imagine that everyone had come to agree with him. Imagine that not only mystics and artists but all great men had done nothing but bear witness as this mystic recommends. Socrates, it is true, had a demon, but it prompted him to ask rational questions and demand rational answers. Aristotle believed in a god that was pure thought thinking itself, a state that moved the universe to love and imitate him as it could. But Aristotle himself undertook, with passion and love, to describe, analyse, and unify the universe intellectually. Einstein had his mystic faith in the intelligibility of the universe and the continuity of human life, but he also invented rational arguments of revolutionary subtlety. Now imagine Socrates expressing his Ideal in song alone, like a witness bird or lieder singer. Imagine Aristotle doing nothing but improvising cool, logical jazz at the piano, or Einstein, unkempt, believing, and exact, doing nothing much but playing the violin in a relatively mediocre quartet. Or change the three men into rhapsodic prophets, and calculate the loss again. Mysticisms differ, I know, but my intuition tells me that if any of them came to dominate the world, it would impoverish mankind materially, intellectually, and spiritually.

Maybe, then, if none of us can have everything, we should end by declaring a reasonable peace and give something known away in hopes of getting something unknown. Sanely mystical and unmystical thought can go on stimulating one another. The world, whose name we have so often taken in vain, is implausibly deep. Kindled mysteriously, its light is too dense to be all caught in mysticism, logic, science, common sense, or the four of them together. The person in the right eye and the person in the left eye may meet, as the *Upanishads* say, in the heart, yet even when joined, they may not see very far. Both the White Stork and the Black Stork can clap and hiss. There are many things to know and not to.

Notes

The Superlative States of Mysticism

1. E. O'Brien, *Varieties of Mystic Experience*, Mentor Books, 1965, pp. 37, 38.
2. O'Brien, op. cit., pp. 103, 105. See also, F. C. Happold, *Mysticism*, Penguin Books, 1963, pp. 204–9.
3. O'Brien, op. cit., pp. 119, 121.
4. D. Knowles, *The English Mystical Tradition*, Harper & Row, 1965 (original ed. 1961), p. 109.
5. *The Life of Saint Teresa*, trans. J. M. Cohen, Penguin Books, 1958, pp. 192 (Chap. 27), 210 (Chap. 29).
6. O'Brien, op. cit., p. 220 (trans. of A. Allison Peers). For a poetic translation, see J. F. Nims, *The Poems of St. John of the Cross*, Grove Press, N.Y., p. 21.
7. G. C. Anawati & L. Gardet, *Mystique Musulmane*, J. Vrin, Paris, 1961, p. 179. See also, pp. 175–83 (*wajd*), 104–6 (*fana*).
8. E. Jurji, *Illumination in Islamic Mysticism*, Princeton U.P., 1938, p. 73.
9. K. A. Hakim, *The Metaphysics of Rumi*, Institute of Islamic Culture, Lahore, third impression (should be 'second edition') 1959, p. 120, note 1 (*Mathnavi* iii, 3670–3).
10. R. A. Nicholson, *Selected Poems from the Divani Shamsi Tabriz*, Cambridge U.P., 1898; reprinted 1952. R. A. Nicholson, *Rumi, Poet and Mystic*, Allen & Unwin, London, 1950. J. Kritzek, *Anthology of Islamic Literature*, Penguin Books, 1964, p. 255 (trans. Nicholson). A. J. Arberry, *Discourses of Rumi*, John Murray, London, 1961, pp. 185, 178.
11. W. G. Archer, *The Loves of Krishna*, Allen & Unwin, London, 1957, p. 43.
12. J. N. Farquhar, *An Outline of the Religious Literature of India*, Oxford U.P., 1920, p. 230.

13. Archer, op. cit., pp. 82–3 (trans. G. Keyt).

14. E. R. Dodds, *Pagan and Christian in an Age of Anxiety*, Cambridge U.P., 1965, pp. 29, 33. A. H. Armstrong, *Plotinus*, Allen & Unwin, London, 1953, p. 160 (*Enneads* VI.9.11).

15. *Shankara's Crest-Jewel of Discrimination* (*Viveka-Chudamani*), trans. Prabhavananda & Isherwood, pp. 141 ff.

16. W. T. de Bary, *Sources of Indian Religion*, Columbia U.P., 1958, pp. 298, 211 (*Bhagavad Gita* II, VI).

17. J. H. Woods, *The Yoga System of Patanjali*, Harvard U.P., 1927, I, 15; IV, 33.

18. W. T. de Bary, op. cit., pp. 59–60 (*Uttaradyayana Sutra* XIX).

19. E. Conze, *Buddhist Texts*, Bruno Cassirer, Oxford, 1954, pp. 92, 93 (selections 84–6, 91, 94).

20. Conze, op. cit., pp. 100, 102, 163 (selections 99, 152). E. Frauwallner, *Geschichte der Indischen Philosophie*, Vol. I, Salzburg, 1953 (for interpretation of early Nirvana). See also, E. Lamotte, *Histoire de Bouddhisme Indien*, I, Bibliothèque du Muséon, Louvain, 1958, pp. 675–77.

21. Lao Tzu, *Tao Te Ching*, trans. D. C. Lau, Penguin Books, 1963, p. 58 (*Tao Te Ching* II).

22. *The Complete Works of Chuang Tzu*, trans. B. Watson, Columbia U.P., 1968, pp. 191 (*Chuang Tzu* XVIII), 77 (*Chuang Tzu* VI).

23. Lu K'uan Yü (Charles Luk), *Ch'an and Zen Teaching, Second Series*, Rider & Co., London, 1961, p. 126.

24. Hakuin Zenji, *The Embossed Tea Kettle*, trans. R. D. M. Shaw, Allen & Unwin, London, 1963, pp. 33–4, 35, 41, 42, 46. P. B. Yampolsky, *The Zen Master Hakuin: Selected Writings*, Columbia U.P., 1971, was published too late for use here. Yampolsky considers Shaw's translation to be inaccurate.

25. H. Dumoulin, *A History of Zen Buddhism*, Faber & Faber, London, 1963, pp. 258, 254.

26. Hakuin Zenji, op. cit., pp. 85–6, 75, 81, 82.

27. *Le Stavicintamini de Bhattanarayana*, trans. L. Silburn, Editions E. de Boccard, Paris, 1964, p. 17. See also, published by the same publisher, *Le Vijnana Bhairava*, trans. L. Silburn, 1964; *Le Paramarthasara*, trans. L. Silburn, 1957.

28. *Le Paramarthasara*, pp. 54, 56. For causes of arousal of mystic experience, see, e.g., *Le Vijnana Bhairava*, verses 70, 73, 77, 83, 84, 96, 111–12, 118; for the effect of music in particular, verses 41, 73.

29. M. Eliade, *Yoga*, Pantheon Books, N.Y., 1958, p. 205. For the whole

subject, see also D. L. Snellgrove, *Buddhist Himalaya*, Philosophical Library, N.Y., 1957; and S. B. Dasgupta, *An Introduction to Tantric Buddhism*, U. of Calcutta, 2nd ed., 1958.

30. W. T. de Bary, *Sources of Indian Tradition*, p. 199. See *The Hevajra Tantra*, ed. & trans. D. L. Snellgrove, Oxford U.P., 1959, Vol. I, p. 93.

31. H. Hoffman, *The Religions of Tibet*, Allen & Unwin, London, 1961, pp. 34-5.

32. Conze, *Buddhist Texts*, pp. 224-39 (trans. D. Snellgrove), esp. verses (quoted) 23-4, 55, 57, 64, 28, 98.

33. H. V. Guenther, *The Life and Teaching of Naropa*, Oxford U.P., 1963, pp. 205-7, 222-3.

Personal and Pragmatic Defences of Mysticism

1. W. Montgomery Watt, *The Faith and Practice of Al-Ghazali*, Allen & Unwin, London, pp. 21-2, 24-5, 33-4, 39, 54-5, 57-8, 60, 61, 62, 65, 64, 79, See also W. Montgomery Watt, *Muslim Intellectual*, *A Study of Al-Ghazali*, Edinburgh U.P., 1963 (mainly sociological and religious background and effect).

2. W. James, *The Varieties of Religious Experience*, Mentor, N.Y., pp. 135-6 (Lectures VI and VII).

3. F. O. Matthiessen, *The James Family*, Knopf, N.Y., 1947, p. 219.

4. R. B. Perry, *The Thought and Character of William James*, Briefer Version, Harvard U.P., 1948, p. 360.

5. W. James, *Varieties*, p. 292 (Lectures XVI and XVII).

6. R. B. Perry, op. cit., p. 365.

7. Ibid., p. 258 (original opening of *Varieties*).

8. W. James, *Varieties*, pp. 388-9 (Lecture XX).

9. R. B. Perry, op. cit., p. 364.

10. W. James, *Varieties*, p. 327 (Lectures XVI and XVII).

11. R. B. Perry, op. cit., p. 253.

Logical and Metaphysical Defences of Mysticism

1. A. J. Arberry, *Discourses of Rumi*, John Murray, London, 1961, p. 162.

2. *The Complete Works of Chuang Tzu*, trans. B. Watson, Columbia U.P., 1968, p. 302 (*Chuang Tzu* XXVI).

3. H. V. Guenther, *The Life and Teachings of Naropa*, Oxford U.P., 1963, pp. 21–2, 27.

4. N. K. Devaraja, *An Introduction to Shankara's Theory of Knowledge*, Motilal Barnarsi Dass, Varanasi, India, 1962, p. 60.

5. E. Conze, *Buddhist Thought in India*, Allen & Unwin, London, 1962, pp. 265–8. See also *The Hundred Thousand Songs of Milarepa*, trans. C. C. Chang, University Books, New Hyde Park, N.Y., 1962, Vol. II, chap. 34, 'The Challenge from the Logicians'.

6. Proclus, *The Elements of Theology*, edition, translation, and commentary by E. R. Dodds, 2nd ed., Oxford U.P., 1963.

7. Nagarjuna, *Madhyamika-shastra*, trans. in Th. Stcherbatsky, *The Conception of Buddhist Nirvana*; quoted in S. Radhakrishnan & C. A. Moore, *A Source Book in Indian Philosophy*, Princeton U.P., 1957, pp. 340–5. E. Frauwallner, *Die Philosophie des Buddhismus*, Akademie Verlag, Berlin, 1958, pp. 170–217. T. R. V. Murti, *The Central Philosophy of Buddhism*, Allen & Unwin, London, 1955, esp. pp. 136–43. A. B. Keith, *Buddhist Philosophy*, Oxford U.P., 1923, pp. 237–41.

8. *Wei Shih Er Shih Lun, or The Treatise in Twenty Stanzas on Representation-Only*, trans. C. H. Hamilton, American Oriental Society, New Haven, Conn., 1938. See also Frauwallner, op. cit.

9. Th. Stcherbatsky, *Buddhist Logic*, Mouton & Co., 'S-Gravenhave, 1958 (reproduced from original ed., Academy of Science of the USSR, Leningrad, 1930, 1932), Vol. I, pp. 108–14, 150–1 (Dharmakirti's experiment); Vol. II, pp. 30–3. See also L. Silburn, *Instant et cause*, Paris, 1955, pp. 237, 399.

10. *The Vedanta Sutras of Badarayana, with the Commentary of Shankara*, trans. G. Thibaut, 2 vols., Sacred Books of the East, 1890, 1896; reproduced Dover Publications, N.Y., 1962, Vol. I, pp. 427, 419 (quoted); Vol. II, pp. 33–4, 14–15 (quoted). N. K. Devaraja, op. cit.

11. J. A. B. Buitenen, *The Maitrayania Upanishad*, Mouton & Co., 'S-Gravenhage, 1962, 1.4/7; 2.1/1; 2.2/2 (last words from the *Chandogya Upanishad* 8.3.4). D. T. Suzuki, *Introduction to Zen Buddhism*, Philosophical Library, N.Y., 1949, p. 70. L. Wittgenstein, *Philosophical Investigations*, paras. 309, 255, 123, 124, 109, 133.

Everyday Mysticism

1. S. Escalona, 'Emotional Development in the First Year of Life', *Transactions of the Sixth Conference on Problems of Infancy and Childhood*, ed. M. J. E. Senn, Josiah Macy Foundation, N.Y., 1953, p. 25. Quoted in T. Gouin Décarie, *Intelligence et affectivité chez le jeune enfant*, Neuchatel, Switzerland, 1962, p. 90. See also, J. Piaget, *The Constitution of Reality in the Child*, trans. M. Cook, Basic Books, N.Y., 1954.
2. M. von Senden, *Space and Sight*, trans. P. Heath, London & Glencoe, Ill., 1960.
3. A.-M. Sandler, 'Aspects of Passivity and Ego Development in the Blind Infant', *The Psychoanalytic Study of the Child* XVIII, London, 1963.
4. R. A. Spitz, *Yes and No, On the Genesis of Human Communication*, International Universities Press, N.Y., 1957.
5. M. S. Mahler, 'Thoughts About Development and Individuation', *The Psychoanalytic Study of the Child* XVIII, London, 1963.
6. P. Schilder, *The Image and Appearance of the Human Body*, International Universities Press, N.Y., 1950, p. 40. For the whole subject see also S. Fisher and S. E. Cleveland, *Body Image and Personality*, D. Van Nostrand Co., Princeton, N.J., 1958.
7. P. Schilder, op. cit., pp. 84-5.
8. J. E. Downey, 'Normal Variations in the Sense of Reality', *Psychol. Bull.* 2:298-9. Quoted in C. Landis, *Varieties of Psychopathological Experience*, Holt, Rinehart & Winston, N.Y., 1964, p. 352.
9. Virginia Woolf, *To the Lighthouse*, in M. Nathan, *Virginia Woolf*, Grove Press, N.Y., 1961, pp. 120-1.
10. M. Isherwood, *The Root of the Matter*, in F. C. Happold, *Mysticism*, Penguin Books, 1963, p. 130.
11. W. L. Wilmhurst, *Contemplations*, in F. C. Happold, op. cit., pp. 137-8.

Creators' Mysticism

1. B. P. Groslier, *Indochina*, Thames & Hudson, London, 1962, pp. 168–87.

2. P. Greenacre, 'The Childhood of the Artist', *The Psychoanalytic Study of the Child* XII, N.Y., 1957.

3. Autobiographies of contemporary English writers: *Writers on Themselves* (a series of B.B.C. talks), London, 1964. General bibliography: C. W. Taylor, *Creativity: Progress and Potential*, McGraw-Hill, N.Y., 1964. Taylor (p. 131) lists five 'personality or emotional traits' of creative scientists, one of which is 'acceptance of mysticism versus denial of mysticism'. For a brief review of some relevant studies: B. Berelson and G. A. Steiner, *Human Behavior*, N.Y., 1964, pp. 226–35; and, more detailed, F. Barron, 'The Psychology of Creativity', in *New Directions in Psychology II*, Holt, Rinehart & Winston, N.Y., 1965, esp. pp. 61–4. For a psychoanalyst's views: L. S. Kubie, 'Some Unsolved Problems of the Scientific Career', reprinted in M. R. Stein, A. J. Vidich and D. M. White, *Identity and Anxiety*, Free Press, Glencoe, Ill., 1960. For 'relatively objective and adequate inquiries': A. Roe, 'Artists and Their Work', *Journal of Personality* XV, 1946–7; A. Roe, *The Making of a Scientist*, Dodd, Mead & Co., N.Y., 1953; B. T. Eiduson, *Scientists, Their Psychological World*, Basic Books, N.Y., 1953. See also F. Bello and A. Roe, in P. C. Obler and H. A. Estrin, *The New Scientist*, Anchor Books, N.Y., 1962.

4. E. Schrödinger, *My View of the World*, trans. C. Hastings, Cambridge U.P., 1964. Quotation beginning, 'We are not', from Schrödinger's *What is Life? and Other Scientific Essays*, Anchor Books, N.Y., 1956, p. 107 ('Nature and the Greeks'). W. H. Cropper, *The Quantum Physicists*, Oxford U.P., 1970, pp. 90–9. M. Born, *Physics in My Generation*, Springer Verlag, 2nd rev. ed., N.Y., 1969, p. 73.

5. P. Michelmore, *Einstein, Profile of the Man*, N.Y., 1962, esp. pp. 75, 76 (a simple book, but containing some new personal information). A. Einstein, *Out of My Later Years*, Philosophical Library, N.Y., 1950, p. 13; 'Autobiographical Notes', in P. A. Schilpp (ed.), *Albert Einstein, Philosopher-Scientist*, The Library of Living Philosophers, Evanston, Illinois, 1949, esp. pp. 3–4, 7, 9; *Ideas and Opinions*, Crown Publishers, N.Y., 1954, pp. 225–7. P. Jordan, *Albert Einstein*, Verlag

Huber, Frauenfeld und Stuttgart, 1969, pp. 290–4. G. Holton, 'Mach, Einstein, and the Search for Reality', *Daedalus*, Spring, 1968; 'On Trying to Understand Scientific "Genius" '—multigraphed expansion of lecture, 18 January 1971, at Conference in Honour of Prof. S. Sambursky, the Van Leer Foundation, Jerusalem. R. Oppenheimer, 'On Albert Einstein', *The New York Review of Books*, March 17, 1966.

6. C. G. Jung, *Memories, Dreams, Reflections*, trans. R. and C. Winston, Pantheon Books, N.Y., 1962, quotations pp. 20, 48, 225–6, 358, 186. See also A. M. Dry, *The Psychology of Jung*, Methuen & Co., London, 1961.

7. P. Valéry, *Œuvres*, ed. J. Hytier, Vol. II, Pléiade, Paris, 1960, pp. 757, 1434, 1508–9. J. Charpier, *Essai sur Paul Valéry*, Paris, pp. 17, 39–43, 82. E. Gaede, *Nietzsche et Valéry*, Paris, 1960, p. 469, notes 323, 322 (*Cahiers VIII*, pp. 103, 473). G. Poulet, 'L'instant, point du départ du temps', in R. W. Meyer, *Das Zeitproblem im 20. Jahrhundert*, Bern & Zurich, 1964, pp. 115–18 (*Mon Faust* quoted p. 11).

8. J.-P. Sartre, *Les mots*, Paris, 1964. 'For anyone', translated from p. 162. See L. Clephane's trans., J.-P. Sartre, *Words*, London, 1964, and also pp. 170–2. J.-P. Sartre, *Nausea*, trans. R. Baldick, Penguin Books, 1965, p. 145. Simone de Beauvoir, *Force of Circumstance*, trans. R. Howard, André Deutsch and Weidenfeld & Nicolson, London, 1965, quoted pp. 385, 451–2. B. T. Fitch, *Le sentiment d'étrangeté chez Malraux, Sartre, Camus et S. de. Beauvoir*, Paris, 1964, Chap. 2. R. D. Laing and D. G. Cooper, *Reason and Violence*, with a foreword by Sartre, London, 1964, esp. pp. 103, 105. J.-P. Sartre, *The Problem of Method*, trans. H. Barnes, London, 1963, pp. 172–4. W. Desan, *The Marxism of Jean-Paul Sartre*, Garden City, N.Y., 1965, esp. pp. 69–70, 88–9.

9. H. R. Graetz, *The Symbolic Language of Vincent Van Gogh*, N.Y., 1963, quoted pp. 173, 99, 295 (*The Collected Letters of Vincent Van Gogh*, N.Y., 1958, numbers 212, W4, 489, 159, 538). Graetz's book has been attacked for naïvety and inaccuracy. See, e.g. Mark Roskill in the letter-columns of the *Times Literary Supplement*, 10 December 1964. But the errors Roskill points out hardly affect the general position, which is supported by many citations from Van Gogh's letters.

10. A. E. Elsen, *Rodin*, N.Y., 1963, pp. 163, 151 (p. 163 quotes A. M. Ludovici, *Personal Reminiscences of Auguste Rodin*, N.Y., 1926, pp. 138–9). Ludovici is reprinted in Auguste Rodin, *Readings in His*

Life and Works, ed. A. E. Elsen, Prentice-Hall, Englewood Cliffs, N.Y., 1965, quoted pp. 158, 123–4. E. C. Geissbuhler, *Rodin, Later Drawings*, London, 1964, pp. 86–7. Rodin paraphrases from Spinoza's *Improvement of the Understanding*.

11. H. F. Peters, *Rainer Maria Rilke: Masks and the Man*, Washington U.P., 1960 (paperback, N.Y., 1963), esp. pp. 90–1. E. C. Mason, *Rilke*, Edinburgh and N.Y., 1963, esp. pp. 19, 47–50, 60–1, 73, 82–4. *The Freud Journal of Lou Andreas-Salomé*, trans. S. A. Leavy, Basic Books, N.Y., 1964, pp. 138, 139, 154–5. R. M. Rilke, *Duino Elegies*, trans. J. B. Leishman and S. Spencer, N.Y., 1939, pp. 119–23 (quotation, 'Later, he thought', p. 122).

12. C. Geertz, *The Religion of Java*, Free Press, Glencoe, Ill., 1960, p. 232.

Mystical Techniques

1. H. C. Warren, *Buddhism in Translations*, Harvard U.P., 1898, pp. 293–6 (*Visudhimagga* iv). See 'After-Image', by H. G. A. van Zeyst, in *Encyclopedia of Buddhism*, ed. G. P. Malalasekera, Fascicle *Acala-Akan*, Govt. of Ceylon, 1963.

2. A. Padoux, *Recherches sur la symbolique et l'énergie de la parole dans certains textes tantriques*, E. de Boccard, Paris, 1963, pp. 112–13, 145, 152–3, 322. A. Bharati, *The Tantric Tradition*, Rider & Co., London, 1965, p. 122 ('The monk'); Chap. 3, 'On Mantra'. M. Eliade, *Yoga*, Pantheon Books, N.Y., 1958, pp. 212–16.

3. C. Luk, *The Secrets of Chinese Meditation*, Rider & Co., London, 1964, p. 83.

4. G.-C. Anawati and L. Gardet, *Mystique musulmane*, J. Vrin, Paris, 1961, esp. pp. 200–7. M. Eliade, op. cit., pp. 216–19. C. Rice, *The Persian Sufis*, Allen & Unwin, London, 1964, pp. 88–97. D. B. Macdonald, *The Religious Attitude and Life in Islam*, 1909; photographic repro., Khayats, Beirut, 1965, pp. 255–6 ('Let the seeker').

5. S. Dasgupta, *A History of Indian Philosophy*, Vol. I, Cambridge U.P., 1932, for a lucid summary of classical Yoga-philosophy. J. H. Woods, *The Yoga Sutras of Patanjali*, Harvard U.P., not always accurate, but translates two old commentaries. I quote or paraphrase from II, 28–55. M. Eliade, op. cit., pp. 53–65, 227–36 ('Place the right', p. 54, from T. Bernard; 'Shut in', p. 60). T. Bernard, *Hatha Yoga*, N.Y., 1944, detailed and honest. For Taoism see H. Welch,

Taoism, The Parting of the Way, Beacon Press, Boston, 2nd ed., 1965, pp. 108–9.

6. H. C. Warren, op. cit., pp. 291–2 (*Visudhimagga* iii). E. Conze, *Buddhist Meditation*, Allen & Unwin, London, 1956, pp. 100–3 (*Vm.* xi quoted), 131 (*Vm.* ix quoted).

7. E. Lamotte, *Histoire de Bouddhisme Indien*, I, Bibliothèque du Muséon, Louvain, 1958, pp. 685–6. N. Vandier-Nicolas, *Art et sagesse en Chine, Mi Fou*, Presses Universitaires, 1963, Chap. 1. H. Welch, op. cit., pp. 123–6. H. Dumoulin, *A History of Zen Buddhism*, Faber & Faber, London, 1963, pp. 126–32 (on the *koan*). Isshu Miura and R. F. Sasaki, *The Zen Koan, Its History and Use in Rinzai Zen*, Harcourt, Brace & World, N.Y., 1965.

8. 'Derwish', *Encyclopedia of Islam*. Anawati and Gardet, op. cit., pp. 208–9.

9. R. H. van Gulik, *Sexual Life in Ancient China*, E. J. Brill, Leiden, 1961, pp. 339–59. H. Welch, op. cit., pp. 120–1. D. L. Snellgrove, *Buddhist Himalaya*, Philosophical Library, N.Y., esp. pp. 80 ff., 206–7. The *Hevajra Tantra*, ed. and trans. D. L. Snellgrove, Oxford U.P., 1959, Part I, 'Introduction'. S. B. Dasgupta, *An Introduction to Tantric Buddhism*, U. of Calcutta, 2nd ed., 1958 ('There is no', p. 164, note). M. Eliade, op. cit., pp. 236–49, 259–72. A. Bharati, op. cit. Eliade is perhaps the best general introduction, though the cited books are all honest, scholarly investigations of a difficult subject. Snellgrove is particularly level-headed. His translation of the *Hevajra Tantra*, an important but incoherent text, includes typical directions for *mantras, mandalas*, sexual rituals, etc.

10. Lao Tzu, *Tao Te Ching*, trans. D. C. Lau, Penguin Books, 1963, p. 116 (*Tao Te Ching LV*). For alchemical re-embryoization see H. Welch, op. cit., pp. 130–3.

11. D. B. Macdonald, op. cit., p. 198

12. M. Eliade, op. cit., pp. 219–77.

13. H. V. Guenther, *The Life and Teachings of Naropa*, Oxford U.P., 1963, pp. xii–xiv, 76–81 (parts quoted), 98 (quoted), 200, 248.

14. F. Barron, 'The Relation of Ego Diffusion to Creative Perception', in C. W. Taylor, *Widening Horizons in Creativity*, John Wiley & Sons, N. Y., 1964, esp. pp. 82, 84.

15. P. McKellar, *Imagination and Thinking, A Psychological Analysis*, London, 1957, pp. 155–6.

16. C. Turnbull, in D. Ebin, *The Drug Experience*, Grove Press, N.Y., 1965, p.108.

17. C. A. Brownfield, *Isolation, Clinical and Experimental Approaches*, Random House, N.Y., 1965, pp. 13–15, 85–7.

18. A. J. Deikman, 'Experimental Meditation', *Journal of Nervous and Mental Diseases*, April, 1963; A. J. Deikman, 'Implications of Experimentally Induced Contemplative Meditation', ibid., xx, 1966, pp. 101–16.

19. D. O. Hebb, 'The Mammal and His Environment', in C. F. Reed, I. E. Alexander, S. S. Tomkins, *Psychopathology*, Harvard U.P., 1958. C. A. Brownlee, op. cit., p. 100. J. H. Woods, *The Yogasutras of Patanjali*, III, 42 and comm.; III, 48 and comm.; III, 26, 51.

20. R. Held, 'Plasticity in Sensory-Motor Systems', *Scientific American*, Nov., 1965. D. P. Schultz, *Sensory Restriction*, Academic Press, N.Y., 1965. J. P. Howard and W. P. Templeton, *Human Spatial Orientation*, John Wiley, N.Y. and London, Chap. 15, esp. p. 393.

21. C. A. Brownfield, op. cit., pp. 131–2. C. G. Costello, *Psychology for Psychiatrists*, Pergamon Press, Oxford, 1966, p. 133. D. P. Schultz, op. cit., Chap. VI.

22. N. N. Das and H. Gastaut, 'Variations de l'activité électrique du cerveau, du cœur, et des muscles squelettiques au cours de la méditation et de l'extase', *International Journal of Electroencephalography and Clinical Neurology*, Supplement No. 6, Masson & Cie, Paris, 1957, as quoted in R. Lannoy, *The Speaking Tree*, Oxford U.P., 1971, p. 350. A. Kasamatsu and T. Hirai, 'An Electroencephalographic Study of the Zen Meditation (Zazen)', *Folia Psychiatrica et Neurologica Japonica*, Vol. 20, No. 4, December 1966, pp. 316–36. N. Calder, *The Mind of Man*, B.B.C. 1970, Chap. 5 (comprehensive popular account). J. Kamiya, 'Operant Control of the EEG Alpha Rhythm and Some of Its Effects on Consciousness', in C. Tort (ed.), *Altered States of Consciousness*, John Wiley, N.Y., 1968. L. V. DiCara, 'Learning in the Autonomic Nervous System', *Scientific American*, January, 1970. R. K. Wallace and H. Benson, 'The Physiology of Meditation', *Scientific American*, February, 1972.

Freud's Psychoanalysis and Patanjali's Yoga

1. According to J. W. Hauer, *Der Yoga*, Stuttgart, 1959, p. 238. The other leading introduction is M. Eliade, *Yoga*, Pantheon Books, N.Y., 1958. For Yoga philosophy see S. Dasgupta, *A History of Indian Philosophy*, Vol. I, Cambridge U.P., 1922, and E. Frauwallner, *Geschichte der indischen Philosophie*, Otto Müller Verlag, Salzburg,

Vol. I, 1953. For the psychoanalytical concepts I have used see O. Fenichel, *The Psychoanalytic Theory of Neurosis*, London, 1946; H. Nunberg, *Principes de psychanalyse* (translated from English), Paris, 1957; and M. Ostow, 'On Human Happiness', in *Drugs in Psychoanalysis and Psychotheraphy*, N.Y., 1962.

2. S. Freud, 'Group Psychology'.
3. Quotations are from J. H. Woods, *The Yogasutras of Patanjali*. Woods, as I have said earlier, is less than completely accurate. The present quotation is from II, 9.
4. *Yogasutras*, II, 7, 8.
5. Ibid., IV, 2, comm.
6. Ibid., II, comm.
7. According to Hauer's interpretation of Chapter IV.
8. *Yogasutras*, IV, 10, supercomm.
9. Ibid., II, 16.
10. Ibid., I, 12, 15.
11. Ibid., II, 54, and comm.
12. Ibid., II, 5, and comm.
13. Ibid., I, 34-6, and comm.
14. Ibid., III, 38.
15. Ibid., III, 51, comm.
16. G. M. Carstairs, *The Twice-Born*, Indiana U.P., 1958.

Psychotic Mysticism

1. *The Life of Saint Teresa*, trans. J. M. Cohen, Penguin Books, 1957, p. 222 (Chap. 31). C. Luk, *The Secrets of Chinese Meditation*, Rider & Co., London, 1965, p. 145. See also E. Underhill, *Mysticism*, London, 1930, pp. 270, 276.
2. C. Landis, *Varieties of Psychopathological Experience*, Holt, Rinehart & Winston, 1964, pp. 329, 327 (from W. James, *Varieties of Religious Experience*, 1902, pp. 151-2); for disorders of time-experience, pp. 200-21. W. A. Stoll, 'Das Zeiterleben in der Psychiatrie', in R. W. Meyer, *Das Zeitproblem im 20. Jahrhundert*, Berne & Munich, 1964, pp. 172-3.
3. H. Werner and B. Kaplan, *Symbol Formation*, John Wiley & Sons, N.Y., 1963, Chap. 16.
4. D. P. Schreber, *Memoirs of My Nervous Illness*, ed. and trans. J. Macalpine and R. A. Hunter, Dawson, London, 1955, pp. 227, 124, 211-15, 47, 197, in C. Landis, op. cit., pp. 125, 126-7, 177, 399, 56,

142–3. Freud's paper is called 'Psycho-Analytic Notes on an Auto-biographical Account of a Case of Paranoia (Dementia Paranoides)'. There have been a number of subsequent studies of the case in psychoanalytical journals, e.g. by W. Niederland, F. Baunmeyer, and M. Katan.

5. C. Landis, op. cit., pp. 283–4, 301.
6. G. A. Ladee, *Hypochondriacal Syndromes*, Elsevier, Amsterdam, 1966, Chap. X. P. Schilder, *The Image and Appearance of the Human Body*, International Universities Press, N.Y., 1950, pp. 138 ff. (depersonalization), 159 ('I run into myself'). T. Freeman, J. L. Cameron, A. McGhie, *Chronic Schizophrenia*, London, 1958, p. 52 ('Do I have a face?'), 54 ('What I was'; 'Gradually'; 'I have lived'). R. D. Laing, *The Divided Self*, London, 1960, p. 118.
7. *Autobiography of a Schizophrenic Girl, With an Analytic Interpretation by M. Sechehaye*, trans. G. Rubin-Rabson, Grune & Stratton, N.Y., 1951, p. 7.
8. I owe much of the formulation in this paragraph to the psychoanalyst, Dr Mortimer Ostow. P. Schilder, *Contributions to Developmental Neuropsychiatry*, ed. L. Bender, International Universities Press, 1964, pp. 339–40, 343 (on giving in to postural tendencies). M. Sechehaye, *Introduction à une psychothérapie des schizophrènes*, Presses Universitaires de France, pp. 36–8. L. Eisenberg and L. Kanner, 'Early Infantile Autism', in C. F. Reed, I. E. Alexander, S. S. Tomkins, *Psychopathology*, Harvard U.P., 1958 (some analogous reactions of autistic children).
9. M. A. Sechehaye, *Symbolic Realization*, trans. B. Würsten and H. Würsten, International Universities Press, N.Y., 1951, pp. 118–19.

Eleven Quintessences of the Mystic State

1. J. G. Fichte, *The Guide to the Blessed Life* (*Die Anweisung zum seeligen Leben*), quoted in R. Otto, *Mysticism East and West*, Meridian Books, N.Y., 1957, p. 220.
2. Fung Yu-lan, *A History of Chinese Philosophy*, Vol. II, Princeton U.P., 1953, p. 295 (the words 'Like a framework', are those of Chi-tsang, A.D. 549–623). E. Conze, *Buddhist Texts Through the Ages*, Bruno Cassirer, Oxford, 1954, p. 160 ('The wise man discerns', *Lalitavistara* XIII). E. A. Burtt, *The Teachings of the Compassionate Buddha*, Mentor Books, 1955, p. 175 ('Bliss consists', Nagarjuna, trans. Stcherbatsky).

3. L. Wittgenstein, *Tractatus Logico-Philosophicus*, 6.41; 6.54; 7. The middle paragraph is in the translation of Pears and McGuiness, as quoted in M. Black, *A Companion to Wittgenstein's Tractatus*, Cambridge U.P., p. 378; the other quotations are in Ogden's earlier translation.

4. *The Zen Teachings of Hui Hai on Sudden Illumination*, trans. J. Blofield, Rider & Co., London, 1962 (Hui Hai was an eighth-century Chinese). For the nature of grasping and the use of hands see *Phenomenological Psychology, The Selected Papers of Erwin E. Straus*, Basic Books, N.Y., 1966, p. 152; and P. Schilder, *The Image and Appearance of the Human Body*, International Universities Press, N.Y., 1950.

5. O Siren, *The Chinese on the Art of Painting*, Peiping, 1936, p. 95 (reprinted in paperback).

6. Lao Tzu, *Tao Te Ching*, trans. D. C. Lau, Penguin Books, 1963, XX (in part).

7. Toukaram, *Psaumes du pèlerin*, trans. G.-A. Deleury, Paris, 1956, 153 (my trans. into English). A.-M. Andler, 'Aspects of Passivity and Ego Development in the Blind Infant', *The Psychoanalytic Study of the Child* XVIII, London, 1963; S. Fraiberg and D. A. Freedman, 'Studies in the Ego Development of the Congenitally Blind Child', *The Psychoanalytic Study of the Child* XIX, 1964.

8. Toukaram, op. cit., p. 92. 'Those who have penetrated to the kernel' are spoken of in the *Zohar* I, 154; see G. G. Scholem, *On the Kabbalah and Its Symbolism*, Routledge & Kegan Paul, London, 1960, p. 54.

9. Nicolaus Cusanus, *Of Learned Ignorance*, trans. G. Heron, Yale U.P., 1954, p. 12.

10. *Meister Eckhart*, trans. R. B. Blakney, N.Y., 1941, pp. 209–10.

11. *Le Vijnana Bhairava*, trans. L. Silburn, E. de Boccard, Paris, 1961, verse 48.

12. Ibid., verse 93.

13. *The Book of Lieh-tzu*, trans. A. C. Graham, London, 1960, pp. 77–8.

14. R. E. Hume, *The Thirteen Principal Upanishads*, 2nd ed., Oxford U.P., 1931 (*Chandogya Upanishad* 8, 1, 1–5, wording modified).

15. W. H. Burnham, 'Retroactive Amnesia', *American Journal of Psychiatry*, 14, 1903, as quoted in C. Landis, *Varieties of Psychopathological Experience*, N.Y., 1964, p. 217.

16. *The Book of Lieh-tzu*, trans. A. C. Graham, pp. 29–30 (also Chuang-tzu XXIII).

17. Henri Michaux, *Face aux verrous*, p. 190, and 'Premières impressions', *Passages*, as quoted in R. Bréchon, *Michaux*, Paris, 1959, pp. 77, 171.

18. Jacob Boehme, *Six Theosophic Points*, U. of Michigan Press, 1959, pp. 167, 170–1.
19. Toukaram, op. cit., p. 160.
20. C. G. Jung, *Memories, Dreams, Reflections*, trans. R. and C. Winston, N.Y., 1962, p. 359.
21. *The Path of Purification (Visudhimagga)*, trans. Bhikkhu Nanamoli, pub. R. Semage, Colombo, Ceylon, 1956, p. 322 (*Vm.* II, 10, 33).
22. A. J. Arberry, *Discourses of Rumi*, John Murray, London, 1961, p. 138.
23. *Meister Eckhart*, trans. R. B. Blakney, p. 203.
24. *The Book of Lieh-tzu*, pp. 70–1.
25. *Rumi, Poet and Mystic*, trans. R. A. Nicholson, Allen & Unwin, London, 1950, p. 133.
26. E. Conze, *Buddhist Meditation*, Allen & Unwin, London, 1956, pp. 8/–8 (*Vm.* VIII).
27. *Le Vijnana Bhairava*, trans. L. Silburn, E. de Boccard, Paris, 1961, p. 98 (verses 52, 53).
28. C. W. Wahl, 'Suicide as a Magical Act', in E. S. Shneidman and N. L. Farberow, *Clues to Suicide*, N.Y., 1957, pp. 28–9.
29. J. Gonda, *Change and Continuity in Indian Religion*, Mouton & Co., The Hague, 1965, pp. 229–83 ('The Guru', esp. pp. 229–30, 278–81), 438–59 (on 'consecration'). *The Path of Purification*, pp. 101–12 (*Vm.* II, 3). H. V. Guenther, *The Life and Teaching of Naropa*, Oxford U.P., pp. 134, 136, 137 ('In meditation'). *Le Paramarthasara*, trans. L. Silburn, E. de Boccard, Paris, 1957, p. 49. *The Hevajra Tantra*, trans. D. L. Snellgrove, Oxford U.P., 1959, Part I, p. 30.
30. A. J. Arberry, *Discourses of Rumi*, p. 35.
31. S. F. Dasgupta, *An Introduction to Tantric Buddhism*, U. of Calcutta, 2nd ed., 1958, pp. 183 (note 4), 184, 187.
32. *Rumi, Poet and Mystic*, p. 152.
33. S. Feldman, *African Myths and Tales*, Dell Pub. Co., N.Y., 1963, pp. 37, 41; adapted from E. W. Smith, *African Ideas of God*, London, 1950.
34. *The Book of Lieh-tzu*, p. 34.
35. Wang Yang-ming, *Instructions for Practical Living and Neo-Confucian Writings*, trans. Wing-tsit Chan, Columbia U.P., 1963, p. 273.
36. G. Feinberg, *The Prometheus Project*, Doubleday Anchor, Garden City, N.Y., 1969, p. 180.
37. C. Landis, op. cit., pp. 287, 285, 287, 33, 391–2 (quoted).
38. Ibid., pp. 37–8, 321, 326, 328, 327, 442.

39. *Autobiography of a Schizophrenic Girl, With an Analytic Interpretation by M. Sechehaye*, trans. G. Rubin-Rabson, Grune & Stratton, N.Y., 1951, pp. 80, 106.

40. C. Landis, op. cit., p. 74.

41. R. C. Zaehner, *Hindu and Muslim Mysticism*, U. of London, 1960, pp. 178–9 (on Sufi pederasty). H. Dumoulin, *A History of Zen Buddhism*, Faber & Faber, London, 1963, p. 309, note 2 (on Zen pederasty).

42. *The Complete Works of Chuang Tzu*, trans. B. Watson, Columbia U.P., 1968, p. 241. (*Chuang Tzu* XX).

43. R. H. Blyth, *Zen and Zen Classics*, Vol. I, The Hokuseido Press, Japan, 1960, pp. 114–15. Lu K'uan Yü (Charles Luk), *Ch'an and Zen Teaching, Second Series*, Rider & Co., London, 1961, p. 201.

44. R. H. Blyth, op. cit., p. 180.

45. *The Hevajra Tantra*, trans. D. L. Snellgrove, Vol. I, p. 24. W. M. Brodney, 'On the Dynamics of Narcissism', *The Psychoanalytic Study of the Child XX*, Hogarth Press, London, 1965.

46. Hakuin Zenji, *The Embossed Tea Kettle*, trans. R. D. M. Shaw, Allen & Unwin, London, 1963, p. 80.

47. See, e.g., P. W. Bridgman, *A Sophisticate's Primer of Relativity*, Harper Torchbook, ed., 1965. Prof. John A. Wheeler of Princeton, as reported in *New Scientist and Science Journal* of 29 July ('Dimensionality').

Index

Some other books published by Penguin
are described on the following pages.

THE SWORD OF GNOSIS
Metaphysics, Cosmology, Tradition, Symbolism
Edited by Jacob Needleman

This collection of essays brings light from ancient worlds to modern man's crisis of the spirit. The authors include Frithjof Schuon, René Guénon, and others whom they have influenced. The subjects they deal with range from Oriental metaphysics to old Lithuanian songs, from the enigma of the koan to the problem of evil, from Islamic art to the seven deadly sins. In these pages the study of metaphysics, symbolism, and spiritual method is seen as a sword with which to cut away the illusions of the present age and open a path for the renewed influence of primordial tradition. Jacob Needleman is general editor of The Penguin Metaphysical Library.

THE UNIVERSAL MEANING OF THE KABBALAH
Leo Schaya

This masterly study of the Kabbalah uncovers deep and universal meanings in the esoteric doctrines of Jewish mysticism. The Kabbalah is an occult interpretation of the Scriptures originally developed by rabbis in the Geonic period. In discussing it, Leo Schaya looks not only at the Old Testament and the Talmud but also at the Book of Splendor, one of the classical sources of Hebrew metaphysics. On this basis he arrives at a synthesis that embraces the multiple states of human existence, from man's earthly individuality to his essential identity with the Absolute.

IN THE PENGUIN METAPHYSICAL LIBRARY

HER-BAK
Volume 1: THE LIVING FACE OF ANCIENT EGYPT
("CHICK-PEA")
Isha Schwaller de Lubicz

This vivid re-creation of spiritual life in ancient Egypt tells
the story of the young Her-Bak, a character created on the basis
of the author's many years' research in Egyptology. We follow
Her-Bak through his education and his training in the Outer
Temple. The reader who accompanies him will gain a detailed
picture of a civilization founded on the search for knowledge

THE YOGA OF THE BHAGAVAT GITA
Sri Krishna Prem

This is an extraordinarily independent commentary on the
Bhagavat Gita. Every Indian teacher who claims the support
of tradition is required to write his own interpretation of this
ancient poem, which speaks with such simple force of the
struggle that leads to immortal consciousness. *The Yoga of the
Bhagavat Gita* was written by a European-born Hindu master.
It therefore reveals the Gita's practical teaching in a way that
can directly penetrate the intellect of Western man.